All About Running

From zero to running hero: a beginner's guide to fitness after forty

Michaela Tagg

Copyright © Michaela Tagg 2023

The right of Michaela Tagg to be identified as the Author of this Work has been asserted by her in accordance with the Copyright, Designs and Patents Act 1988.

All rights reserved. No part of this publication may be reproduced, stored in any retrieval system, or transmitted, in any form or by any means without the prior written permission of the author, nor be circulated in any form or binding or cover other than that in which it is published and without similar condition being imposed on the subsequent purchaser.

The information in this book has been compiled as general guidance on health and fitness. It is not a substitute and not to be relied upon for medical or healthcare professional advice. The advice and strategies contained herein may not be suitable for your situation. If you have an underlying medical condition or you are taking medication, please consult your doctor before following the plans in this book. You are advised to consult a doctor on any matters relating to your health, and in particular on any matters that may require diagnosis or medical attention. So far as the author is aware, the information given is correct and up to date as of 27th November 2023. Practice, laws and regulations all change and the reader should obtain up to date professional advice on any such issues. The author disclaims any liability arising directly, or indirectly from the use or misuse of the information contained in this book.

Book Cover illustration is AI generated, with cover design using Canva

Illustrations purchased from Shutterstock

First Edition 2023

https://www.35dayrunningchallenge.com

Dedication

To my parents, whose guiding light helped me get to here. For the ever-present support from my brothers and sisters, and in memory of Robert, who we miss every day. To Arthur, mijn koning en liefde van mijn leven.

Contents

Preface	IX
Introduction	XV
Part One	
1. Nought-y Forty – Starting from zero	3
2. Why do I hate exercise?	7
3. Why running?	15
Part Two	
4. Run for your life! Why our bodily systems LOVE running	21
5. Brain, spinal cord, nerves and neurons – Our nervous system	27
6. I heart you lungs	39
7. Feeding the mind, body and soul – Our digestive system	51
8. You'd be nothing without me – Skeleton & muscle	59
9. Regulate! – Our endocrine system	65

10.	Running for weight loss	71
11.	Other bodily benefits	83
12.	Running for our mind	93

Part Three

13.	Absolute Beginner	103
14.	Making running a habit	109
15.	The kit – How to choose shoes and other clothing considerations	125
16.	Back to my routes – The Base Route	139
17.	I'm me and you're you - Running style and technique	143
18.	Fuelling the habit – Food and hydration	149
19.	Building Fitness	167
20.	Dodging the running rut - Taking our training to the next level	173
21.	No one needs to get hurt... Avoiding injury	181
22.	Safety first - Running safely	241
23.	Running myths	245
24.	Bringing it all together – The happier, healthier you	257

Part Four

25.	Training schedules	269
26.	Race-day preparation	285
27.	Meal ideas	293

28. Are you with me?	303
Notes and references	307

Preface

I started running, properly running, as a knobbly-kneed nine-year old. In fact, as the fourth child in-line (one of eight in total) and with competition at home pretty fierce, I was running not long after I'd learned to walk. But it was while representing my school in a kilometre long run that the natural talent I'd been honing, precisely thanks to my extremely active childhood, was discovered.

My running story begins one summer afternoon, crowded behind the start line in Oxford's South Park, one of a group of carefully selected 'sporty' school girls tasked to run as fast as we could around the edge of the hilly park. There were two factors at play that day: firstly, as a generally obedient child, I followed the instructions: "at the sound of the start-gun, one lap of the park"; secondly, and much more powerfully, I knew that I had no option but to win that race (or risk the goading from of my older brothers at home that night, who in the well-rehearsed words of Queen, had "No time for losers").

On a clear day, South Park will provide one of the finest views of Oxford's dreaming spires, but on that particular day, when the gun released the firecracker like sound, the only view I was interested in seeing was an empty one, with precisely zero people in front of me. I flew from the start line like a sprinter out of the blocks; the first twenty metres crowded with other girls with the same 'must win' mentality, splaying arms with sharp elbows were used in a clear bid to take no prisoners on the way to victory! After fifty metres the numbers were thinning out; logic said that to win I had to be at the front and stay at the front; if I wanted a hero's welcome at home that evening, the challenge was on to see just how much I could get from my little legs...

At halfway, and no longer able to hear the sound of the eager breathing through gritted teeth behind me, I had a quick glance over my shoulder to check how close my opponents were. 'I've got this', I thought to myself; 'just keep going and I can take first place!' And on I ran... As I approached the finish line and having had a few more cursory glances over my shoulder to check there were no late challengers for my title, I felt my shoulders relax and the exhilarating bliss of complete exhaustion set-in. It was to be my first experience of pushing my body beyond what I knew it was capable of and the magnificent feeling of strength in how my body and mind respond. Running providing me with this life-enhancing sensation and this knowledge was mine to keep forever!

Winning the race, I was asked to join the local running club, which I did only because my friend (who finished second) was also asked, meaning my parents could share the driving to and from the training sessions twice a week. At that young age I remember the training sessions as being fun; it was more about routine and the discipline of turning up and doing the work. We tried different events: hurdles, high jump, long jump, sprinting, relays and laps of the running track; everyone was welcome, many came and went.

Autumn and winter were about cross-country; a hilly run through muddy fields and forests, finishing the race with legs blue from the cold and covered in mud. If the ground was frozen that day, at least it meant avoiding having my legs hosed down with cold water at the end, numbing any last sensations in my adolescent limbs. Approximately three-quarters of the way through each race I would find myself questioning why I had thought it was a good idea to climb out of bed early on a Saturday morning and subject my body to a torturous muddy contest to find the fastest girl among us. But the rewards did come and within a couple of years, now training three times a week and sometimes a gym session midweek too, I was winning the 800 metres at county level at every outing for my age group. In my early teens, competing in the English Schools' Athletics Championships, I was one of the fastest 800 metre runners in the UK for my age.

I knew at the time that I wasn't training as many times per week as some of my peers; my parents had always been adamant that I wouldn't be over-trained while my bones and body were still growing. But looking back, I realise that I was also lacking some of the drive my rivals had. In this day and age we talk about the best of the best being 'obsessed' with winning; waking up each day with a singular focus on how they are going to improve themselves and their next performance. I can see now that this level of drive, to commit my whole being to an extremely fragile life in athletics, was missing for me. And it is one of the reasons why, aged seventeen and having been diagnosed with glandular fever and unable to run for a number of months, I ended up quitting.

I couldn't stay away from running for long however and in a bid to get back into shape while in my first year at University, I joined an early morning running club and was quickly reminded what it is that I love about running. Eight marathons later and close to 3,000 training runs, spread across six of the seven continents (I'm still building up to do the Ice Marathon), I've been enjoying running purely in the name of keeping fit and without the pressure of having to be the best.

Running has so often symbolised a new beginning for me; the thing I always go back to with renewed energy when I need new focus in life. Requiring both mental and physical strength in itself, it has helped me through all of my life challenges; grief, heartache, the knocks and disappointments. It has always kept me on a path that allows me to keep moving forwards, helping me make the difficult decisions and to grow as a person. And running has always been much more to me than simply providing relief from a stressful job, or trying to stay fit and in shape. Most of the regular runners I speak with in fact, tell me that running has become so important to their having a balanced, happy existence that life feels out of kilter when they're unable to run for one reason or another. Harmony is missing from day to day life.

The headspace I access during a run helps to provide a calmness to my life when I need it most. Trying not to sound too woo-woo, it is a way for me to connect with the universe, which is a feeling I get when I push my body and mind to do difficult things; when I know I am doing things today that are going to make my life a bit better tomorrow.

I should be clear that I am not a doctor and am in no position to provide medical advice; instead I have studied and researched what's going on in our body and our mind while we run very simply because improvement demands it. I feel how each step of every run I do challenges my body; I notice the different phases my energy levels go through and how my mind reacts to the peaks and troughs. I've worked with my body to recover from injury, overcoming the upset when it lets me down by investing the time in making it stronger again. But most fascinating of all, I have experienced the positive impact that running has on every other area of my life.

My inspiration to write this book has been the ambition that I might be able to help others enjoy everything great that running can add to our lives. I've sought the wisdom of friends who run, as well as those who don't, hoping to inspire everyone to pull on their running shoes and get outside, whether it is for regular walks, or setting a goal of being a healthier human being in a year's time.

I appreciate that running is something that many people will have written-off during a painful sports day years ago and are now unable to imagine that their body could ever build enough strength to be able to run again. But if we remove expectations as to what it means to be a runner and treat our own experience as having a unique starting point and a goal that's individual to us and just get out there, how much better might our life be? By making this commitment to ourself today and then putting one foot in front of the other, how much will our quality of life improve over the next two, ten, twenty, thirty years? And so before you say "no way", I ask you to first read this book before deciding whether running is for you or not. Read it in its entirety (including the 'Notes and references' section at the end). Then maybe even sneak on your running shoes and give it a little go.

Let's get the whole world running.

Introduction

Just suppose that I could make you love running. Just suppose that despite the fact that you haven't run since you were at school and you can't think of anything worse than running, I could make you passionate about getting out and pounding the pavements twice a week. Maybe the idea of running is so very alien to you that you genuinely believe it is a hundred times more likely a pig will fly past your window than it is you will ever pull on a pair of running shoes and head out for a gentle jog?

So here's a thing: why, when we happily run around the playground as a child, following a football, playing tag, chasing our first crush, why do we suddenly stop running? An activity which our complex body is built especially for, with amazing muscle formations, bones - which ounce for ounce are stronger than steel, and these clever joints with a perfect range of movement to allow us to move our skeleton from one place to another. And this is all happening without us even having to think about it. When we want to stand up from our chair, we don't have to instruct each bone in the role it needs to play in elevating us, we don't have to concentrate on keeping tension in the right muscles to prevent us from immediately collapsing on the ground, nor are we having to prepare our joints with a series of warm-up exercises to make sure we can hit an upright position. In fact within a fraction of a second of making the decision to stand up, the brain's cerebral cortex formulates a plan and sends instructions all around our body making sure each and every cell is doing what it should so that we can lift ourselves out of our chair. Muscles, tendons, heart, lungs, eyes, ears, bones, joints, blood; every part of our body receiving messages and then sending a message back to our brain to let it know everything is working A.O.K (or if it isn't, giving the brain a sign that we're in trouble). Pretty damn amazing, right?

But how often do you think about the thousands of different processes that are happening within your body each minute, every day, right under your nose? Maybe when you're ill and feel unwell? As a newly pregnant woman, or curious dad-to-be? Or perhaps the answer is simply "I never think about what is going on inside my body", which would be of absolutely no surprise, because - there is no need for us to do so. Our body gets on with what it needs to do, when it needs to do it, so that we can go about living.

OK - great, so with that knowledge safely confirmed and tucked under our belts, we don't need to worry about not worrying, right? Well what about if I were able to instill in you a newfound appreciation for the complexities of our body, and then persuade you that with only a little bit more maintenance each week, we can live a significantly happier, healthier life, and - for longer? That a little bit of time invested in looking after ourselves today is going to help make our future life more satisfying, with continued independence well into old age?

How about if no matter when we last exercised, no matter what our body shape is today, or how old we are, we were all able to learn to love something that we never thought we would; something that is going to dramatically enrich our lives in every single way imaginable? Not overnight, but within a matter of weeks of focused attention.

This is my hope with this book and my reason for pouring my passions into this long-term project. I'm really curious to see whether, if we are to take our extraordinary body less for granted and if we start to appreciate the mind-blowing processes that are happening within us (as covered in Part Two), this can motivate us to take better care of ourselves? Could this be a trigger to reestablish an activity that had been written off many years ago as unnecessary, or painful, perhaps even embarrassing, but that is actually the simplest way for all of us to give our body the tender loving care it needs so that we can all live our very best lives?

When I speak to people about running, I get the sense as to just how many barriers need to be broken down so that they might try running, or see it for what it is (easy access for all) and also dispel some of the unhelpful myths around running, particularly the first question I'm asked when I tell people I enjoy running: "but isn't it bad for your knees?"

So it is a dream of mine really that everyone who is physically able to would spend thirty minutes, twice a week, running. That we would pass people in the fields, in the park, playground, woods, on the beach, on the pavements outside our houses, people who hadn't run in years, out for a jog. That people would build jogging into their lives, and after five weeks, three months, a year, everyone would be stronger, healthier, fitter and much, much happier as a result. Less fear of getting old, more confident of remaining mobile and independent until the end, and living a more comfortable and considerably better life in the meantime.

I know it isn't as simple as it sounds, because of these barriers we put up for ourselves: "I'm not a runner; I'm not built for running", "I'm not sure how to run; where do I start?" "Running is hard and my life is tiring enough"; "I don't want to injure myself"; "I'll look like an idiot"; "I don't have the time to invest in a long-term project such as running" etc. etc. These barriers that we've built and then reinforced over time make knocking through them extremely difficult. But - another thing about us humans is that when we put our minds to something, when we want something badly enough, we've proven to ourselves over and over again that we're capable. We can make a change, even if it is only a small change, we have the power to make it happen. This is the start point I'd like you to consider. As you go into Part Three of this book, start with a completely open mind, believe that within a relatively short period of time, you too could be going out for a jog, and actually enjoy it. Dump all the negative stuff for now, the reasons you give for having zero desire to go out running and imagine yourself in a years time, jogging non-stop for thirty minutes, feeling better than you have done in years, stronger in every way and super proud of yourself for everything you are doing to give yourself your best possible future life. I wonder if we can build up from here, perhaps following one of the training schedules included in Part Four, and have you looking back in a year's time, amazed at just what you've achieved?

Part One

Chapter One

Nought-y Forty – Starting from zero

Holy guacamole – what the sweet baby cheeses happened to my body last night?! Yesterday I was so svelte and slim, looking all cute and sexy in my skinny jeans and skintight top, today I've got overspill from my trousers and my arms are trying to Incredible Hulk out of my favourite shirt! How did this happen?

Welcome to your forties.

It has been more than twenty years since exercise formed any part of your life. You climb out of bed following yet another broken night of sleep, your body feels stiff and sore as you transition through the seven stages of Neanderthal to human body shape on your way to the bathroom. When did this happen? Why do I wake each morning feeling like I need just one more hour of good sleep? When did it become painful to even get out of bed? Why does it take half an hour each morning before my body starts to do what my brain is telling it to? Is this all I have to look forward to now? A slow decline in mobility? A steady increase in aches and pains? Is this what middle-age looks and feels like?! Isn't there anything I can do to feel better....?

So – here we are. Forty-plus years old. Slappidy-slap-slap in the face - the realisation that youth is leaving the building... The spring is sprung. The beat of the Duracell bunny's drum is slowing. The morning brain fog lingers longer. The call for coffee comes from a place of necessity rather than pleasure. Lifts, not stairs, car not bike. Muscles hiding under a layer that wasn't there a few years ago. Bones crunch, joints creak, exertion forces exclamation "ahhh", "oooh", "ouch", "****". Digestion is slow, the post-lunch slump creeps and seeps up to the end of the afternoon. When will I poo again...?

Denial remains rife, despite all of the signs. The weighing scale hasn't been used in so long that even if you stood on it, you wouldn't be able to read what it was proclaiming under the thick layer of dampened bathroom dust. "Pointless standing on that old thing; I'm sure its broken and won't give me an accurate reading...". "Trousers have clearly shrunk slightly in the wash, but maybe my shirt will fit again once I have time to go on that diet and have a few days watching what I eat". "My brain fog will clear once I have a holiday and can catch up on some sleep". "My anxiety about all of this will go away once I...."

Get fit...?

There it is. This thought, or feeling, that I'm sure almost all of us have deep down: if only I could enjoy one kind of exercise. If only there was some form of sport that I got pleasure and happiness from doing that would mean I didn't get out of bed each day feeling like I am slowly falling apart. That saves my neck from this laptop-induced stiffness, which feels like my bones are slowly fusing together.

Perhaps you have felt slight envy when you see someone your age exercising, and enjoying exercising? Why isn't that me? Why was I not built and wired to enjoy exercise? I know it would be good for me to do more. I know that I enjoy looking at my step counter at the end of the day and seeing the magic '10,000', or just knowing that I've been on my feet all day. I know I feel more in touch with myself, with my life, with the world, when I've done a bit of exercise and I get that sense of life running through my veins, and that being alive is an amazing thing! So why? Why can't I make exercise a habit of mine? Why don't I ever persevere? Where do Mr and Mrs Motivation disappear to every time I even consider putting my sport shoes on?

Chapter Two

Why do I hate exercise?

If we know that exercise would do us good and would ultimately make us feel better about ourselves, why is it that we have such an unhealthy relationship with exercise? Why does it feel like a chore? Why does the prospect of doing exercise feel as attractive as self-flagellation with a thick new leather buckled belt, or some equally out-there extreme punishment? What early learning has instilled itself in our brain such that the thought of raising our heart rate through anything other than practicing the horizontal mambo fills us with dread? At the very idea of physical exercise the curtains come down, the barrier is raised, the alarm starts flashing and wailing inside our head "Exercise is bad, no exercise today. Away, away – oh evil thoughts of putting my poor body through such things…" Then the feeling of relief washing over us: "Whoa – that was close; I don't really have to exercise; no risk of pain or discomfort for me today! The lady on my social media feed doing a downward facing dog may mean well, but there really is no reason for me to have my butt elevated above my head on this fine day".

And yet – once we're at home, relaxing on the sofa after a long day, there's still that niggling feeling: "damn – I wish I'd done just a little bit of exercise today". "What have I done with my little bit of free time instead? I have scrolled through my phone, watched twenty minutes of depressing news headlines and now I'm half-watching some re-run on TV while I try and exorcise thoughts of chocolate biscuits from my head". "Dammit – why didn't I go out for that twenty minute jog / go to the gym / try that new Pilates class / login to the fitness App I downloaded with '20% off' last month and still haven't used?"

Why do so many of us have an almost allergic reaction to even the thought of exercise? How much comes down to wanting to avoid the physical discomfort and pain exercise causes us? Or the uncomfortable feeling of being self-conscious, the fear of feeling like a failure, or not being good enough?

Unlike childbirth, or the tough times in a loving relationship, or even going to the dentist, the pain caused by exercise can easily be categorised as 'unnecessary pain'. The agony of giving birth results in the amazing gift of a child. The argument we have with our partner that ultimately leaves us with a better understanding of each other and culminates in a passionate making-up session. The visit to the dentist that is five minutes of comparative pure hell but ultimately means we know we will have a healthy set of teeth for the foreseeable future. What does exercise do that makes the pain worthwhile?

Exercise is one of those discussion points that we can easily argue ourselves out of giving serious consideration: "I survive perfectly well without exercise; in fact – neither my grandma, nor my mum, did anything other than a bit of walking and my grandma was ninety years of age when she passed away, and my mum is still going strong, apart from the normal aches and pains of someone of her age. Sure – I feel a bit slothful at times, my back is sore in the mornings, I am a little creakier these days and I can't climb a flight of stairs without feeling my heart pounding through the wall of my chest by the time I get to the top; but – I am doing just fine without the punishment of exercise in my life".

And the argument continues: "Besides - I can't exercise for five minutes every day and expect to make a difference. Exercise takes ongoing, concerted effort before it even starts to make a dent in the figure that appears on the scales these days (or would do, if I ever stood on the scales). That means the pain is ongoing. Ongoing discomfort of putting myself on display to the world as 'that women who clearly hasn't done any exercise for thirty years and is now trying to get fit'". Hands up if you know how this story ends...

The inner voice, oh the critical inner voice. This voice that wants to protect us from stepping into the unknown; that shouts at us "what the hell do you think you are doing?" the moment we try something new. The well-trained reaction to quickly quieten any possible disobedience to the early learnings that put us firmly on this path in life. On our path in life. "I wasn't built to exercise". "I'm not one of those people who actually enjoy running. If my destiny in life was to become a yoga guru, I would be able to get past my knees when I try and touch my toes". Perhaps even: "I was supposed to work my way up the career ladder so that I can feel proud of my social status; it doesn't matter that I have no time for exercise and looking after myself; this is just the way things are supposed to be". Or "sometimes you have to look at the gifts you were given in life; I was not gifted with the grace of a springbok when it comes to jogging, and I will save the world from the sight of my 'Tired-Tellytubby trundle'". (Which – by the way – happens to be my running style when I'm nearing the end of my run...).

Is that right? Are we really destined to the dustbin of the hundred-metre dash once we get into double digits? Jilted to the jogger's junkyard because we're no longer a juvenile?

Is our future firmed-up by the time we're a full-grown adult?

Well, no. I like to think that I am living proof of this (currently trying to disprove this anyway...) Hard-working with a successful career to date and a promising path ahead of me, yet with this nagging voice somewhere in the back of my head: "is this job challenging me in such a way that I feel fulfilled after a day's work? Am I really investing this time and energy is making the world a better place in some way?" And "why is this voice that is calling me to try something new starting to get so shouty?" So – after more than one winter of discontent, and having saved enough money to give myself some breathing space, I finally I stepped off the hamster's wheel. Naturally – my legs and feet were still desperate to keep the wheel motion going; it was all they really knew, it was what they felt comfortable doing. And it took some time to find my feet, like shaking off the feeling of sea legs. But I changed the pattern; stepped out of the comfort zone that had been neatly sign-posted since I'd launched myself onto my career path and here I am now, writing a book. Something I'd wanted to do for as long as I can remember and had dreamed about doing ever since I became aware that there were other worlds out there, similar to those that had sucked me in as a child as I joined Mrs Pepperpot on her latest adventure.

Anyway – I digress... My point is that from the 'truths' we're told at a young age, and following our subsequent 'successes' or 'failures' according to these truths, we find ourselves on a path in life; career, relationships, social life, exercise etc. If this path is one that we're 'supposed to be on' (whatever that might mean) then we are generally considered 'successful' and therefore everything is fine and dandy with our life. Right? OK – but how did everyone know what would be best for me aged zero to sixteen that put me on this path to where I am now? Did I myself even really know when I was eighteen years old? As a woman, the toughest years of my life were between the ages of sixteen and eighteen; I was terrified of going out into the adult world and being a failure because I couldn't find this damned path to success!

It is never too late to question why we have a certain belief about the way we choose to live our life, what we allow in, and what we choose to ignore, or omit from our life. When we accept that we have a belief about something because it has been instilled in us from an early age and if we are prepared to question whether that belief is really true, or actually something that we told ourselves so long ago and have just accepted as fact ever since, then we can choose to pull down the barriers we have put up for ourselves. We can ignore the 'straight-ahead only' sign, we can question the directions we were given as a fourteen, sixteen, eighteen year old that were going to help us find our destiny in life and we can make a choice to stop. Only once we stop can we really see what else is around us.

Back to the point of the story: perhaps you stopped exercising while you were at school because you 'weren't good enough' at sports to make it worthwhile continuing? Destined, even by your teenage years to believe that by not being a sporty person, keeping fit is automatically out of reach? Who would run if there is nowhere to run to? Or - perhaps you still hold on to the belief that the pain caused by exercise is bad? Akin to punishment, and self-inflicted at that? "Just why would I put myself through the pain? I'm not cutout for exercise, and just how much time and effort would I have to put in before I saw any real results? There is no short-term gain, only short, medium and long-term pain!" "Yes – there are times when I wish I was one of those people who loved working out, but as I can get by without it and avoid the discomfort of exercise, I can sweep those fleeting thoughts of pulling on my sports shoes for a brief jog right back under my favourite TV-watching armchair from whence they came!"

But (and firmer butt…) ask yourself this: "What if within this notion of 'them and us' (runners and non-runners), I realised that by starting tomorrow I could be 'a runner'? What if I could challenge this notion that exercise is torture and change this long-standing mindset that exercise is to be avoided at all costs? What if I could recognise the pain as a good thing, a sign that my body is changing for the better? What if I could trust that I have the ability to rebuild the strength of my body again instead of being afraid something else is going to fail me tomorrow? What if I were able to find short-term pleasure in exercise such that I could reap the rewards over the longer term too? A happier, healthier me. Might this be possible?"

Yes – and here comes the point (finally): we need to change our mindset. We have to consciously stop; we have to delete the beliefs that have been instilled in us between the ages of zero and sixteen. These are no longer true.

Then we have to examine the unknown; "what if there is another truth than the one I've been living by, one where I learn to enjoy exercise?" "What if it allowed me to enjoy being active and to appreciate this extraordinary body I have been gifted with?"

I hope, I really hope, that the contents of the following chapters are going to help you to stop, question your beliefs about exercise and then have a completely different outlook on getting fit again. One that gifts you a new feeling of responsibility to become the healthiest version of yourself!

Chapter Three

Why running?

Let's start by agreeing that just because you haven't run in a long time, it doesn't mean that this option is closed off to you forever (please refer to previous chapter). Your body, while perhaps a little creakier these days, is still perfectly capable of making a gradual switch from its usual walking pace to a jog. The choice is now yours to make: do you want to try something new and difficult, that will improve your quality of life immeasurably? Or - will you continue to live a life where your body slowly becomes weaker each day, allowing Mrs Old Age to sweep you along her chosen path, just hoping that she doesn't have an imminent 'surprise' for you in the form of an injury, or illness?

Let's say that you choose the former. Let's say that your interest is piqued enough by now and you love the idea that you can slow down the ageing process. Let's say that you love the sound of the fact that by starting to exercise now, you can even reverse some of the ageing that your body is experiencing. Let's say then that you are willing to take up this challenge to become a runner. Push away the doubt that running is not for you and that you could never get into it seriously in the long-term. Instead cling to the thinking: "wouldn't it be great if I could be more active and get that feeling of 'vitality' back in my life!"

With that agreed, now I want you to close your eyes and imagine you are the superhero version of yourself...

Embracing your inner superhero is important in this mission; we can say that walking/running are "only exercise" like it is nothing special; "you choose to do it or not", but if we haven't exercised in a long time, it is going to require the superhero version of yourself to get started again. Maybe it has been a while since your superhero self came out to play? It could be months, or even years since you tried something that required you to be really brave and try something that you didn't have complete trust in yourself that you were capable of? How long is it since you polished your superhero badge with pride as you were congratulated for doing something that required you putting your ego on the line but you did it anyway? We are all capable of being this version of ourself; of trying things that we have previously convinced ourselves that we can't do; we will need to draw on these hidden powers as we set-off on our mission to build running into our lives. With this in mind, I'm not going to launch straight into the "how can I get started tomorrow?" Instead I'm going to begin with the 'why' you are going to want to get into this running thing.

Of all the different types of exercise we could choose, running is going to provide us with everything we need to be a healthier version of ourselves. We don't need a lot of equipment (a pair of running shoes), nor do we need a lot of preparation. Yet – providing we ease into our running and don't push it too hard, too fast, the benefits for both the body and the mind are unequalled.

The reality is that running is really, really tough on our body. If we think about it, unlike walking, where we always have our weight supported on at least one foot as we push ourselves forwards, when we're running we have to spring and push all of our weight up off the ground. In fact, when we gain momentum there is a brief moment in time when neither of our feet is touching the ground. Add that to the fact that we are moving at a faster pace than when we're walking, and it is easy to imagine how much stronger our feet, ankles and legs need to be, as well as all of the other muscles we are using, the length of our body.

To give an idea of how much more effort is required for running versus walking, we could have a detailed look at Newton's second law of motion...

Or maybe I'll just explain it by saying that 'the effort we have to exert in order to move our body forwards, increases the faster we go'. Or – even more simply: 'we're going to become stronger and burn more calories if we run instead of walk'.

One of the reasons running will make us fitter, stronger and ultimately healthier, is that it really is working every bit of our body. All of our bodily processes have to work together; the very definition of 'a finely tuned machine'. Of course – it won't feel like this in the beginning; our body will predominately feel like each part is battling against each other to start with. However – with time, and continued training, we can soon achieve the feeling of our body working like a well-oiled machine, and this, I can assure you, is an amazing feeling!

But it does take time, and if we are just starting out with running, patience and persistence are what will take us to running nirvana. To better understand why this is, and to use this knowledge to then motivate us, we need to understand a bit about how the body works, and importantly – how it all works together.

Part Two

Chapter Four

Run for your life! Why our bodily systems LOVE running

Did you know that we have more than 600 muscles in our body, 78 organs and between 60,000 to 100,000 miles of arteries, capillaries and veins supporting our eleven bodily systems (skeletal, muscular, nervous, endocrine, cardiovascular, respiratory, skin, hair & nails, lymph and immunity, digestive, urinary and reproductive)? Of course – one of the things that makes our body so amazing is the fact that our systems generally always work in perfect harmony. When we run however, we are activating everything all at once and at a high tempo. The rate at which our heart is pumping blood around our body increases, our lungs are working harder; our brain firing instructions, hormones are produced and levels regulated - all of these things go into 'superhero mode'. The rate at which our body reacts to being asked to run and the extra effort it has to go to in order we can keep moving forwards is the ultimate work-out for body and mind. It helps to keep our body 'in-tune' with itself. If we compare it to learning how to play a piece of music on the piano, we would practise the piece over and over again. At first it would be full of gaps; we might get frustrated, stopping and starting as we worked through the entire piece, but our fingers would start to learn where they had to move next, the messages to our brain would remind us how the next note should sound, and each time we practised the piece, we would get better and better. With running, the first time we get out there, our body basically knows what it needs to do, but it hurts and we get out of breath really quickly. The next time is still tiring, our feet are still dragging towards the end, our body again starts to sag forward as we near home and there is still this frustrated screaming voice in our head – "why isn't this getting any easier?"

However - our body simply needs more practice. From our nervous system, our breathing, our muscles (including our heart muscle), the release of hormones that support exercise, and - the list goes on. This is why, much like learning to play the new piece on the piano, to get all of the different elements of our body working together in perfect harmony, is going to take practise, patience and persistence.

Far more than just a temple

Our body is quite simply – extraordinary! Beyond comprehension in many ways (literally). If we examine how all our bodily systems work together, from hormones, to nervous system, organs, blood flow, getting rid of waste, our muscles, limbs etc. If we really look at everything that is happening within our body on a second by second basis, then if we add in movement as well, or look at certain times of the day, or monthly cycles, before eating, after eating etc. etc. it is truly MIND-BLOWING! This is even before acknowledging the fact that there is still so much that we don't know and don't fully understand about how our body works. Many of our bodily processes are so intricate, and form a part of a chain reaction of messaging within our body, that it often makes it difficult for us humans to understand cause and effect. Add to this the complexity that our body behaves and reacts in a slightly different way to the next person, and then in relation to our environment as well and we can start to see why opinion varies in terms of how best we should be looking after our body. In fact these differences between you and me are one of the reasons why we are seeing a move into the development of medicines and treatments that will be specific to an individual. But better still – we would have an improved understanding as to why some people are more susceptible to diseases, illnesses, or even injuries than others. What is genetic, what is specific to our environment, and also what our body is 'deep learning' without our realising it (both for the good, also to our detriment, becoming more difficult to address over time)? Prevention is, after all, better than a cure.

We can look at the pictures in any book or website about human biology and marvel at the sophistication of the composition of our body. Perhaps you've already spent time wondering how a specific process works within your body and done some casual reading up on it and have already realised just how amazing our body is? However - unless you got lost down the rabbit hole as you looked up the answer to your question, perhaps what you won't have realised is how incredible it is that all of the elements of our body work together in such perfect harmony.

But I manage perfectly fine without exercise...

Yes – ok, but does the thought ever creep into your mind that your life could be even better with exercise? How you would feel if you slept well every night, clocking up your seven or eight solid hours sleep? How about being able to climb several flights of stairs in one go, without being out of breath when you got to the top? What about knowing you are slowing down the ageing process of your muscles and bones, significantly increasing your chances of being fully mobile right up until your last day on this beautiful planet of ours? After all no one wants to get to the stage in life where they're reliant on their partner or a carer to get out of bed each day, or to stand up from their armchair, or have a shower, or go to the toilet; right?

What about knowing that getting fitter will have a knock-on effect to diet and to eating better? What would it be like to feel good about your body, every day? Because when you are exercising and you know that you are putting time and effort into looking after yourself, damn – does that make a difference to how you feel when you get out of bed each day! Really, really, really!

Trying to get pregnant? The acceleration of oxygen rich blood-flow induced by exercise is going to help here too, feeding and thickening the uterine lining, ready for implantation of the embryo.

This is not where the list ends; the day-to-day improvements to our life that we experience through regular exercise are endless, and many of the things going on in our miraculous body we might not have linked with exercise before.

Having been a runner almost all my life, having been 'marathon fit', then post-injury unfit, being fit but not performing well, then days of feeling 'on-fire' (also for no obvious reason), I have always been fascinated by the human anatomy and physiology. I am not a doctor, but I have studied the effects on my body from a runner's point of view. In all my years of running, but particularly since I started running marathons, I have observed everything that I'm aware of going on with my body as I run. When I've had pain, or unexpectedly had an 'off day', or when I'm running well and I simply have the energy to observe; I love reading and learning about what might be going on in my body in these different states.

In the next few chapters I will look at some of what I've learnt about what is going on in our body when we exercise and just how far the benefits of exercise extend through our entire body. The challenge in doing this lies in the fact that our body is so complex, with everything working in such perfect equilibrium, it is difficult to break everything down into individual parts. Let's see how I get on...

Chapter Five

Brain, spinal cord, nerves and neurons – Our nervous system

The control centre: our mysterious brain

Our wondrous brain, the most complex of all of our organs, forms a part of our central nervous system. Our central nervous system, working together with our interconnected peripheral nervous system and automatic nervous system, controls and coordinates all of our body's activities. If we begin to look at what is going on in our brain when we run and how running improves our overall brain health even as we age, we can start by looking at coordination. Coordination is defined as 'the ability to use different parts of the body together smoothly and efficiently'; it is the brain running the show here!

Our brain is composed of billions of neurons, with messages being pinged to our brain, around our brain, and from our brain to every other part of our body, non-stop. Our brain controls the non-conscious stuff going on in our body (regulating our heartbeat, making sure our body stays the right temperature), as well as coordinating our conscious movements and actions (for example – arm and leg movement when running). Our brain enables us to think, learn, and makes everyday life possible in each of our different states of consciousness.

Our 'control centre' brain connects to every part of our body in one way or another; controlling hormone levels, breathing, balance, co-ordination, regulating nutrient levels, blood pressure; it is also where feelings and emotions are initiated: for example, hunger, feeling full, thirst, anger and fear. The brain is always awake and alert; even when we sleep our brain ensures our heart keeps beating, that our breathing rhythm is maintained and that it can still detect incoming sensory information and activate the brain into action if necessary (to things that go bump in the night!).

Apart from when we're really concentrated on solving a problem, pretty much everything else that is going on in our brain we take for granted. Thanks to our automatic nervous system, which helps maintain constant conditions in our body ('homeostasis') as well as enable our body to react to sensory nerve messages (for example, receiving messages from the muscles and joints, and relaying instructions to produce precise, coordinated movement), we're free to just get on with our lives. In fact if we were to try and think about everything that is going on in our brain, each micro second, it could literally blow our mind (even for the smartest brain scientists ever to have lived).

Also – perhaps you already refer to using the left, or the right side of the brain for certain activities (the left side typically being associated with logical thinking, and the right side with creative tasks), however our brain can be split into four main structures, including the large cerebrum with its left and right hemispheres. Some processes are controlled by only one part of the brain, however a lot of the stuff happening in our brains requires information to be sent from one part of the brain to another before we can make sense of it (for example, emotions, memory, sight, sounds, smell).

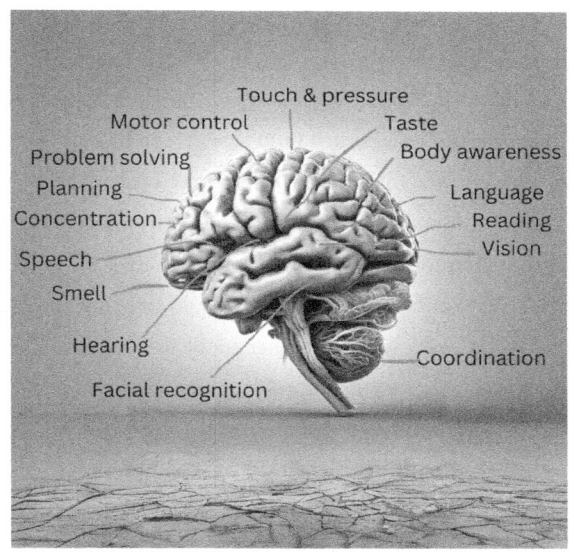

Our remarkable brain, a complex network of billions of neurons, tirelessly orchestrates a symphony of messages. These signals travel to, from, and within the brain, reaching every part of our body. This intricate communication allows us to function effortlessly in our day-to-day lives, autonomously directing bodily actions without our conscious instruction

The brain can also be mapped according to which part of our body it is receiving information from; emotions such as fear are initially processed in one part of the brain, whereas being able to understand what someone is saying when they speak to us is controlled by another part of the brain. Even more fascinating is that there is a separate part in our brain (the putamen) that stores 'subconscious memories' that are formed through repetition. This means that when we repeat certain actions over and over again, our brain stores this ability in a different part of our brain, so that over time, the action becomes 'automatic' to a large degree. The brain is even picking out what information needs to be transferred to 'short term' stores, or to 'long term stores', without us even having to think about it (and if we want to keep something in the long term store, for example learning a new language, then we have to repeat and repeat the new words and phrases until they move from our short-term, to our long-term store).

With help from our putamen, our long-term store is where we want to get our exercise and running habit to reside in our brains. Through repetition and consistency our 'muscle memory' for a given activity becomes stronger, meaning that each time we run it becomes easier to do and recovery is also more efficient. Plus - if we have to have time-out from running for any reason, our body knows what is being asked of it when we restart and we can get back into our running groove much easier and faster then before. This is why we have to keep pulling on our running shoes and getting out there. Even if we don't run very far, or very fast, the frequency with which push ourselves out of our front door each week is what makes our brain recognise running as a regular activity, making it easier to do each time we get out there.

> The brain is this amazingly complex centre of everything in our very day-to-day existence. It also needs a constant, good strong flow of blood and 'food' (glucose) so that it can operate at 100% all of the time, subsequently ensuring that our body is working as efficiently and effectively as is possible.

> In fact, our brain forms only 2% of our bodyweight, but consumes approximately 20% of the body's oxygen via its rich blood supply (without which we'd quickly lose consciousness!)

How does running and exercise help our brain health? The network of blood vessels running throughout our brain is vast, threading through every part of our brain, supplying all of the oxygen and glucose that our brain needs. Not only does running help to maintain the health of these blood vessels, but a good run will also get our blood pumping at a much faster pace than it does when we are sitting down. This accelerated pumping of oxygen rich blood and glucose through these healthy blood vessels is going to help 'feed' all of the nooks and crannies of our brain, meaning that simply by making running a habit, we can continue to live our lives blissfully unaware of all of the crazy stuff our brain has to deal with each millisecond so that we can continue to move/talk/listen/learn/remember etc.

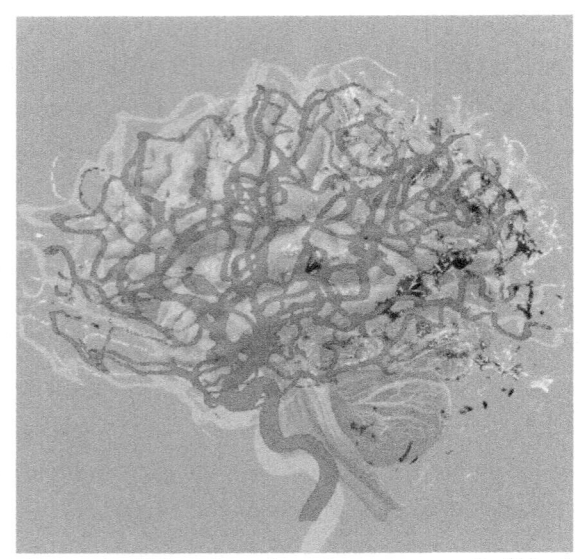

Oxygenated blood flows through a vast network of blood vessels in our brain. When we exercise blood is pumped through at a faster rate; perhaps even helping us to think more clearly?

Be Alert!

With our brain running the show, our nervous system, alive with non-stop electronic pulses, runs through the entirety of our body, sending and receiving messages about what is going on both inside our body but also about everything that is happening externally too. Being alert to what is going on around us not only helps to keep us alive (think not getting run over while crossing the road) but it also enables us to soak up all of the sensory superbness that the world has to offer (think of everything that you love seeing, smelling, feeling, hearing and tasting...) Running outdoors is great for our being more alert. There are two parts to this: first up is the brain stimulus resulting from all of the information our senses are sucking up while out on our run. Our eyes constantly monitoring what lies ahead, noticing the coloured leaves on the ground, how brightly the sun is shining, a discarded banana skin, to be avoided as we adjust our stride slightly so as to step over said skin. Our ears: listening out for cars approaching from behind, hearing the birds calling from the trees as we notice the sound our feet make on the gravel path. Also – feeling our feet rhythmically make contact with the ground, the tension up one leg and then the other. All of this is food for our senses; fitness for our brain. The more we train our brain by exposing it to all of this sensory information, and also if we combine this with moving our body at running pace, which requires us to process information much faster than if we are walking, this is going to improve our levels of alertness in every day life. Why is this useful? Well for starters we know that feeding our brain with sensory information helps in the fight against cognitive diseases as we age, but it also enriches our lives today, for example with on-the-spot decision making. Being able to react quickly to a given situation, and with information flowing faster and more effectively, decision-making will be improved (making the right decision on the spot).

What exactly is going on in our body when we run that is improving our ability to process information quickly? Every second, millions of tiny electrical impulses race through our body's nervous system carrying information about everything that is going on inside our body, as well as processing the information about what is going on around us, external to our body. All of this data is whizzed from the receptor directly to our brain at such a speed, by the time you've thought about how fast this is, already a million more pieces have information have been sent to your brain for processing! The next mind-boggling fact is how quickly our brain can analyse this information and make a decision, without us even having to think about it. We feel a chill and our body shivers, or our knife slips while we're chopping the veg and we pull our hand away in a split second to avoid cutting ourself. Many of these reactions are unconscious and our body just gets on doing what it needs to do (heart rate adjustment, blood pressure control), but there are others where the message is sent to the brain, which then require a conscious reaction, for example: 'danger', or 'hot'. These reactions: 'jump out of the way' or 'pull my hand back' are why we want to ensure our senses and brain remain in tip-top shape. By feeding our body and brain with as much external information as is possible (sight, sound, smell, touch, taste), and at a running pace, this is only going to help the brain stay fit and ready to react to anything!

> Our marvelous brain is processing everything that is going on in our nervous system. Smell and taste are signals relayed through our nose, and mouth; the sense of touch comes from microscopic receptors under our skin, or deeper in our tissue. We react to light, cold and pain as the messages are sent along our spinal cord to the 'touch centre' in our brain.

As with our brain, the rest of our nervous system must have a good supply of oxygen and nutrient rich blood feeding it and keeping it in good working order. If we think of our five senses, our eyes, ears, tongue, nose, and the sensory receptors for touch, these are all filled with tiny blood vessels for which a good supply of blood is essential for our ability to see, hear, taste, smell and feel physical sensations. Raising our heart rate through exercise is going to pump our blood to the very corners of these sensation rich destinations in our body, helping to ensure we're able to interact with the world around us in the most fulfilling way well into old age.

Our nervous system: what happens when things go wrong?

So if it isn't convincing enough looking at the benefits of exercise, how about looking at what can happen if we don't maintain our body and keep it healthy? What if I told you that exercise can help reduce the risks of having a stroke? Or - that exercise can help stave off dementia?

A stroke is caused by disruption of the blood supply to nerve cells in the brain; the result is a loss of function of the body parts those nerve cells serve. Prolonged high blood pressure can damage the tiny blood vessels in the brain, ultimately causing a blockage in the blood flow and then starving the nerve cells of their 'food'. With the body's message centre out of order, the body stops working properly. The result may be weakness or numbness on one side of the body, slurred speech, blurry vision and losing balance; the impact of a stroke can be life-changing.

Exercise is the most effective way to keep our blood pressure under control. Not only does running help to keep these blood vessels supplying our brain fit and healthy, but our blood is pumping much more efficiently around the whole of our body as our fitness improves. Running also helps to improve the composition of our body in terms of muscle mass versus fat; burning calories through exercise and increasing muscle strength will help relieve the strain put on our heart, which in turn will help to keep our blood pressure under control. Running is also proven to reduce stress levels, which is again vital in our quest to keep our heart pumping at a healthy rate and our blood flow at an optimum pressure.

There is a lot of ongoing research into dementia and why some people seem to age 'normally' (occasionally misplacing car keys, struggling to find a word but remembering it later) and those who develop dementia (lose ability to reason, or problem solve, not being able to complete tasks independently). However it is known that poor heart health, high blood pressure and high cholesterol can all increase the risk of developing dementia. It has also been proven that keeping our brain active in problem solving and giving it regular stimulus ensures that the right electrical pulses are firing across our brain, helping to stave off cognitive decline. If we consider that 'regular use' is effectively exercise for our brain, we know that:

Exercise = fitness, and fitness = health

How does running help in all of this? Regular exercise plays a significant role in brain health. Aside from the benefits to keeping our heart healthy and our blood pressure under control, think of all the different stimuli we come across, even when we go out for a walk. The smells, the sounds, the freshness of rain on our skin, the sight of the sun; our senses being awakened, our brain stimulated by sensations from every part of our body. Pulses firing through our brain; information,

information, information. This live intelligence about what is going on in the world around us helps to keep our brain and mind firing on all cylinders. And the exercise we are doing, whether it be walking or running, is going to get our heart rate up, our blood flowing faster, providing oxygenised blood to our brain at an accelerated rate. A double-whammy of goodness! And – if you think about it, you must already know how invigorated you feel after a walk in the open air?

Current research suggests that chronic migraines are also linked to the brain and a disturbance in the activity of brain chemicals. It is thought that the brain rewiring causing this disturbance happens over time, with stress being a major contributing factor. Stress is often also the trigger for the onset of a chronic migraine (nausea, blurred vision, vomiting, being bedridden). While there is no cure and medication doesn't help, it is known that finding ways to reduce and manage stress can cut the risk of migraines. With regular exercise proven to help in how we deal with stress, and even reduce stress levels, getting fit is going to help keep those migraines at bay! Could it reverse the disturbances in the brain altogether? Perhaps; but at the very least it may help to prevent the brain from further rewiring itself.

Chapter Six

I heart you lungs

I see you: C.V. (cardiovascular system)

The heart, oh how I love the heart! Our entire body is of course amazing, however the heart, the sophisticated little pumping system and the way in which it partners perfectly with our lungs, always leaves me in awe of this special temple we inhabit!

Every single cell of our body relies on the steady circulation of life-giving blood; providing oxygen and nutrients, and removing carbon dioxide and waste products from those same cells. Good, healthy blood circulation, pumped around our body by a strong healthy heart is going to help ensure that we live a long, healthy life. Having just seen some of the reasons why having an oxygen rich supply of blood pumping through our body is vital for keeping our brain healthy and our nervous system in good working order; it is also vital for the health of our heart itself. More than that still, the blood pumped around our body by our heart feeds our respiratory system, digestive system, muscles, bones, skin, hair, nails, immune system, and reproductive system. Put very simply, our heart is in itself, worth thirty minutes of exercise a couple of times a week.

Our cardiovascular system is powered by our strong, pumping heart muscle. This incredibly powerful organ of ours forces oxygen rich blood through our tough, elastic arteries, which divide into millions of tiny capillaries, the walls of which are so thin that the oxygen and nutrients can pass out of the capillaries to the cells and tissue in our body. The 'waste products', including CO2 (carbon dioxide), which our body doesn't need and can be harmful to us if allowed to accumulate, are then collected from the cells, passing into the blood via these same tiny capillaries. The blood containing the waste products flows from our capillaries, into our veins and our veins carry the waste products to the appropriate organ so that they can be expelled from our body. Once the waste disposal has been completed at the appropriate organ, the blood flows back to the heart via our veins, where the blood will be re-oxygenated. So repeats this cycle, every heartbeat, approximately 100,000 times every day, for the rest of our lives.

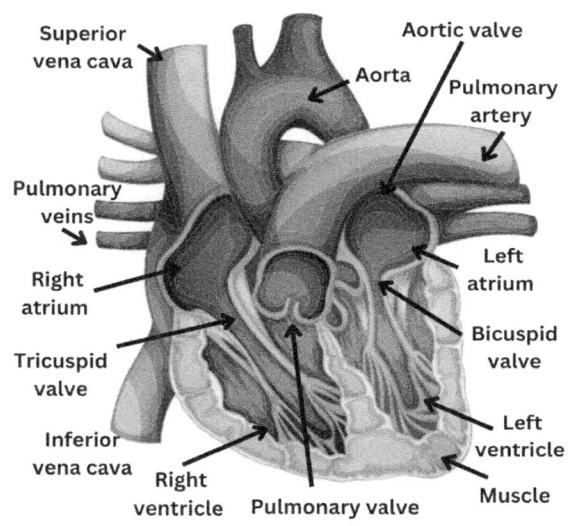

Divided into four chambers, the left and right sides of our heart don't communicate. Oxygenated blood from the lungs enters the left atrium (via the pulmonary vein) and deoxygenated blood from the body enters the right atrium (from the vena cava). The heart muscle relaxes to allow the blood to flow into the corresponding left or right ventricle and then contracts to force the blood out of the heart and around the body. Clever valves prevent the blood from flowing back the wrong way

Fun fact? The network of arteries, veins and capillaries in our body extends for more than 100,000 km, or 60,000 miles, meaning that if we laid our blood vessels end-to-end in one continuous string, we could wrap it around Earth two and a half times! That is a phenomenal distance for our heart to be pumping our blood with every beat, and if we want to be living a healthy and active life into old age, is precisely why we want to keep our heart to be tip-top condition!

Our heart is only about the size of a clenched fist, and its muscular wall is constantly active. Twenty-four hours a day. And unless something has gone wrong, it will never stops beating until the day we die. As well as having its own electrical system to control its rhythm, the heart has its very own blood supply, carrying the oxygen and energy needed to make sure the heart can keep beating. It is so important that this blood-flow to the heart itself continues uninterrupted, that there are 'emergency' connecting vessels between our coronary arteries (arteries that supply blood to the heart muscle). If one of these arteries becomes blocked, there is an alternative route for the blood to flow.

Blockages in blood vessels can starve tissue of oxygen and can cause issues anywhere in the body; a blockage in the blood flow to the heart is known as coronary artery disease (or coronary heart disease) and is caused by plaque buildup in the wall of the arteries. The plaque forms gradually, with fatty deposits and cholesterol two of the main culprits. The result is that over time arteries become more and more narrow until eventually the blood can't flow anymore. We're talking heart attack, angina, embolism, thrombosis and strokes.

Regular exercise and a healthy diet help to reduce our risk of heart disease. Obviously by reducing the amount of bad fat and bad cholesterol we consume, we also reduce our risk of heart disease in the first place. However exercise plays many roles in both helping our body process any cholesterol and fats we're eating today but also in ridding our body of any excess cholesterol that has already accumulated over the years. Ideally we want to be exercising until our heart rate is such that our blood is pumping so fast around our arteries, there is less opportunity for the plaque to build up in the first place. And if cholesterol levels in the body are already high, exercising until we've worked up a good sweat is a good sign that the battle against the bad stuff is in full swing! So – if you're a fan of a Full English Breakfast, lesson number one is to not eat it too often (so limiting the amount of bad fats and cholesterol we're ingesting in the first place) but lesson number two is that regular exercise is going to help reduce the health risks associated with enjoying the occasional F.E.B.

'Vigorous exercise', where we are raising our heart rate to two, or three times more than our resting heart rate, will look different for each of us (depending on age, current level of fitness etc. etc.). However elevating our heart rate for a period of at least twenty minutes, is what we want to slowly work towards. This is what is going to help keep our arteries clean, and both our arteries and our heart healthy and strong.

While our heart primarily consists of cardiac muscle, which is only found in the heart and is different to skeletal muscle because it contracts and relaxes automatically, it is still muscle. So despite the fact that cardiac muscle never gets tired and (assuming there's a good, healthy blood supply) our heart will keep on beating away without any conscious effort, it is still very much within our power to make it stronger and 'fitter'. Again - we can do this through exercise that raises our heart rate, ideally maintaining a higher heartbeat for at least twenty minutes with each exercise session we do.

Over to you O2

Oxygen, oxygen, oxygen... Where would we be without oxygen? Well

– very simply, we wouldn't. Essential for life, we breathe air in through our nose and mouth, and our respiratory system takes the oxygen from the air and transfers it into our blood (where our cardiovascular system can distribute the oxygen around our body). What actually happens to the air in our lungs when we breathe in and out and how the heart and the lungs work in perfect harmony, is – again – exquisite.

For us, it isn't complicated; we breathe in and the air travels down our trachea (windpipe) into our lungs. We breathe in oxygen from the air and we breathe out carbon dioxide. So what is this magic that is happening in our body, 'transforming' oxygen into CO_2?

> Our lungs are sponge-like structures, with the air flowing in through a primary bronchus (airway) and from there travelling to tiny bronchioles, before arriving into one of the millions of microscopic alveoli (air sacs) that we house in each lung. This is where the magic happens! It is via the millions of alveoli and the surrounding capillaries that the oxygen from the air we breathe diffuses into our blood, quickly bonding with the haemoglobin in our red blood cells. At the same time the CO_2, travelling in our deoxygenated blood as a waste product from our cells, is dropped off by our pulmonary arterioles; the CO_2 will effectively swap places with the oxygen that we have just breathed in, and pass back from the alveoli into the lungs ready for exhalation. In the meantime, the freshly oxygenated blood is whisked away along the pulmonary venule, through the pulmonary vein and into the heart, ready to be circulated around the entire body.

Trachea
Bronchus
Heart
Right lung
Left lung
Bronchiole
Alveoli

Diaphragm

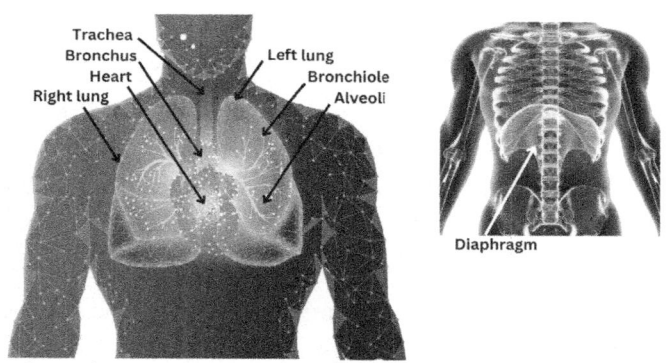

The trachea (windpipe) divides into two bronchi which enter the left and right lung before dividing into smaller bronchioles. These then divide into millions of alveoli (air sacs) where the dense network of capillaries allow the exchange of oxygen for carbon dioxide. The diaphragm is a large, dome-shaped muscle located at the base of the lungs and the top of the abdomen. When we inhale, the diaphragm contracts and flattens, expanding the chest cavity and allowing the lungs to fill with air. Upon exhalation, the diaphragm relaxes and returns to its dome shape, helping to expel air from the lungs

In fact, when we breathe in, while our lungs are responsible for the gas exchange of oxygen in place of carbon dioxide, it is our diaphragm, a large dome-shaped muscle which sits at the base of our chest, working together with the muscles that sit between each rib (our intercostal muscles), which form the body's main breathing muscle.

The underlying need to breathe is regulated by a non-conscious process happening in our brain, according to the amount of oxygen and CO_2 we have in our blood. When we are 'at rest', the rate at which we breathe is largely controlled by our diaphragm; we breathe roughly twelve to seventeen times every minute and approximately half a litre of air shifts in and out with each breath. When we exercise however, we shift to what is known as 'forceful inhalation'. This works all of our breathing muscles much harder, but also enlists the help of our neck and chest muscles to ensure that our lungs have enough room within our ribcage to stretch and allow in more oxygen. In fact, when we exercise, we can suck in an extra two litres of air with each breath. If you then consider that forced exhalation expels almost as much, it means there is more than four litres of air moving in and out with each forced breath. If you add in the faster rate at which you breathe while exercising (perhaps increasing up to 36 – 51 breaths per minute), the total air exchange can be twenty times more when exercising than when at rest.

Why is this a good thing? With our breathing relying on the muscular diaphragm and intercostals, through regular exercise and pushing our breathing to the point of exertion, we can strengthen these critical muscles and make them more flexible. So for starters, this means no more getting out of breath after climbing a flight of stairs, as well as being able to run for longer than a minute without having to stop and gasp for breath. Deep, or forced breathing has also been proven to be good for our nervous system; working our phrenic nerves (which controls our diaphragm), stimulating our vagus nerves (digestion, heart rate, immune system, mood etc.) as well as improving how different areas of our brain communicate with one another (good for our coordination, among other things).

The muscles of our diaphragm (contracting and relaxing), intercostals (making ribs swing in and out), sternocleidomastoid (neck), scalenes (connecting the vertebrae to the top two ribs) and pectoralis minor (pulls up third, forth and fifth rib) can all be trained to become more flexible. Similar to trying to touch our toes every day for six months, just spending a couple of minutes each day, reaching for our toes and trying to get a millimetre closer, after a few months we'd be closer to touching our toes (if not touching them already); the same can be said for expanding our lung capacity. Through exercise we are training these muscles to be more flexible; allowing more air (and oxygen) in with each breath, our cardiorespiratory system becoming more efficient, so enabling us to be more active without getting out of breath. In fact – the improved efficiency as we get fitter even means our rate of breathing slows down when we are resting. This is good. This means that when we are at rest, our body really is able to 'take it easier', our heart rate slowing, we feel more relaxed and less 'on edge'.

If we want to visualise what is happening as we're making these muscles more flexible each time we go out for a run, or push ourself to the point where we're out of breath but keep going anyway, we can imagine an uninflated balloon that we've just taken out of a brand new packet. When we first take out the new balloon the plastic feels thick and stiff, it is difficult to stretch and if we try and blow air into it the balloon barely inflates. Now we stretch the balloon before trying to blow air into it, pulling it by each end until the plastic stretches a bit more each time. Now when we blow into the balloon, it immediately inflates and we can blow more and more air into it, until no more air fits. The stiff, new, uninflatable balloon is equivalent to our respiratory system if we haven't done any exercise for a long time. There is enough air and oxygen getting into our body to keep us alive, but if we do anything that raises our heart rate and increases the need for oxygen (so speeding up our breathing), we get out of breath almost immediately. So – just like the balloon, we need to make the muscles in our respiratory system more flexible. We do this through repeated exercise, running until we're out of breath and then trying to run a little bit further.

This is the key to our being able to get fitter and by pushing ourselves just a little bit further, we strengthen our respiratory muscles and improve their flexibility. Our breathing steadily becomes more efficient as a result; we take more air and oxygen into our lungs with each breath, our blood is richer in oxygen and therefore in a resting state our heart doesn't have to work so hard just to keep us alive. Why is this good? Well – it means lower blood pressure for one thing, with our heart able to pump all of the oxygen that our body needs to function properly in fewer beats per minute.

The perfect partnership

Good lung and heart health are vital if we want a long and active life, and with our respiratory system and our cardiovascular system working in synergy to provide oxygen to each individual cell in our body, we must look after both. If we let either weaken, the other will also weaken faster as we age. On the flip-side, keeping our lungs healthy and in 'regular training' (with regular exercise) means that all of the tiny bronchioles stay fit and healthy, as will all of the capillaries and arterioles in our lungs. This will help maintain the strength of our lungs and the muscles in our chest. Everything will be easier as we age: carrying shopping, climbing the stairs, playing with grandchildren, hitting the dance floor… Likewise with our heart, if our lungs are more efficient with the amount of oxygen we can transfer into our blood with each breath, our heart doesn't have to work so hard just to keep us alive. And lower blood pressure means no heart palpitations after a small amount of activity, it is easier to relax, easier to get to sleep, and we can sleep more deeply and possibly for longer (if we so wish).

Healthy lungs and a healthy heart really do go together hand-in-hand. And although feeling out of breath after running for only a minute is frustrating, if we keep 'stretching at the balloon', exercising until we are out of breath and then exercising a little bit more, we will soon be able to go for longer. And – if we keep repeating this week after week, for a period of a few months, our breathing will continue to become more efficient; our heart rate and breathing slow down while still providing our body with all of the oxygen it needs. Once we have achieved this level of fitness, all of our daily activities become easier and less tiring.

There is also the 'muscle memory' element to consider; once we have noticed that our resting heart rate has slowed down as a result of our improved fitness, our muscles will be at the stage where they are better able to maintain their strength. So if for any reason we can't exercise for a couple of weeks, while the first run we do after the time-out will be more difficult than it was when we were at full fitness, it won't be like starting from scratch. In fact, when we go out for our second run, because our muscles 'remember' all of the work that went in prior to our time-out, we will feel like we're almost back to our previous fitness levels.

Chapter Seven

Feeding the mind, body and soul – Our digestive system

Unlike some of our bodily systems, we are much more aware of what is happening with our digestive system (or at least parts of it). Our digestive tract is approximately nine metres long from our mouth to our butt. It is responsible for digesting the food we eat and ensuring that our body extracts all of the nutrients it needs to keep us active and functioning, then finally for expelling any waste. Another part of our fully-integrated 'smart body', our digestive system doesn't work in isolation but is fully dependent on the right hormone messaging as well as a strong, healthy supply of blood.

To kick the whole digestive process off, we need to jump to our endocrine system and a hormone called Ghrelin, also known as the 'hunger hormone' for the logical reason that it stimulates our appetite (although it also has many other vital functions within our body). Basically when our body recognises that it needs food, Ghrelin is secreted by our stomach; this hormone messenger then signals to our brain (nervous system) that it is time to eat. We might experience 'hunger pangs', a grumbling stomach, and the sight of food may even make us dribble a bit as our saliva glands kick into action...

Once we've succumbed to the sounds of our hunger, the food we eat passes down our oesophagus into our stomach where the process of breaking down the food to a 'semi liquid' begins. This semi liquid then passes into our small intestine, where it is further broken down and all of the nutrients from the digestible food can be absorbed into the blood and lymph (we'll come on to our lymphatic system shortly). Finally, our large intestine (colon), which is home to lots of important gut microbiota, gets to deal with the indigestible leftover waste product, eventually expelling it from our body.

Food travels through our digestive system by muscular contraction, which is an automatic process within our body, again requiring a healthy blood supply to these muscles, but also a healthy, balanced diet to keep these muscles strong (fibre gives these muscles a good workout and is therefore essential to our diet). This isn't where our digestive processes stop however; our liver is also involved, as is our gall bladder, and our pancreas.

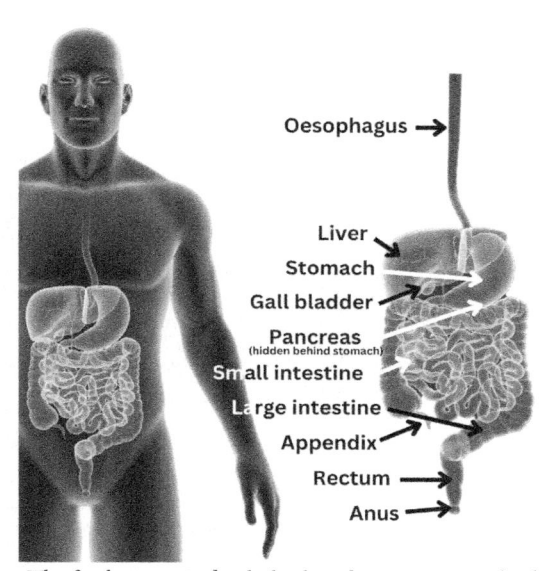

Oesophagus
Liver
Stomach
Gall bladder
Pancreas (hidden behind stomach)
Small intestine
Large intestine
Appendix
Rectum
Anus

The food we eat is slowly broken down as it travels along the nine-meter long digestive tract, with the nutrients absorbed by the dense network of blood capillaries that form part of the small intestine. Waste products from the food we eat that our body can't use, pass into the large intestine before being expelled from the body

When we exercise, our body needs more nutrients. Our muscles need more energy, our brain is more stimulated (particularly if we are running outdoors); our heart is beating faster, sending blood pulsing through our body and to our lungs at a higher rate; all of this burns through considerably more calories than sitting on the sofa does! As the food we eat passes through our small intestine, our blood absorbs all of the nutrients we need to power the cells in our body enabling us to exercise. In fact we continue to burn through these energy stores in our cells even after exercise; as our muscles cool down we are still burning calories at a faster rate than normal.

This process of converting the nutrients in our food into energy that our body can use to power itself is a 'metabolic process'. After eating a healthy meal, our intestine delivers the nutrient rich blood to the liver (the body's largest internal organ). Our liver converts sugars into glycogen (providing energy to our cells), makes amino acids (proteins for our cells), as well as processing all of the vitamins.

The liver is also our body's own super-detoxing machine, removing harmful substances from the blood, for example alcohol and metabolic waste products, but the list of functions our liver plays, essential for maintaining our overall health, is a long one, even including recycling our red blood cells. In fact, the often underrated liver, which receives not one, but two blood supplies via our 'hepatic portal' circulation, is vital in deciding what happens to our food once it has been digested. When we exercise our cells are more active and our body demands more amino acids, fats (needed for the cell membrane) and glucose (the 'simple sugar', providing energy to the cell). Any surplus glucose that our body doesn't immediately need is converted into glycogen and stockpiled. If we don't use this stockpiled energy (by burning calories) then our body will convert this excess glucose into body fat (watch out for the weight gain!). However – if the body is running low on glucose (we're using more than we're consuming), it can use these stored fats to power the cells in our body instead (how we lose weight). So the weight-loss equation of 'calories burned being greater than calories consumed' is indeed confirmed:

Calories burned > calories consumed => weight loss

(Assumes no underlying medical condition impacting weight loss)

Lovin' the Leptin

Did your parents ever tell you to "chew your food properly" when you were growing up? Ok – probably partly because they didn't want us to choke to death on our Brussels sprouts, but also so that we would actually taste the food that they had so lovingly prepared for us. Aside from these reasons however, eating more slowly gives our body the opportunity to let us know that we're full. Leptin is the hormone at work here and is released by our body as a signal to the brain that we've consumed enough fuel and we should stop eating. If we eat too quickly, we can easily over-eat before our body has the chance to send the 'stop' signal. It is also possible to just ignore the signal, and carry on eating anyway (roll-on full bloaty-bloaty feeling for the next two hours!) There is still a lot of research being done on leptin and the role it plays in our bodily functions but when respected, it is definitely our friend. When our levels are balanced and in-tune with our body, it helps with mood regulation and brain function; when leptin becomes less efficient in our body, it can play a role in weight-gain, mood swings and brain fog.

The amount of leptin in our blood is directly proportional to the amount of fat in our body, and the best way to keep our leptin in check is through exercise and eating a healthy, balanced diet. To warn against crash dieting as a way to lose weight, the way leptin works in our body means that dieting can actually make our body think it is starving and a feeling of intense hunger is stimulated. This can lead to difficult to ignore cravings, which may actually then result in increased food consumption and in our gaining weight rather than losing the pounds we'd hoped to. This is one of the many reasons dieting is so difficult to maintain over a long period of time and why we're much more likely to keep our weight where we want it to be if we are exercise regularly.

Staving off the Lymphatic System lymp

The lesser-known lymphatic system consists of vessels ('veins'), nodes, ducts, patches, as well as our spleen, tonsils and thymus. It is vital in maintaining our health and well-being, keeping our digestive system in good working order as well as the homeostasis of our body (keeping the systems in our body in balance).

Our lymph vessels transport 'lymph', a fluid that circulates slowly around our body, helping to distribute nutrients and collecting fats from our digestive system as well as the stuff our body doesn't need. The lymph fluid transports immune cells but also removes waste products (including bacteria and viruses) such that they can be expelled from our body and so plays a key role in our immune response but also in cleansing our body of toxins.

> Our lymphatic system plays an important role in weight loss, absorbing digestive fat from our small intestine where it can either be used as energy or removed as waste. It also helps maintain fluid balance in the body, preventing the buildup of excess

> fluids that could lead to tissue swelling (edema). In contrast, a poorly functioning lymphatic system, which doesn't properly deal with dietary fats, can lead to weight gain and difficulty in losing weight.

Lymph transport around our body, which works by peristalsis (alternate relaxation and contraction of the muscular vessels that carry the lymph, squeezing it along the tubes in our body), is pretty slow and sporadic. In the average resting person, the flow may be as little as 125ml per hour, or an estimated four litres per day. However - when we exercise, the flow of lymph is elevated several times over, and working together with our circulatory system, helps our body drain excess fluid, get rid of any toxic waste as quickly as possible, deal with dietary fats as well as promote immune system health.

> Have you heard of lymphatic tapping? The idea is that by using our hands we tap (slap) along the lines of our lymphatic system in such a way that we stimulate the flow of lymph, boosting our immune system and our blood circulation. Running is going to boost the flow for us anyway, however I can highly recommend giving the left and right sides of your neck a good rub (top to bottom) in the shower each morning to help shake off the post-sleep sluggishness. Perhaps try using a daily exfoliating cleanser on your neck at the same time and kill two birds with one stone?

So - with the lymphatic system involved as well, our complex digestive system is directly reliant on messaging and support from our nervous, muscular, cardiovascular, respiratory, lymph and (as we'll see) our endocrine system; all working together so that we can function and survive.

Chapter Eight

You'd be nothing without me – Skeleton & muscle

Dem bones

Did you know that as an adult we have 206 bones in our body? How about the fact that our bones are at their peak mass and peak condition in our early twenties? Or that once we're in our twenties our skeleton is constantly breaking down and renewing itself, with most of the adult skeleton replaced every ten years? As well as providing protective housing for everything sitting inside our body, one of the most vital roles of our skeleton is the fact that in our long bones we have spongy bone marrow tissue containing stem cells, which produce our blood cells; red, white and platelets. These bones are actually also packed with a network of blood vessels, which provide the nourishment essential for their maintenance and for the continuous renewal and restructuring of the bone tissue.

Unfortunately we don't yet know how to hit the 'stop' button on bone ageing and by the time we hit the age of forty we slowly begin to lose bone mass. While genetics and our environment contribute to bone health and it is well known that vitamin D is vital for keeping our bones strong, exercise is also critically important in maintaining a strong skeletal system into old age. In fact, contrary to what some people say, running actually helps stave off osteoporosis in later life. This is multifaceted; first we have the improved flow of oxygen and nutrient rich blood flowing through our bones (literally right through them), but assuming we're wearing the right running shoes, there is also significant benefit to our bone density, which according to Wolff's Law is a result of the impact our feet make with the ground with each stride we take.

As we age, decreasing oestrogen levels mean women are more prone to osteoporosis, however men will experience a decline in testosterone levels, which can also lead to loss of bone mineral density and weakened, fragile bones. Running, coupled with a diet including plenty of calcium, vitamin D, magnesium, vitamin K and protein, can help maintain good bone mass as we age. Having optimal bone health as we get older is going to help reduce the risk of age-related bone loss and any annoying fractures (or hip replacements) that reduce our mobility or mean we become dependent on having a carer.

What about our joints? Amazingly our body has more than 300 different joints, most of which are freely moving synovial joints, with the ends of the connecting bones covered by the connective tissue, cartilage. The cartilage is kept well-oiled and nourished by synovial fluid, which is secreted by the synovial membrane in the joints. Cartilage is the 'shock absorbing' material that sits between our joints and whether we exercise or not, our knee cartilage naturally becomes thinner as we age. However the joints that we use while running, in particular the knee, are stabilised by external ligaments and supported by the surrounding muscles. By running, we can build the strength of the muscles surrounding our joints, and if we wear the right footwear, running is more likely to help delay osteoarthritis than be the cause of it. With this degenerative joint disease affecting many people after the age of about sixty to some degree or another, we are less likely to suffer pain in our joints if we're active and keeping fit.

While cartilage can help to promote the healing of bones, it has a limited ability to repair itself. Research is ongoing as to how re-grow cartilage in the joints, particularly with a view to helping people who suffered bad sports injuries at a young age, in the meantime we do have to take very good care of our bone cartilage and keeping the muscles around our joints good and strong is going to help.

The hustle with our muscle

Our skeletal system would be useless without our muscle tissue, but our muscular body system does so much more than just help us move around. Muscle powers our heart, breathing and our digestive system (to name but a few of the vital bodily processes for which we need strong muscles). How do we keep muscles strong and healthy? Through regular use and training.

We have 640 muscles in total in our body, split into three main types: skeletal muscles (helping us to move), smooth muscle (e.g. blood vessels and airways) and cardiac muscle, which forms the walls of the heart. Our muscles rely on our nervous system for instructions and on a healthy blood supply to provide the oxygen and the energy they need to contract.

Since our skeletal muscles can only contract (pull) or relax, they must work together in pairs that act in opposition to each other, with the movement produced by one of the muscles in the pair reversed by the second. In reality, we rarely just use the two muscles to move but whole teams of muscles are engaged to achieve the precise movement in a given direction.

> How do our muscles know when to contract or to relax? Our muscles, ligaments and tendons have tiny sensors in them, which send messages to our brain, so our muscles know exactly what they need to do at any one time. This is how our body senses its own position, posture, and movement, and is known as 'proprioception'. (Note that kinesthesia is closely related to proprioception but specifically focuses on the sensation of movement). These signals sent from our muscles to our brain integrate with information sent from our eyes and ears, and from this combined package of information we know how quickly we are moving and we can stabilise our body as well as coordinate our movements. As confounding as it is clever, right?

With all of the work that our muscles and tendons do for us and the much-improved quality of life they provide us with when fit and healthy, we must take extra special care of them. When we are exercising, and if we want to avoid injury it helps to understand why we might strain a muscle and what is going on with the muscle as it is damaged. This is covered in Part Three.

Unfortunately most of us now live a life that means we're at high-risk of becoming a patient of the 'sitting disease', with our work life demanding that we sit at a computer seven or eight hours a day, five days a week. We might stand up and go for lunch, or walk fifty metres to go to the bathroom a few times each day, otherwise our muscles sit cold, lazy and flaccid, using just enough strength to hold us upright in our office chair. Given what our body and our muscles are capable of and how quickly we can build our strength with just a little concentrated effort, this lifestyle that we've designed for ourselves is really quite depressing. It is depressing for our body too. How frustrating for our muscles that we allow to them to wilt to the point where we can't even carry heavy bags for more than a hundred metres, or have the strength to lift an object from a shelf above our head. No wonder either that we're quickly put off the idea of exercise when even walking for an hour leaves us feeling tired and our legs complaining for three days afterwards.

With our newfound running habit, coupled with exercise to complement our running, thankfully we don't have to be this person. By looking after ourself and keeping our body strong, our future self can still carry shopping bags and has the strength to do the spring clean and go for daily walks; we're able to remain mobile and self-sufficient until our dying day.

Chapter Nine

Regulate! – Our endocrine system

Of all of our eleven bodily systems, working together to maintain the health and efficiency of the entire body, the skeletal system, the muscular system, the nervous system, cardiovascular etc. one we might not so readily appreciate is our endocrine system. Consisting of glands and glandular tissues, our endocrine system is where our hormones (or 'chemical messengers') are produced and is responsible for regulating the hormone levels in our body.

Our knowledge of hormones and the role they play in keeping us fit and healthy is steadily improving, however the massive importance of hormonal balance on our overall well-being, and how both internal and external factors are at play with our hormones still isn't getting the attention it deserves.

Hormones circulate in our blood (and other fluids) and help maintain the optimal internal environment for our body. Think of melatonin, which regulates our sleep; think oestrogen and progesterone (regulating the menstrual cycle, supporting pregnancy and oestrogen is also important for bone strength); think testosterone, which is the primary sex hormone in males. But the endocrine system is much more than the titillation arising when we see someone we fancy the pants off, our thyroid gland plays a vital role in the maintenance of body weight, how quickly our body uses energy but also our heart rate. Our stomach secretes hormones that digest our food, our kidneys secrete a hormone that helps produce red blood cells in our bone marrow, and our adrenal glands regulate metabolism as well as producing adrenaline. The pancreas regulates blood sugar levels and also makes sure our cells have the energy they need. The list goes on:

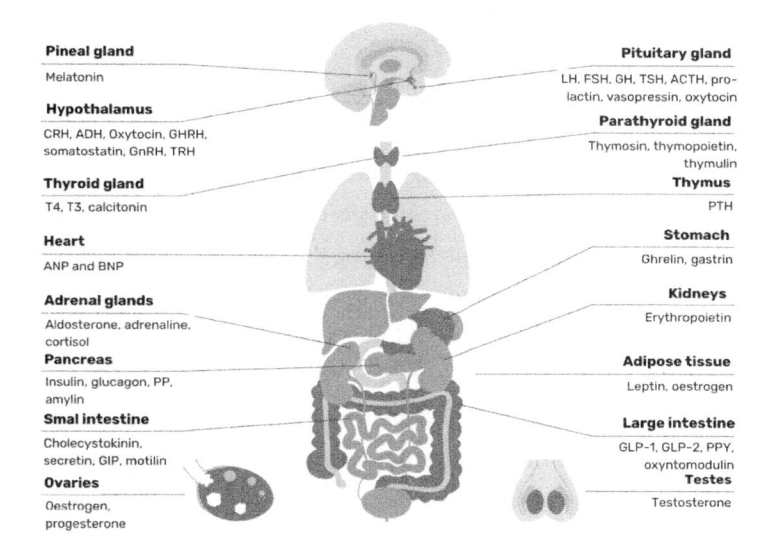

Pineal gland	**Pituitary gland**
Melatonin	LH, FSH, GH, TSH, ACTH, prolactin, vasopressin, oxytocin
Hypothalamus	**Parathyroid gland**
CRH, ADH, Oxytocin, GHRH, somatostatin, GnRH, TRH	Thymosin, thymopoietin, thymulin
Thyroid gland	**Thymus**
T4, T3, calcitonin	PTH
Heart	**Stomach**
ANP and BNP	Ghrelin, gastrin
Adrenal glands	**Kidneys**
Aldosterone, adrenaline, cortisol	Erythropoietin
Pancreas	**Adipose tissue**
Insulin, glucagon, PP, amylin	Leptin, oestrogen
Smal intestine	**Large intestine**
Cholecystokinin, secretin, GIP, motilin	GLP-1, GLP-2, PPY, oxyntomodulin
Ovaries	**Testes**
Oestrogen, progesterone	Testosterone

Hormones and the endocrine system are integral components of the human body's internal communication network. Hormones are chemical messengers produced by the endocrine glands and secreted directly into the bloodstream where they travel to various organs and tissues and play crucial roles in regulating metabolism, growth, development, reproduction, and mood, among other things

As a woman, we have to allow for some heaviness in our legs for a day or two around our period and as our hormone levels shift around. This is actually a good time to go for a run if we're able to however because it just keeps everything in check and moving along as it should do. Giving our hormones a little

> 'HIIT training' at our time of the month and also making sure we have a good oxygen supply to the new cells that are forming and replacing the cells we have lost is only going to be good for our reproductive system

Because hormones are carried in the blood, we come again to the fact that we need our blood flow to be strong and healthy; pumped to each tiny corner of our body, ensuring the chemical messaging can happen at the right time and in the right way such that our body can continue to function as it should. But aside from helping to ensure our hormones are carried to the required destination within our body, exercise also stimulates the production of certain hormones. Examples include: growth hormone, testosterone and insulin-like growth factor-1 (IGF-1), which help to regulate metabolism, enable muscle growth and improve bone density (to name a few). Also the hormone prolactin, which plays a role in our reproductive functions, immune system, glucose homeostasis, insulin secretion (reducing the risk of type-2 diabetes) as well as behavioral responses (again - to name but a few of the currently known roles this hormone plays). "Exercise can help reduce stress levels" – yes, but not just because we're getting out into the fresh air and gifting ourselves some headspace; the small spike in cortisol released while exercising has been proven to suppress the cortisol response to every day stresses ('fight or flight' response), so promoting 'stress resilience'. This ability to better regulate cortisol reduces the risks associated with sustained high levels, such as weight gain, high blood pressure and immune system dysfunction. Improved energy levels? Yes – going back to the thyroid again, exercise can help to regulate and improve thyroid function and how our body uses energy.

Perhaps better advertised is the fact that exercise is also known to increase the production of endorphins and our levels of the chemicals serotonin and dopamine. Known for their mood-enhancing and pain-relieving effects, these help induce a sense of well-being and reduce the risk of depression and other mood disorders.

Do we need any more evidence that exercise is more than just a workout for our muscles? Are we going to wake up each morning thanking our endocrine system for all it does to keep us in good working order and promise that we will look after it equally in return by getting out these each day for some exercise? Perhaps we should all begin our day with the mantra:

Endocrine exercise = endocrine fitness = good endocrine health = superhero self

Chapter Ten

Running for weight loss

Aside from helping us to sleep better and keeping our hormone levels in-check, running is a great way to lose weight. However - as with any long-lasting changes that we want to make in our life, we will have to be persistent with our mission over a longer period of time.

Why do we eat? As human beings, it is well documented that our relationship with food has changed over time; what we eat, how often we eat and most of all, how much we eat. However the need to feed our body with enough energy so that it can continue to operate (heart beating, breathing, thinking, moving) is the very basic reason why we need to eat. If we didn't eat and our body wasn't getting the simple energy that it needs, we'd waste away and eventually we'd die.

If we look at what has changed and why, we go to our taste buds and the messages that these juicy fellows send to our brains, which combined with the smell of the food we inhale as we eat, we have this complex experience of flavour. In a split second, our brain is processing the smell, taste and 'mouth feel' of food as it touches the tongue. We might also be influenced by how the food looks before we put it in our mouth and some people even think that the sound of eating certain types of food may send messages to our brain about whether we like a food or not.

We are also very good at storing this information in our memory banks and if you ask anyone what food they dislike, or for their list of favourite foods, these would likely roll-off the tongue. When we like a particular food, our combined senses can set-off a rush of dopamine (our feel-good hormone), which is in itself an addictive feeling.

Some chefs have used this knowledge to experiment and figure out what gets us going with the whole eating experience. We can now go to their restaurant's and have a 'multi-sensory' meal, where colour, clever flavour combinations and smell take us to a happy place. Or – how about eating in the dark? Just how important is sight when it comes to enjoying what we put in our mouth?

This new-found level of eating being an experience in itself is all very well if we make an effort to make a flavour-full vegetable dish that gets our taste buds tingling at the mere thought of it. However - in a world where 'man-made' ultra-processed foods are often cheaper than fresh fruit and veg, this new knowledge we have about what makes certain foods addictive has been abused in creating stuff we eat that has no nutritional value at all. Aside from the couple of seconds of pleasure we get from eating junk food, we are putting our long-term health at risk (while making some big company and a couple of people at the top of that company a tidy profit along the way). Ultra-processed foods with high levels of added sugar, salt, fat content and E-numbers to make the flavour more appealing are the real danger foods. When reaching for the packet of sugary biscuits, the sausage roll, the crisps, the fast-food burger or the average chocolate bar, remember that these have been specifically made to trigger an addiction by way of dopamine release in our brains. With such high levels of salt, sugar and fat, coupled with the fact that these foods are made to make you want to eat more of them, it is a double-whammy of bad calories! So when eating a sugar or fat-laden food we should always ask ourselves "is this really going to make me happy when I eat this, or is it a moment of pleasure and afterwards I'll feel rubbish for having indulged?" If it is that second of pleasure we were looking for, we can take a minute and imagine how we'll feel after we've given in to temptation and if it is really worth the ongoing feeling of guilt that we've just eaten half a chocolate bar in one go, or snuck into the fast-food restaurant for a quick/easy/dirty burger?

It is also important to know that we can actually wean ourselves off certain food and drink if we so choose. Because our smell and taste neurons regenerate every few weeks, over time we can train ourselves to avoid certain foods and to appreciate other (hopefully healthier) flavours more. Following this theory, if we can abstain from a certain food until we forget the pleasure it brought us then it will get easier to say "no" to in the future. This sounds less challenging than it is however, as anyone who has tried to give up a food or drink they enjoy will know. Getting through the initial cravings in the first fortnight, then the "one won't do me any harm" mindset during the next couple of months; depending on our willpower, realistically it probably takes about a year for our taste buds to forget the pleasure of a given flavour. Even then we have to be aware of certain triggers that may make us relapse, or putting ourselves in a situation where we have no choice but to eat the very food or drink we've worked so hard to give up. However

- it is possible that by abstaining from a certain food or drink over a longer period of time, our preferences change and we don't enjoy that food or drink as much as we used to (and therefore have much better control over our consumption of it).

There is no doubt that for many people good food has become one of life's pleasures (it has been the case for much longer in certain parts of the world). Food is a way to travel and experience different cultures without leaving our home, it is about creating memories with loved ones, trying something new and learning about different flavours. These are all good things to have come from our improving knowledge about what we eat. Now we just need to find the balance between our basic reason for eating (nutrients to keep our body in working order) and seeking out this pleasure and eating too much of the wrong foods.

'We are what we eat'

The food we put into our mouths is the food that our body uses as its energy source. It is also what ends up on our hips, or expands our waistline if we eat too much of the wrong stuff or even too much of one thing. It is what accumulates on the inside of our blood vessels if we eat more fatty foods than our body can process in a safe way, slowly putting us at increased risk of a heart attack.

On the flipside, from a positive standpoint, if we are eating a healthy, balanced diet, this can have a massive impact on how good we feel hour-to-hour, day-to-day. If we include our weekly exercise in the equation, we're going to feel more energised, more confident in our appearance and very likely – happier. In fact - exercise plays a vital role in helping us to feel good about our health and wellbeing; simply watching our diet and being careful with what we eat and drink will have a much more limited effect (and calorie counting can often just leave us feeling stressed). Also - making a commitment to look after our health is one thing, actually achieving this and persisting with it for a period of time is much more difficult to do and if we can achieve this, we can feel really proud of ourselves.

But how relevant are calories in all of this? Have you ever heard someone say "they never put on weight; they must have a fast metabolism"? Generally this is in relation to children and the fact is that when we are children we do use a lot more energy just by 'being'. A high proportion of the additional energy we require as children is because we are growing but we are also much more active when we are younger. In adulthood our energy requirements decrease quite considerably. In fact on average, a growing child may burn through 1,800 calories per day (girls) to 2,200 calories (boys) and if you add in some sport and exercise, these figures increase by 200 – 400 additional calories per day, so as a growing girl or boy we were burning as many as 2,200 – 2,600 calories respectively.

In contrast, while the published guidance for calorie consumption for women and men is 2,000 and 2,500 calories per day respectively, the problem with these figures is that once we hit the age of forty, if we're not exercising, our calorie requirements drop by as much as 20%. A woman in her forties, who goes about her daily life, going to work, then coming home and getting on with family life before going to bed and doing the same thing day after day, will only need the energy equivalent of about 1,800 calories per day. If said woman were to consume any more than 1,800 calories per day, she would put on weight. Take away family duties and this figure drops even more; add in post-pandemic home-working and daily calorie requirements could be as little as 1,600 per day for a forty-year-old non-exerciser. The same is true for men, who burn between 2,000 and 2,200 calories per day going about their normal daily lives; if they were to eat and drink more than this, the weight will go on. So unless we are regularly raising our heart rate through exercise, the fact is that we just don't burn as many calories as we grow older and while we may have got away with doing very little exercise up to the age of forty without putting on much weight, we now have a choice to make if we want to avoid the ever-expanding waistline (and the health risks that come hand-in-hand). The only way to increase the number of calories we burn each day once we hit the big Four-O (to more than 1,800 for women and 2,000 for men) is to get active! Or – the other option - we reduce our daily calorie intake to less than 1,800 calories. Every. Single. Day. Yikes.

Personally I love my food and counting calories every day would just take the enjoyment out of eating. That said – I do think about what I put in my shopping trolley and I do plan healthy, balanced meals. But I also love to be able to treat myself with a guilt-free piece of cake every now and then, or the occasional Full-English Breakfast on a weekend morning (portion size monitored and avoiding second helpings!). So for me - I much prefer working on the 'calories burned' side of the equation by making sure I am getting regular exercise.

The fact that we can run our normal daily lives using fewer calories as we get older also means that if we are running two or three times a week, we don't need to increase the amount we are eating. Sure – if we are trying to bulk up with muscle, we would eat more protein in our diet and we might shift the mix of our diet between food groups, however we don't need to increase our calorie intake if we are only exercising for a few hours each week.

The good news within the weight-loss equation (if calories burned is more than calories consumed => weight loss) is the fact that as we get fitter and are able to exercise for longer, or more intensively, not only do we burn more calories while we are exercising (with our body using the energy from our food to power our muscles, heart rate, blood flow, breathing, coordination etc.) but our body will continue to burn calories faster even after we finish working out. Several factors contribute to this 'afterburn effect', including our body having to work to 'repay oxygen debt' and to cool itself back down to its normal temperature. Another major factor in the afterburn effect is that because we push ourselves during an exercise session and demand more from our muscles, the cells in our muscles not only consume more energy to keep us moving but once we stop moving, our muscles go through a cycle of 'rebuild and repair'. While this may infer that we have broken something, which would normally be considered a bad thing, in this instance the 'breaking down of our muscle' that occurs during exercise (depleting the energy in our muscles cells), then the rebuilding that happens after exercise, is actually making our muscle even stronger (meaning we can run faster, or further next time). Knowing what we now know about our body, we can well imagine that this post-exercise repair of muscle takes energy in itself; and so we can understand why we continue burning calories at a faster rate even after we've finished exercising.

How do we know when we are pushing ourselves out of our comfort zone and therefore setting off this snowball effect with our calorie burning? Basically we know we're doing well if we're exercising with a raised heart rate for an extended period of time, which also manifests as deep, heavy breathing or feeling out of breath. These are both signs that our body is calling out for more oxygen to ensure that it can keep working effectively.

But the snowball effect of our improving fitness on calorie burning continues and we can further improve our metabolic rate if we are building muscle as a result of the exercise we're doing. Building muscle, and maintaining the health of muscle cells consumes more of our body's energy, so having more muscle will mean we burn more calories per day, even when 'at rest'. This does however require us to make an effort to maintain our muscles by exercising regularly, and if we don't use the muscles once we've built them up, the muscle will deplete and we will become weaker.

In fact weight loss through bodybuilding on its own is difficult to maintain. Bodybuilding tends to work on very specific muscles and as soon as we stop weight training, these muscles degenerate. Also - because bodybuilding involves increased calorie intake to support the muscle growth, if this isn't decreased once the weight training stops, there is a risk of over-eating and subsequently to gaining weight. In fact a professional sportsperson has to be very careful about putting on weight once they retire from their sport. One day they are training for several hours per day, the next day, nothing. If they haven't adjusted how much they are eating at the same time, or if they don't make an effort to continue with some form of exercise, they risk putting on weight, at least until they have adjusted their diet to fit with their new, less active lifestyle.

Reassuringly, when we exercise we can build up muscle as quickly as we might lose it, and muscle memory means that our body knows what it needs to do to re-build any lost muscle and it is easier to get back into the swing of things than when we first started our new exercise regime.

More on the mones

Hormones are our body's messengers, powered by our endocrine system and firing information via our bloodstream to our organs and tissues; our hormones are vital in every major process happening inside of us. It is well documented that the functioning of our endocrine system changes as we age and our hormone levels start to shift around.

For women, our estrogen (estradiol) levels start to decline, not only leading to a slow decrease in our bone mineral density but also the ability of our body to regulate our metabolism. This means that as well as needing less calories as we get older, our body also becomes less efficient at burning these calories and breaking down fat and is why we find it much more difficult to keep the extra pounds from accumulating around our midriff.

In men, testosterone levels start to drop with age. In fact as we learn more about hormones and their impact on our body, more men are being diagnosed with 'Low-T', where the body isn't producing enough testosterone and the effects of which are detrimental to both physical and mental well-being. Physically, not only does testosterone play a critical role in muscle growth and maintenance for men, but low testosterone levels are also associated with increased fat mass (particularly around the belly). Also - because muscle burns more calories than other tissues, if muscles aren't purposefully maintained to counteract the fact that they naturally degenerate as testosterone levels decrease, the amount of calories required reduces, perhaps by as much as 300 – 400 calories per day (c. 15 - 20%). Without exercise therefore, not only will muscle mass decline with age, decreasing the number of calories burned on any given day, but the body fat resulting from any excess calories consumed tends to accumulate in one place, giving birth (or a sort of 'reverse-birth') to the 'beer belly'.

How can we keep the bulge at bay? Well what isn't yet properly understood is how much our naturally being less active as we age contributes to the changes in our hormone levels versus how much is actually just due to the slowing down of our body as we age. However - what has been proven is that regular exercise helps to slow the decline of these vital hormones. So by watching what we put in our belly in the first place, plus maintaining muscle strength through regular hormone-boosting exercise, combined with reducing stress levels and getting enough sleep (both of the latter being consequences of our regular exercise), we can avoid the ever-expanding waistline (and the health risks associated with the podgy paunch).

And so it is that as we age and the levels of our 'sex hormones' start to decrease in both women and in men, regular exercise is vital in helping our body re-tune itself and adjust to the fact that we no longer have oestrogen and testosterone playing such a controlling role in our weight. Exercising once we hit the big Four-O is going to pick-up some of the slack; keeping our metabolism in check and maintaining muscle strength it is also going to help counter the decreasing levels of hormones. Of course there is also the offset of our post exercise 'happy hormones' to be considered as we adjust to a life lived more often in the middle lane than the fast lane; there's no better way to counter low mood and energy levels than the natural boost of dopamine and endorphins that follow a run! Plus – if we're running outdoors, studies suggest this helps optimise melatonin levels, regulating the sleep-wake cycle and the quality of our sleep.

Exercise has also been listed as one of the best ways to help women manage through the adjustments and transition happening in our body during menopause. With menopause messing with hormone levels, which in turn can impact quality of sleep; add to that our slowing metabolism (how much energy we burn at rest), we might well be feeling a bit sluggish, or 'blocked up'. The effects these symptoms have on us are a consideration when scanning our body for anything out of the ordinary when running and exercising too ("why do my legs feel so heavy today?!") As a regular runner, or with regular cardiovascular exercise, the effects on sleep and on feeling low on energy can be better regulated; exercise will certainly help alleviate the 'blocked-up' feeling and subsequently help us to feel better in ourselves.

As well as all the good stuff that comes with exercising in terms of counteracting the natural changes in our hormone levels, we can scare ourselves a bit and look at what happens if we don't exercise as we age: the almost inevitable weight gain can lead to insulin, ghrelin and leptin resistance, making over-eating more likely and making it more difficult for our hormones to regulate themselves. This vicious circle of hormone (in)activity might be the tipping point as to when weight gain can start to feel out of control.

Therefore - any exercise that gets our blood pumping and our heart rate up for twenty minutes or more, two or three times a week, is going to help keep our hormones in-check. And – it is never too late to start building and slowly strengthening our muscles; if you're an octogenarian who let things slip a bit during the pandemic, just start very slowly and easily; you'll be surprised how much strength you can regain with a little time and effort each day.

Chapter Eleven

Other bodily benefits

The zeds: sleep and exercise, exercise and sleep

All of this physical exertion, which is fine-tuning everything that is going on in our body and making sure each of our bodily systems are supporting each other as we push ourselves to a point of exhaustion, is also going to help us sleep better. Personally I try not to exercise too late in the day because immediately after exercise I feel very awake with all of the exercise hormones flying around my body. However on a day that I do a good cardiovascular or gym session (and at least two or three hours before bedtime) I know that I will fall asleep faster and sleep deeper than on a non-exercise day. This deeper sleep gives our body (and mind) the chance to rejuvenate.

As anyone over the age of forty will appreciate, a good nights sleep can really make the difference with our mood, how we deal with stress and generally with coping with whatever life throws at us on a particular day. Sleep is one of our best friends, and by raising our heartbeat through exercise and giving our body a cardiovascular workout, we can help ensure this is an enduring and healthy relationship.

How about the fact that a good nights sleep of seven or eight hours is vital for keeping our weight under control? Not only are we more likely to eat less healthily when we are tired (who isn't guilty of grabbing a sugary mid-afternoon treat to try and counter the post-lunch slump?) But being sleep deprived can also disrupt the balance of our hormones, which in turn can screw around with the messages being sent (or not being sent) to our brain. In fact our levels of ghrelin (the hunger hormone) increase with sleep deprivation, and our levels of leptin (the 'I'm full' hormone) decrease. Added to the fact that our metabolism slows down when we aren't getting enough sleep and our body can't run these vital metabolic processes as efficiently as it can when we're fully energised, it is easy to see why not getting enough sleep can lead to weight gain.

Another hormone that has been proven to increase if we are sleep deprived is cortisol. Cortisol helps regulate our response to stress and is vital in our 'fight or flight' response. It also plays a role in controlling how our body uses fats, proteins and carbohydrates, as well as regulating blood sugar; if cortisol remains at too high a level, it will prompt our body to store fat.

Immune system benefits

The average adult human body contains between nine to twelve pints of blood (4.5 – 6 litres). The blood that we have in our body doesn't just carry oxygen, glucose and hormones (via our red blood cells), our white blood cells are part of our body's defence (immune) system, protecting the body against infection from external microorganisms. Almost all of our blood cells are produced in our bone marrow; unlike red blood cells however, white blood cells can grow and mature into different types of white blood cells, each of which has a different function in our immunology and protecting our body from infection. So here again, getting the blood pumping around the body through exercise means that our white blood cells are carried to exactly where they need to be to fight off any infections.

Exercise has also been shown to reduce inflammation in our body, improving immune function and helping to combat health issues associated with chronic inflammation, such as arthritis, diabetes, bowel disease and psoriasis (to name a few). Plus - running improves the diversity of our gut bacteria, which we now know plays a vital role in our immune function. And of course exercise helps reduce stress and anxiety, which have been proven time and again to have an adverse effect on our immune system and how much energy our body has left to fight infection and illness.

All of these benefits come with the proviso that we don't overdo it and push ourselves to the point of exhaustion for long periods at a time, or run when we can feel we're already coming down with something. If we suddenly decide to do a two-hour intense training session, pushing ourselves to the limit and then pushing some more, we're at risk of depleting our immune system and opening ourselves up to getting sick as a result. As for exercising when we're feeling unwell, a good run can aid the recovery from a cold, but only once we're over the worst of it. We can do ourselves more harm than good if we exercise in the first few days of an illness; it is better to wait until we can feel we're coming out of the other side and then go for a run to help clear our system of the toxins floating around in our body after our illness and getting our body back on track.

A win with the skin

Back to the subject of oxygen and oxygen-rich blood flow to all of our cells, how about throwing in the anti-ageing benefits of exercise for our skin? Our skin is not just a waterproof, protective barrier for our body, it is actually a complex organ (the largest of the body) and consists of a variety of specialised cells. Our skin contains thousands of sensors that are sensitive to touch; it also contains sweat glands as well as cells that produce hair and nail tissue.

Our skin is full of blood vessels, playing a vital role in regulating our body temperature but also providing nutrients to our skin. Fun fact: one inch of skin consists of nineteen million skin cells, contains a thousand nerve endings and twenty blood vessels!

How do we make sure each one of these blood vessels is being filled with oxygen and nutrient rich blood, feeding our skin as well as supporting healthy collagen, elastin, hair and nail growth?

Exercise.

In fact if we think about the purpose of a facial at a beauty parlour, part of that facial is to massage the skin and encourage the blood to the surface of our skin. Exercise does exactly this, but with a superior blood flow being pushed all the way from our heart to these tiny vessels, the blood pressure helping to keep these vessels active and strong so serving this function of a beauty salon facial in a far more effective (and cheaper) way.

Cardiovascular exercise such as running is in fact fabulous for ensuring that our skin, nails and hair remain in tip-top shape. By keeping the tiny blood vessels under our skin pumped with oxygen and nutrients, we provide all these cells with everything they need to stay healthy. At the same time, the strong blood flow to the skin helps us to sweat out some of the waste products from our body, so cleansing our body from the inside out.

Not the traditional baby making exercise...

What of our fertility system? Yes – while exercise will not resolve any underlying issues with fertility, it can absolutely optimise our chances of a successful pregnancy. A good, strong supply of oxygen rich blood will aid the thickening of the uterine lining preparing it for implantation of the embryo. In the first weeks of pregnancy, before the placenta and umbilical cord have formed, the embryo is fully reliant on this blood flow to the lining of the womb. Even once the placenta has taken over, a healthy supply of oxygen and nutrients to the growing fetus is wholly dependent on the blood supply to the uterus, so maintaining a strong, healthy blood flow is also necessary for a healthy birth.

While walking will normally always be recommended in any stage during pregnancy the generally available advice is not to start a new exercise regime once pregnant. It is better to get fit before becoming pregnant, then (assuming the doctor gives their "OK"), maintaining this level of exercise for as long as comfortable through pregnancy, finally reverting to walking (or marching) when it is the only exercise our body will allow of us.

Again – we're all different and our doctor's advice around exercise will vary person to person, depending on the perceived fragility of the pregnancy. Always ask your doctor for help with exercise plans covering before, during and after pregnancy. One thing is for sure though - it is also a good idea to do arm and core workouts pre-pregnancy; holding a baby for hours on end requires strong arm muscles as well as a strong back and core!

Detox

Not only does our body process what we eat at a faster rate when we exercise, it also gets rid of the waste by-products more efficiently, speeding up our body's own detoxing processes. So although it may take some serious self-persuasion to convince our body that it wants to go out for a run the day after a night of one too many drinks, raising our heart rate is going to help clear the toxins from the body much faster. In fact the same can be true for any bodily detoxing; by going for a run and speeding up our metabolism, waste products will be cleared from the system faster. I can also recommend using running to help 'cleanse' our body after being on a course of medication and wanting to get rid of any remnants left in our system, or perhaps we've eaten something that has left us feeling bloated or 'clogged up'; a good run will help clear this problem up (or 'down' as the case may be here...)

Assuming we are drinking enough water (which is needed to help smooth the way along the digestive tract), then running is as good a detox as we'll get and is great at getting rid of the even the last bits of waste that might be trying to hide in a little nook somewhere along our pipes.

In terms of 'enough water', the recommended amount is 1.5 litres per day (about three pints), but spread out during the course of the day as much as possible (don't drink that amount in one go). A proviso here is that it is likely that we'll feel more thirsty on the day we go for a run, or do some cardio exercise, in which case we may need up to 2 litres of water (approx four pints) during the course of a day.

Detecting illness

I will start by saying that obviously running is not a fail-safe way to detect all of our illnesses. However – because of the demands put on our body while running, it does mean that we are more easily able to sense when something 'just isn't quite right' within ourselves during, or after the running session. This does require that we have been running regularly enough and for long enough that we know how we feel during a run when everything is 'normal', and are therefore able to recognise an off-day. But if we are well in touch with our body and notice that on consecutive runs we're feeling off-colour, perhaps a lot more tired than normal, a feeling of heaviness, or not able to go as far without stopping, this provides us with knowledge we wouldn't otherwise have so that we can address this and figure out if there is something more serious than just fatigue going on.

An illness may present itself as a feeling that our body is struggling more than it normally would and we're unable to pinpoint anything else that has changed in our life that might signify why. If we pay attention to what's going on in our body when we run (when running, we have little choice but to really listen to our body!) this is when running can help identify hidden health issues which otherwise might not be picked up until much later on.

If we think about how finely tuned our body needs to be to deal with the demands of running; our body demanding more oxygen, our breathing getting faster and deeper, heart-rate increasing, our brain (nervous system) gathering the incoming data from our body (endocrine system) and then pinging messages around our anatomy to make sure each of our cells has enough oxygen, food and water. All the while the liver is hard at work helping to cover any additional energy requirements, either through our energy stores, or via our fat cells; plus the liver and kidney are simultaneously dealing with waste by-products resulting from all of this burning of energy. Together with what is going on with the skeletal system and muscular system, this is still a mere fraction of what is going on with our cleverly synchronised bodily processes. But it goes some way in explaining why running is so demanding on our body and also therefore why running will help us sense when there is a fault (weakness or illness) developing somewhere in our body. If something has gone out of whack with our body's fine-tuning and we're trying to push our body to a point of exertion when we run (by running at a tempo that has us breathing much more deeply than normal for an extended period of time), we are going to feel that something is off. It will feel like our body can't cope with the exercise, whereas normally it wouldn't complain, and if this happens consecutively for a period of two to three weeks, without any other external factors at play (e.g. lack of sleep, or a sudden change in eating habits), then it could be a sign that there is something else going on in our body (meaning that our body doesn't have as much energy resources to expend on running or exercise). The hope is that in recognising this relatively sudden shift in our physical abilities during a period of a month or so and quickly seeking medical help, as little time as possible is lost on early treatment and quality of life can be restored in full.

Having myself had running to thank for help identifying burn-out (I could still run, but my legs felt like I was dragging two logs of wood around with me), I have experienced the power of communication within the body when something feels 'off' when we push ourselves close to our limit. In my mind, and if I really over-simplify the workings of our body for a moment, the message that something is not quite right might be comparable to a car that has a loose screw in a key component in the engine. If the car only ever goes at 20 – 30 miles per hour, the car might drive for months without the problem ever becoming evident. In the meantime there could be knock-on damage being done elsewhere in the engine because the root cause takes so long to diagnose. If the car was regularly being driven at 70 mph, the chances are that the issue of the loose screw would become apparent within a few days and could be quickly fixed before any other damage was done to the rest of the car.

Obviously our body is much more complex than the mechanics of a car so comparing the two doesn't do our body justice. Nonetheless, the key advantage of a prompt diagnosis lies in reducing the likelihood of lasting damage and long-term health consequences. Furthermore, running has the ability to serve as a catalyst for identifying health issues that may otherwise go unnoticed.

Chapter Twelve

Running for our mind

There are a lot of triggers in our lives these days that provide us with a short, sharp hit of pleasure; food, drink and buying new stuff can all give us a little dopamine 'hit'; but as we're slowly beginning to realise, they don't actually make us feel any happier in the medium or longer term. Running on the other hand can provide both immediate pleasure and a route to feeling consistently happier in ourselves. As a boost when we're feeling down, a tool for our toolbox to lessen anxiety, running is well-documented in helping manage and alleviate the symptoms of depression.

When we run, our body releases hormones called endorphins and ß-endorphin is one of the neurochemicals associated with the phenomenon known as 'the runner's high', a short trip into a deeply euphoric state.

As well as endorphins, our body also releases the hormones serotonin, norepinephrine and dopamine during exercise. Serotonin helps to stabilise our mood and well-being, but together with norepinephrine (a hormone that increases heart rate and helps break down fat) these chemicals combined, help to combat depressive episodes and boost energy and alertness.

As well as being essential for mood, serotonin also aids healthy digestion, good quality sleep, our brain function and our circadian rhythms (our sleep-wake cycle and how our energy levels change during a twenty-four hour period).

Ninety-five percent of our body's serotonin is produced in our gut, and our gut bacteria play a key role in this. What we also know is that regular exercise helps to boost the diversity of our gut microbiome, meaning that there's this accumulating affect of:

Exercise + balanced diet = healthy gut = serotonin = We're feeling good!

As for dopamine, as well as being a motivational neurotransmitter, dopamine provides us with the pleasure sensation that keeps us coming back for more (for some people, to the point of addiction).

When pleasure leads to happiness

OK – great news that we can achieve this short-lasting hit of pleasure by heading out for a run, but what about feeling happier, on an ongoing basis?

What makes you feel happy? Do you feel good after you have done something that you know benefits your health? After a relaxing holiday? After eating well for a week, or cutting down on your drinking for a period of time? If we read any book about achieving happiness it will tell us that it comes from within, and that lasting happiness can be achieved through having the right state of mind.

Most of us have the ability to train our mind to identify the positive in all situations, even when shit happens. This takes time and effort to achieve but there are things that we can do to help us accelerate to this (almost) permanent happy state. This isn't about not feeling sadness or grief either; in fact it is vital that we allow ourselves time to sit with these emotions as part of the healing process of trying to deal with events that were out of our control. A good run can help draw these feelings out even and certainly help us through the sadness. But in the day to day, when non-life-changing events threaten our mood and we have a choice whether we allow something to suck us under or we laugh it off, we can practise seeing the positive challenge, rather than the negative. If we recognise also that happiness is a 'by-product' of the things we do each day, it is easy to see how we can achieve a happier, more positive state of mind through exercise.

Firstly, going out for a run will make us feel better about ourselves; the fact we are making this commitment to ourselves to get fitter, stronger, and healthier. Just taking twenty or thirty minutes within our day, to do something difficult but that we know is doing us good, is something we can feel really proud about. This is also true when we've made the commitment to ourselves to make running a habit, week-in, week-out; when we can look back and say – I've done at least one run every week for the past two/three/twelve months. Creating new (good) habits is in itself something that should fill us with pride, but is often overlooked as the massive achievement that it is. When we're tracking the time or distance of our runs and we notice that we're slowly improving, or that we've run a bit further in total this month than last; this is also going to have a really positive impact on how we feel about ourselves and all of the hard work we're putting into looking after our mind and our body.

Going for a run is also an opportunity for some time-out for our head. A kind of meditation, with our mind wandering where it wants to go before slowly coming back to the rhythmical sound of our feet hitting the ground and awareness of what is going on in our body. Gifting ourselves these moments of calm provides time and headspace to help us address what is happening in our every day lives. An opportunity to cleanse our mind; a moment of clarity that provides the solution to a question or problem we've been battling with all week, or to see the other side of an argument that enables us to approach an ongoing discussion with a slightly different perspective. There is a peacefulness to be found in the 'being in the now' that going on a run provides; taking time to be in nature and observing the natural beauty around us.

Achieving a 'moment of bliss' while out on a run, when everything feels alright with the world, has a lasting effect; not only lifting us for the rest of the day but as a snapshot of a happy place we can refer back to when we need a booster shot of happiness.

All of the above provide us with an inner-strength that also mean that when the shit does hit the fan in our lives (which is inevitable, no matter who we are), we are better able to deal with the situation and come out the other side with our positive attitude still in tact. And confidence breeds confidence; over time we become more resilient so that no matter what happens, we know that we will be able to find a way deal with it and that we will come out of the other side even stronger.

Eventually anxiety, fear and the worry about 'what might, or might not be' will become so insignificant in our lives that we feel ready for anything! The positive attitude that we can achieve by living in the now will impact every area of our lives; better sleep, more space for compassion, patience, generosity (with ourselves and with others); all of which are factors known to improve feelings of lasting happiness.

Of course we still need to make sure we direct our mind to the positives, and certainly that we recognise but then let go of negative emotions, no matter how tired or fed-up we are feeling! If a negative thought, feeling or memory comes into our head, don't give it the time to grow into something it isn't. Again – this is a conscious decision to instead find the positives, perhaps something that directly contradicts the negative thought, or remind ourselves that we have never found value in holding onto the negative. If we struggle with this, take the time out, go for a run, draw on the strength of our body that will get us through the run and help us get through the day in a positive way. Tomorrow will be another day, and we will be stronger tomorrow.

Mastering this powerful tool of focusing on the positives, rather than letting negative thoughts take over, is easier to do when we're doing something good for our physical and mental well-being, such as running. Once we master this when exercising, we can carry this to all other elements of life, again improving our patience, compassion and empathy, and at the same time eliminating negative emotions that drain us as we deal with the challenging situations life throws at us.

It is difficult to summarise just how beneficial running is to both our mind and body, firstly because our body is so magnificently complex, but also because up to a certain age our body does just manage to tick-on even without intervention (apart from food and water on a regular basis). This will often bring us back to the argument "my body is looking after itself just fine, why do I need to exercise?" Thankfully - in terms of looking after our mind we are now recognising that times have changed; our lives are so complex, with so much choice and so many decisions to make all of the time, the only way we can get through life is to take time to focus on ourselves to help manage what is going on inside our head. But if we know this is good for our mental health, can we also begin to appreciate that our body also needs an extra helping hand in this day in age too (or better still that the two are intrinsically linked?) While we may not always be so aware of what's going on in our body as we are what's happening in our head, much has changed over time; diet, activity levels, sleep patterns, as well as external environmental factors. With this is mind, we should be giving our body more attention than ever in an effort to stay mentally and physically fit well into old age.

Perhaps a daily mantra might help to get us out the front door for our run, something to the effect of "I have an amazing body and an extraordinary brain and for my own sake and for those I love dearest I am going to do everything within my power to maintain the health of both, giving myself the opportunity to live my best life, for as long as possible".

What should be obvious by now is that running isn't just a choice we make in order to lose weight, or to try and achieve a certain body shape so that we think we look good in the eyes of other's. Running is a choice we can make for ourselves to take good care of our complex body; a choice that is going to enrich every waking (and sleeping) minute of our lives, for the rest of our days.

Part Three

Chapter Thirteen

Absolute Beginner

There are no two ways about this, the first five weeks of our new running schedule are going to be really, really tough. It is going to be tiring, it is going to hurt, it will feel like we're not seeing any results from our efforts, however – if we can just get to that five-week mark (35 days), having run at least three times per week, this is when our commitment to the hard work starts to pay-off.

When we first start out running, it will probably take about ten seconds before we feel completely out of breath. Neither our lungs nor our diaphragm have had to work this hard in a long time. In fact – if we remember that same new, un-inflated balloon, the rubber still super stiff so that when we first try and blow into the balloon, we can barely get any air in there; this is our lungs when we first start out running. And so it goes that similar to what we need to do to inflate a new balloon, warm it up and make the rubber more flexible and conducive to allowing in more air, we need to challenge our breathing apparatus a little more with each run, slowly improving our lung capacity and making our lungs more efficient with each breath we take.

If you look at any beginner's training schedule or 'Couch to 5K' plan online, the first week consists of alternating between 60 seconds of jogging, and 90 seconds of walking, for a total of 20 minutes, two or three times per week. Week two builds to 90 seconds of jogging alternating with two minutes walking, and so the slow build continues week after week. This carefully thought through schedule recognises that this is probably all our lungs will allow, while also acknowledging that our muscles, including our heart, are new into this game and also need time to adjust. This is why it is important that we're patient with ourselves and accept that we're going to have to build up our running very slowly over a number of weeks.

When we run, our muscles demand more energy to power them and our heart begins to beat faster, pumping the oxygen in our blood from the lungs to our muscles more quickly. At the same time, our body is having to work harder to get rid of the extra carbon dioxide. Because our lungs are still gaining in fitness, this limits how quickly our body can get the right amount of oxygen to our muscles. However - by regularly 'stretching' our breathing capacity through frequent extended cardiovascular activity (exercise that makes us feel out of breath for at least twenty minutes), running three times per week, pushing it a little more with each run, by the end of the fifth week we can be jogging continuously for the full twenty minutes.

When we get to this stage, we'll be able to walk further, or up more stairs, without feeling out of breath. Our muscles will hurt less after exercise and, if we're managing to eat a balanced diet and watch our portion size, at this five week landmark we'll be feeling really damned good within ourselves. Then with our metabolism speeding up again, helping us feel more energised in our day-to-day life, plus our muscles growing in strength with each run, continuing our newfound running habit beyond week five is when the magic really starts to happen. (Check out the '35 Day Running Challenge' in Part Four and see how you can sign-up).

> Our body is so amazing that it will react reasonably quickly when we push ourselves a bit more each run, but we do need to allow our body a full five weeks of regular exercise before we start to feel the difference. It is important to take our time and not think we can cut corners by pushing ourselves really hard for only two or three weeks; it will take the full five weeks, even if we're motivated to run more than three days per week.

And – remember to take the time to stretch after exercise (covered in the chapter 'Avoiding injury'). This is going to help us recover faster and protect us from any muscles strains.

Getting Started

One of the reasons I'm such an advocate for running over any other form of exercise is that anyone can do it, anywhere, anytime. As with many things however, making that first step is the hardest part. In order to conquer our fear of giving this thing a go, we need to remind ourself of all of the good this new running habit is going to do for our mind and our body. Then we need to use this positive energy and take that first simple step; to set ourselves a goal. Whatever this might be, having a clear objective in our mind is going to give us something to aim for. Everything after that is easy. Ok – the running itself is still tough... But once we have set our goal, then all we need to get going are some simple clothes, a pair of running shoes and a running route. There is no reliance on any equipment, it takes a minute or two to get changed, we probably have a route outside our front door (zero travel time) and this simplicity makes it an activity we are much more likely to persevere with.

Setting ourselves a goal

Maybe you're starting out on this running journey with a specific goal in mind: to be able to run for 20 minutes without stopping, or to complete a 5K? Perhaps you've got your sights set on being able to run a full marathon, or maybe you simply want to be more active? Maybe you've done your Couch to 5K and then got stuck on the 'what's next?' Maybe you jumped straight in with marathon training and having devoted four months of your life to it, saying no to social events, giving up alcohol, watching your diet, you got to the end and just felt like you wanted to claim your life back? This isn't an uncommon theme in people who weren't runners and set their first running goal as marathon distance (zero to 26.2 miles in only a few months). Often the pressure to build up to that level of fitness in a short period of time means that any enjoyment of training disappears about two thirds of the way through the schedule; then it is just another chore. In fact for many within this group, once they cross the finishing line they quickly vow 'never again'. But what a shame if after all of the training and building fitness up to such a level, the running shoes are hung-up for good because there wasn't the time to learn to enjoy running before training for one of the toughest running challenges out there!

Running a marathon is a massive time commitment and does require lifestyle changes if we want to give it our all. This is why I'd advise against the zero to 26.2 within four months, but instead set a more easily achievable running goal. If we're going to make running a habit, it is important that we enjoy each step in the journey to achieving our goal. Once we have achieved our initial running target and we realise that we get as much from our weekly training runs as we did from ticking the box after our 5K, we're firmly on the road to being able to successfully maintain this mission to run.

Your goal may simply be: "to continue being generous with the time and effort I dedicate to looking after my body", or "to continue gifting my mind with this 'me time'". Perhaps "to persevere with this commitment I made to myself to make sure that I will be as fit, healthy and as mobile as possible until my final day on this great planet of ours". The journey is then every run that we go on; hopefully something in every outing that we can take pleasure from, with the longer-term project helping us attain the fiercely sought-after by-product that is happiness.

Chapter Fourteen

Making running a habit

How do we get to the point where running is a normal part of our weekly lives? How do we get to the stage where even if we've had a couple of weeks without running, it is just 'normal' that we come back to it again as soon as we're able to? Perhaps even driven back to it by the fact that we miss it when we're not able to run for a period of time? In short, how do we build a running habit?

Ultimately this is about planning and prioritisation, motivated by a strong desire to make our future life better than it would be otherwise. 'Building' is a wholly appropriate term; a positive habit takes time, effort, perseverance and stamina to engrain into our daily life. What makes it tougher still is that we are building a positive habit for our future self, often not seeing any obvious immediate benefits of all of the hours we are investing.

With a mission to become a regular runner, the likelihood is that when we are first starting out we experience only pain, or we quickly lose confidence in ourselves that we should be trying something new ("why would I put myself through the humiliation of having to start from square one with this activity?!") These very natural thoughts and emotions, plus the fact we have to very purposely plan the new activity within our already jam-packed life, make building a new habit extremely difficult to do.

There are some hacks we can employ however so that we give ourselves the best chance of success in building a habit, for example if we build our running habit off the back of a much easier habit and maintain a certain level of planning each week, the building work can begin. (More on this later in the chapter...)

Planning and prioritisation

One of the first thoughts we will have about incorporating running into our weekly routine is "where I am going to find the time?" We may be struggling to find thirty minutes to ourselves as it is and when we do have a small window of time to relax, that's the only thing we feel we have the energy to do, to sit and switch off completely. This is where the conscious prioritisation and planning comes in.

For the foreseeable future, running needs to be priority number three in our life. Family, work, running. Then, within these three life priorities, we need to be really strict about not letting one eat into the time we set aside for the other. If you already partake in another sport on a regular basis and are reluctant to give up this time to running, how about trying to commit to running for five weeks (just enough time to build it into the routine)? After that you can incorporate both into your weekly planning and you'll be fit enough that it won't feel like starting from square one every time you run.

The second, really important action we're going to take, is to tell our partner, family and people at our work that we're on a mission to get fit and we will be building regular exercise into our weekly routine. This commitment to ourselves, and to the people around us is incredibly difficult to do. The human instinct is to think that by telling people our dreams and ambitions, we've now got this massive pressure on us not to 'fail' at the task at hand.

We need to get over this fear and just spout it out: "I will be taking time to myself over the coming months because I have decided I want to improve my fitness. I would really appreciate your support with this by allowing me to carve out this time in my weekly schedule". Even saying these words to another person is a measure of courage and can be ticked-off as our first success. Yes – there is more to do, but we shouldn't only view success as an end result of doing something but instead we need to recognise and congratulate ourselves on all of the steps we're taking towards our goal.

Our first walk, jog or run is a success worth celebrating; seriously – this is a big deal, so congratulate yourself! The second time we go out for our walk/jog/run, putting ourselves through the pain again in spite of how we felt after our first run, is also a major success; nice work! And if we can keep going, even if we're only going out running once per week, this is success. We've succeeded in trying something new, which probably made us feel very uncomfortable in itself, plus we've put ourselves through the pain of working muscles we haven't used in a long time - and we've not given up!

As for the fear of 'failing' once we have vocalised our intentions to others, we shouldn't ever let our own sense of success or failure hinge on what we believe others might think of us. This fear will stop us trying something that we might find we really enjoy doing, or that we know is really good for us; it could even stop us finding our true purpose in life. The inaction resulting from this fear can lead to extreme levels of pent-up frustration, annoyed that there's an 'invisible hand' holding us back; it can also lead to regret, and as time passes, all we are left with is a "what if...?"

So – if you're still thinking "but I'm not a runner, that's for other people" or if you're scared to make the commitment of building a running habit by saying it out loud to other people, remind yourself that it is tremendously courageous and requires great determination to take ourself out of our comfort zone. Create the space in your life to give yourself the chance to give running a go. Then make time to recognise all of the other successes you're achieving; from the moment you made the decision to try and make your future life better by starting to exercise, to actually getting out there each week and doing your walk/jog/run.

And so the planning begins

Taking the time to plan is a massive factor in making this mission a reality. It isn't a plan that you can just keep in your head either, it needs to go down on paper, or in your phone (with reminders) at the start of each week. It doesn't need to take long; a simple seven-day table split down by hours of the day will work well, and it will get quicker and easier to do each week. It isn't necessarily about getting the exact timings right, but instead saying, for example, "I will do my run on

Tuesday at lunchtime this week, my Thursday run immediately after work, and my Sunday run will be before I do anything else that day".

	Monday	Tuesday	Wednesday	Thursday	Friday	Saturday	Sunday
A.M.					Yoga / swim (before breakfast)	Core exercises (at home - as soon as I get out of bed)	
Work/ Family/ Other							
Lunchtime				Run 30 mins (block lunch hour)			
Work/ Family/ Other							
P.M.	Pilates (class / App)	Run from work (40 mins)	Resistance (gym)				Long run (1 hour)
Dinner							

A very simple example of a weekly exercise planner. Split into morning, lunchtime and early evening blocks of time for each day of the week. Work, family and dinner time are assumed as unavailable

I would recommend taking five minutes on a Sunday evening to draw up your weekly plan. Look at the diary for the coming week and block out an hour on the two or three days we will run, making it clear to family that these are the times during the week when they need to be self-sufficient, or you need help from your partner. If you're running before work, immediately after work, or in your lunch hour, make sure your work diary is blocked so that nothing is going to interfere with you having an hour-long lunch on Tuesday, or finishing work exactly on the dot on Thursday. Stick your plan up where people can see it, and then protect the times you've set aside for your running through any means possible! We will be saying "no" to stuff if it looks like it is going to interfere with our planned runs, being very clear that we are on a mission, and this is our scheduled time for exercise. As soon as we start to give the time we've planned for ourselves to others, it is very difficult to get it back again. And once we lose the discipline in protecting the time we have purposely created for ourselves, it can quickly become very messy, with the people we most need support from then continually trying their luck, asking us to move things around to suit their needs. Once this happens, reaffirming our strict running schedule with the people around us becomes more difficult.

Planning and then sticking to our weekly running schedule will be easier for some than for others. Some people are very singular-minded anyway and find it easy to immerse themselves into something once they have made the decision to do so; everything else would naturally fall away to make space. In my experience, men generally seem to be better at this valuable skill of protecting their time and blocking out any other distractions than women are (particularly, and not surprisingly, compared to women whose daily duties include running a household). So for most of us this level of planning, very purposely avoiding distraction and strictly adhering to the times we have set aside for running is going to give us the best chance of success in getting out for a run two or three times a week.

There is also something about this level of planning and having made this commitment to ourselves that means when the time comes, we're in a better place to just get out there and do it. When we realise how precious our time is and how few opportunities we have per week to take thirty minutes out to dedicate to our health, we will be more likely to just get on with it. Of course, some procrastination is still highly likely, particularly if work is busy and we begin to wonder if we should give up our running time so that we can spend the thirty minutes on work stuff instead. Then of course there is the "do I really feel like going out for a run now anyway?" kind of deliberations. These we need to address with habit hacks, because going out for a run is rarely seen a special treat beforehand but if we can just take that first step outside, we will soon be beaming with joy.

How detailed does the planning need to be? It depends just how much you've got going on and how much help you are going to need from others so that you can protect your three sessions per week. Planning down to the last hour each day might actually make finding time feel overwhelming. But if there are unavoidable, important events that have been planned for the week ahead, perhaps a parent's evening, a dentist appointment, your best friend's birthday party, then add these to the weekly planner. Once we have key events detailed on our planner, we can begin to schedule a time (or time window), three times a week, which we commit to ourself to do our running. These will sit around our working hours and our family obligations (recognizing that family time is impossible to plan down to the last minute and that we will need to be more strict about keeping to meal times and to bed times). If we are really strict about our scheduling of family time (including any household chores within this), hopefully when we look at our weekly planner we now have two or three timeslots we can allocate to running. Add these very clearly to your weekly planner.

Having this plan for the week doesn't mean to say that efficiencies shouldn't be introduced, and in particular that we make sure that family responsibilities are shared out as much as is possible. Perhaps draw up a rota of who is cooking dinner on which nights, who is putting the rubbish out, who is doing the food shopping, and who is responsible for children each morning, or evening. Only this level of planning is going to give us the best chance of having this time (and the energy) we need to build our new habit. We will need to trust our partner to do the tasks at hand and to stand our ground and not revert to the attitude of "I'll just do it myself so that it's done". During a busy week, we may need to get creative with when we run, or where we're running, but we must plan it into both our work diary and the rota at home; then we have to do everything we can to stick to this commitment.

This is how we will achieve our mission. This is how we give ourselves the best chance of being able to look back in three, six, twelve months times and say to ourselves "I did this. Against all odds. I am a legend". Then all that time planning and looking out for yourself will have been worth it, and I guarantee it will feel good.

Scheduling

If you're following one of the standard training schedules (as include in Part Four) then you can simply choose which days are going to suit you best for each of the training runs specified for the relevant week. But what about if we're not working towards a specific goal but want to continue this running habit for ourselves; what does a training schedule look like then? It looks like two or three runs a week, one of which would be at a pace where we feel we're 'pushing it'; it won't be particularly far, and may only be twenty or thirty minutes long but we've raised our heart rate pretty quickly and kept it high for the entire run. The second run would be at a steadier pace, and we would run until our legs are aching a bit and our body is feeling tired, but not exhausted. If we're still building fitness this could be between three and five miles; if we're already half marathon, or marathon runners, this could be eight, or perhaps ten miles some weeks. If we also then include a Pilates, yoga, core strength or resistance training session along the way each week, our body is going to be so finely tuned that we can feel the harmony of everything that is going on inside our body.

In terms of preferred time of day, the only hard and fast rule is to leave at least two hours (preferably three) between eating and going out for a run. If our body is still expending energy digesting food, we're going to feel really sluggish on our run, and very possibly give ourselves an uncomfortable case of indigestion.

Running first thing in the morning, before we do anything else, is great for clearing our head and setting us up for the day ahead. Running before breakfast is also really good for burning fat. Having effectively been fasting through the night, our body is probably already in fat-burning mode by the time we wake up; if we then exercise before eating anything, we continue burning fat at a faster rate. However - depending on how well our body is trained to exercise early in the morning, we'll probably only be able to run for thirty minutes to begin with, and we'll need to train ourselves to go for up to an hour without food. We definitely can't expect to break any records if we haven't eaten anything yet! And for some people, running on an empty stomach won't be an option and the lack of sustenance could lead to feeling faint or unwell. I'd suggest that if you are running before eating breakfast, take an emergency granola bar with you just in case you need a quick hit of energy along the way. Also - eat breakfast as soon after finishing running as possible.

Another consideration with running first thing in the morning is whether your 'morning routine' might require some attention. For some there is the risk of being caught out mid-run; the hare and the turtle-head, frantically searching for the nearest toilet. Preferable is to try adjusting your routine, avoiding coffee and drinking plenty of water in the twenty-four hours before running and eating a well-balanced dinner the evening before (carbs, protein, fibre and healthy fats), avoiding having too big a portion. Otherwise – if your routine is set in stone, unchanged for many years, perhaps have a coffee and some water as soon as you wake-up, use the bathroom and then head out for your run. Although eating just prior to running is not normally advised, you may need to nibble on a cereal bar before heading out in this instance, just to give your body a small energy boost and deal with your now completely empty tank!

Weather is a secondary consideration in our scheduling if we have the luxury of picking the day and time for our run. If we're running regularly, we're never going to be able to completely avoid running in the rain, and actually there is something very satisfying about hauling our butt out the door when our natural instinct is to shy away from getting wet. However - running in blazing sunshine, really strong winds, torrential rain, hail or sliding around on ice, is not so much fun; try and plan your weekly runs around this if possible.

Even if you're not crossing an actual finish line, take the time each week to congratulate yourself on persevering with this super challenging habit. Choosing to run, an exercise that we know makes every demand of our body yet we continue get ourselves out there each week anyway because we know the mental and physical benefits are unparalleled, is a remarkable feat. Share your progress with the people around you; tell people when you've got a new 'personal best' and you've run further than you have before, or ran the fastest ever time for a given distance, or that you're super proud of yourself because you're still running regularly after so many weeks, or months.

Success in building a habit is about every little thing we do along the way in making the habit a reality. It is about overcoming the voice in our head which is telling us that we can't, or that other people are judging us, worrying that they'll think we're a failure. We shouldn't ever let our own sense of success hinge on what we believe others might think of us. Instead we need to recognise that every change we're making, big or small, is its own success story and each is a step towards building a new long-term habit.

Habit hacks - Tips to keep you true to your new routine

Creating the conditions: Ideally we should plan the exact time of day we want to head out for our run. If for example our plan is to run immediately after work on a Thursday, we write this into our agenda for 17:30pm and we make sure we're ready changed so that we can head out of the door on the dot. Or if we plan to go home first and then go for a run, if we know the journey from work takes thirty minutes, we would plan the run for 18:00pm. Get home, get changed immediately (or better still, change before leaving work) and then head-out before anything else can distract us from our cause. Don't work late that day. Block the evening in our work diary. Be militant about leaving on the dot. (If we're doing our hours across the week, no one at work is going to say anything about leaving work on time to go for a run).

Joining forces: If possible, we need to be brave and plan to run with someone. Make a commitment to meet a friend, or running buddy at a given time. Then don't let them down (and tell them off if they back-out without good reason). It will feel really good to make this commitment to each other and to your running cause. As well as the additional motivation to get out there, the whole experience will be more enjoyable if we're mixing it up so that we're not always running on our own.

The easy way (to get) out: Create a difficult habit off the back of an easy habit. A difficult habit is going out for a run two or three times a week. An easy habit is changing into our running gear as soon as we get home from work and then stepping outside the front door and locking it behind us. Some days we may just unlock the door and go back inside immediately. Other days we'll persuade ourself to go for a walk around the block. What will happen more often than not however, is that we will end up going for our walk-jog-run. But the sole focus in that moment is to put on our running clothes and step outside our front door; that is our only goal. Having got ourself out of the front door and into the fresh air, something else takes over. We are out of our cage and free from all of the thoughts crowding out our positive intentions "wouldn't it be nice just to sit on the sofa instead?", "maybe

I'll just sit on social media for five minutes and see if that helps my motivation". Just get out the front door and resist putting yourself in that situation where thirty minutes passes and you think to yourself "Dammit – I could just be finishing my run now if I'd only gone out when I promised myself I would". Commit to the easy habit (putting on running gear and stepping out of the front door), then use it to break down the barrier around this difficult habit.

Be creative: Where there's a will, there's a way and sometimes our planning will involve getting creative so that we can fit our running into the week. One thing that makes all the difference for me, is replacing a journey I've got to make anyway with a run. Running to work, or home from work, whether that be the whole distance, or getting off the train one or two stations before my destination (it is a good reason to leave the laptop at work too). Or if the week is so chock-a-block, perhaps I'll end up running back home from an evening out seeing friends. Having enjoyed an alcohol-free drink and a friendly catch up, I'll then set off home, a small running rucksack on my back, equipped with a slightly smug satisfied feeling that I'm the one leaving the pub early to do some exercise.

Think of the trips you do in your car or on public transport each week and see if any of these can be replaced with a run instead. Perhaps running home from the school drop-off? Maybe putting the children on bikes to school and running alongside? Or ask to share the weekly school runs with another parent so that you can alternate days having the extra time to exercise instead (after all - who's going to say no to this if it frees-up some time?)

Guard your space: Set a reminder for the time you've set aside for your run, stop whatever else you're doing when it goes off and switch into run mode. A very simple habit hack is to have a reminder ping up on our computer screen, our phone or our watch, thirty minutes before we're due to go for a run, and then again with five minutes to go, giving us time to get changed and making it less likely that we lose track of the time. Don't ignore the reminder; even if you have to come back to whatever it is you're doing later, guard this time you've set aside for your run.

Pomodoro Technique: Are you easily distracted from the task in hand? Evidence suggests that in this age of mobile phones, we feel the urge to pick them up to see what's going on an average of 58 times per day (with statistics suggesting it could be as many as 344 times per day for some people!) The desire to seek-out a quick burst of dopamine via our favourite Apps on a regular basis is killing our ability to focus on any one thing for any period of time. This is where the Pomodoro Technique comes in handy and we're going to use the principle behind it to help us get out for our run. Developed by Francesco Cirillo in the 1980s, the idea is that we work in chunks of time of twenty-five minutes, then give ourselves a five minute break; twenty-five minutes, five minute break, repeating this four times before taking a longer break of twenty to thirty minutes. Then begin again, until our work for the day is done. Strictly focusing on the task in hand for a twenty-five minute period, without allowing any distractions (door closed, phone on flight mode), then taking a short, timed break is going to improve our efficiency at getting things done. How do we use this time management technique to help us get out for a run? For the twenty-five minutes, running is our only task in-hand, our sole focus. All other distractions can wait until after the twenty-five minutes are up. Practise this technique across different areas of your life; it is a great way to keep the flow going throughout the day, improving how productively we use our time and reducing the amount we waste on meaningless rubbish.

Be in the now: We made it out for our run, nice work! Now we can use this time to focus on all the good stuff that is going on in our body while we're exercising; notice the things around us and feel good about being alive! Let our mind wander if needs to. Say "no" to any negative thoughts that pop into our head and any 'what-if...?' anxieties; they are not welcome now, thank you. Don't think about how far it is to the end but focus only on putting one foot in front of the other. And remember – pain is only pain and it will pass and leave us stronger.

Building a running habit is extremely difficult to do. Only by purposely carving out time in our agenda for the week ahead (and if possible, for the upcoming fortnight) and then sticking to our guns and ruthlessly prioritising and protecting this time for ourselves will we be able to build a new habit. It won't be easy to start with and there will be occasions where we let this time slip away from us. But – it will get easier as time goes on as we rewire our mind and body to know that running is now a normal part of our life.

It is most important that we don't let one or two missed runs dishearten us and leave us feeling like we've already failed and should therefore stop altogether with this silly idea that we might actually stick at something new. Don't do this. In fact – don't do this even if you've missed a month of running. Instead we should be patient with ourselves; reminding ourselves that we won't change our lives for the better in a day and the reason that we'll keep going is because our future self doesn't care that we missed one run, it cares that we got back out there and continued on our mission to create this new habit.

Chapter Fifteen

The kit – How to choose shoes and other clothing considerations

There are a few basic items of clothing we need and with running shoes being the most important, it is worthwhile investing in the right pair. That said – if you don't want to make the investment upfront, if you have a pair of trainers with a sole at least two centimeters thick at your heel, you can use these for your first few runs while you get into the swing of things. Also – if you are new into this and don't want to spend any money on new kit just yet, you can use any pair of shorts and T-shirt to get started. Once we're a few weeks into our new running habit however, we should take a bit of time to select the right pair of running shoes and make this investment in looking after our joints and muscles (a very worthwhile investment in ourself!). 'Right pair' of running shoes doesn't mean expensive, but we're looking for a good fit and shoes suitable for our running mechanics (how our body moves when we run).

Running shoes

To protect our body when running, a good pair of running shoes is the most important piece of equipment we'll buy when we first start out. The definition of good running shoes is 'comfortable, and best suited to our personal running mechanics'. Comfort comes in wearing the right size running shoe, which will generally need to be at least a half a size bigger than our normal shoe size (maybe even a full size bigger, as is the case for me). The increased blood flow to our feet when we run, plus if we're wearing running socks (which tend to be very slightly thicker than our everyday cotton socks), mean our feet need a bit of extra space. We'll also need to take into account if we have wide, or narrow feet. Frustratingly, shoe sizes can vary from brand to brand, which makes it all the more important to try before you buy. In fact I highly recommend booking an appointment and going to a specialist running shoe shop when buying your first pair of running shoes. Once we've found a brand we like and figured out the right size and support, it is easier to replace these in the future, without necessarily having to go back to the shop for a test run every time we need new shoes.

There seem to be a good number of specialist running stores that offer 'gait analysis' and can help to find the right running shoe. In fact I have seen that free online gait analysis is offered by some specialist retailers, however I would recommend going in person if possible and trying on a few different pairs of running shoes while you're there. Also - let the store assistant know what your budget is upfront so that you are comfortable with the price of the shoes they give you to try on.

The purpose of gait analysis, as well as finding a shoe that feels good on your foot when running, is to look at our running mechanics. When we run, we each have an individual running style. There is no right or wrong to this, but how our muscles, bones, joints and tendons work together will vary person to person depending on many factors from genetics, to how much sport we did when we were younger and how our movement developed as we were growing up.

Gait analysis looks at how our foot hits the ground when we walk or run and whether our foot 'pronates'. As things stand today, we can all be grouped into one of three categories when it comes to pronation:

'Overpronation' is when the foot rolls inwards slightly when it hits the ground. As a result more weight passes through the inner ankle when the foot hits the ground and pushes off again. Often with overpronation the inside edge of the sole of the running shoes will wear out more quickly and the shoe may also develop a bulge along the inner anklebone. In this instance the running store assistant will likely recommend running shoes with more stability built in. This won't stop the overpronation completely but will offer more support to the inside of the foot and to the ankle, which in turn helps relieve any imbalances up the leg and through the rest of the body.

For a 'neutral runner', the foot lands on the ground and pushes off again with the hip-knee-ankle-foot movement working together in a straight line. The foot hits the ground with the pressure centering through the ball of the foot and with an even distribution of the pressure through the foot, ankle and leg as we push off again. In this instance a 'neutral' running shoe will be recommended.

If we underpronate (supinate), the foot rolls out very slightly when it hits the ground. Here the sole of the running shoe tends to wear out faster along the outside of the shoe and a bulge may develop in the shoe material around the base of the little toe and the outside edge of the shoe. With underpronation a 'high cushioned' neutral shoe is recommended; this will compensate for the foot's lack of natural shock absorption on the outside edge of the foot.

Gait analysis takes about fifteen minutes in total. The store will probably start off with a neutral shoe and ask you to jog on the treadmill (or a small track) for twenty seconds or so and will then judge if you need a shoe with more stability, or if a neutral shoe is most suitable. It is then a simple question of trying on three or four pairs within budget and seeing which feels most comfortable when you run. To ensure you're buying the correct size, be sure to wear a proper pair of running socks when trying on the shoes.

Gait analysis is one of those things that feels intimidating no matter if we're a seasoned runner or a first-timer. It is well-worth grinning and bearing through the one-time exercise though, knowing that once we've found 'our shoe' we can replace like-for-like in the future. If you're feeling daunted at the prospect, find your local running store, or contact the virtual gait analysis clinic online and have a chat with them about the process to start with. A really good assistant is going to immediately make you feel more relaxed about the whole process and the fact that serving you and making sure you buy the right shoes is an important part of their job. It is a competitive shoe market out there today and one of the ways physical retail need to differentiate itself versus shopping online is outstanding customer service so if you don't feel like you're being treated like a valued customer, search around until you find someone who gives you the attention you deserve.

Undergoing a gait analysis session at a running shoe store doesn't obligate you to buy the shoes on the spot. It is perfectly acceptable to go away and think about which shoes to buy and to shop around for the best price. Perhaps you want to do some more research online and read other runner's reviews about the shoes you're thinking of buying?

If you normally wear corrective insoles of any kind in your everyday shoes, be aware of putting these into your running shoes, particularly if you've bought running shoes with extra stability built in and then you try doubling-up on the support. I'd advise speaking with your podiatrist, showing them the new running shoe and asking their advice on whether you need inserts or not. If you are post foot surgery of any kind, you may not have a choice but to change to your prescribed insole. Otherwise it will also depend on how far you're running and how fatigued your supporting muscles become; perhaps the spring in the new shoes plus the spring in your step completely counteract the need for additional support.

Our feet work together with our ankles, legs and hips, all supported by our upper body; the way we run is then just our 'natural movement'. Trying to change or adapt the way our body naturally wants to move is a long, slow process, requiring months of targeted muscle work with the help of a specialist physiotherapist. A stability running shoe to support lower arches or flat feet should be sufficient, and as long as we're replacing our running shoes at the right time, a neutral shoe should be fine to support any underpronation.

In terms of replacing running shoes, the general rule is that we should replace them either roughly every 300 – 500 miles, or every nine to twelve months, whichever comes sooner. The variability depends on what surface we run on (running on roads will take the bounce out of the sole faster than running on grass) and also on our weight (a twenty stone muscle-man will wear through his running shoes faster than a ballerina). Once we get used to the feel of a shoe and the cushioning it gives us when we run, it becomes easier to tell when the sole of our running shoe has lost its bounce and feels overly soft, or 'deflated', compared to when we first bought the shoes. Other times we can see that the sole of the shoe is completely worn down in a particular area, or the shoe is bulging so much in one area that it is no longer giving the support we need. These are all signs that it is time to invest in a new pair of running shoes.

While it is ok to wash running shoes in a cold wash if they get really muddy, it will affect the bounce in the sole and will age the shoes faster. Ideally we let the mud dry and then just brush it off. However if the shoes have to go into the wash, a short, cold wash will get the worst off. Then when drying running shoes, stuff them with newspaper and rather than put them directly on the radiator or heater to dry, just place them close to the heat source. This will stop them drying too quickly and shrinking.

Once you're done with your running shoes, recycle them. Use them in the gym, then they could be used in the garden; alternatively some running stores will take old shoes and recycle them for you.

Running socks

Good, 'breathable' trainer socks are a very worthwhile investment. Proper running socks are going to make your run more comfortable and reduce the risk of any blistering. Most running socks have little or no cotton in them because it absorbs moisture, trapping it against the skin, making our feet feel really hot. Cotton socks also tend to stretch with the material rubbing between our foot and shoe and causing blisters. Again – running socks don't need to be expensive to do the job well but proper socks are slightly cushioned in the right places and the material is moisture-wicking, taking the sweat away from the surface of the foot, through the breathable material.

If you suffer from shin splints during or after running (pain along the shin bone), wearing compression socks can help alleviate this. Of course it is best to try and tackle the root cause of the shin splints, which could be due to wearing worn-out shoes, only ever running on very hard surfaces, or weakness in the muscles of the lower leg (see the chapter '…Avoiding injury' for some strengthening exercises).

Running shorts or trousers

To avoid any chafing between the thighs, I'd recommend going for skintight lycra (polyester) shorts or leggings. It is of course possible to buy decent non-lycra running shorts, which tend to be 100% polyester and are lightweight and more breathable but which don't provide the same protection against the chafe. Some people like to double-up, with lycra underneath and running shorts on top; generally I end up mixing and matching, depending on the weather and how far I'm running.

Make sure the waistband isn't too tight as having any squeezing pressure on our stomach when we run can leave us feeling a bit queasy after a run, or worse still, with stomach pain. Most running shorts and trousers have a pull string around the waist as well as elastic, so as long as they are skin tight around the leg (if we're protecting against the chafe), we can even opt for a slightly larger waist measurement than we would normally wear, just to make sure we're not 'strangling' our tummy when we run.

Also - while we might want to go for brighter colours for the rest of our running kit, a human's propensity to sweat while exercising means that we may choose to buy black or navy shorts and trousers.

Running top

There are two main considerations when choosing a good top for running. Firstly, we don't want something that is going to chafe our armpits, so even with a skin-tight top, there should be a bit of air between the material and our underarm. Also be aware of where the seams sit against our body; if we have a lumpy seam sitting right under our armpit, once we start running longer distances this is also going to cause the painful chafe. Secondly, the material should be breathable, wicking the sweat away and allowing the heat to escape from our body. Again – because cotton absorbs moisture, holding it against the skin as well as making the t-shirt heavier, it is not a good choice of material if we're pushing ourselves to the point where we're working up a really good sweat. (Men – beware of nipple chafing! If you're going for a long, sweaty run, put some extra-strong plasters on your pecs beforehand).

When doing a walk-jog, we will want to make sure we stay warm, particularly if we're sweating and our body is trying to cool itself down. However if we're going to be continuously jogging or running, even if it is cold outside, our body is going to be really warm after five minutes, so if we're wearing a long sleeved top, bear in mind that we might feel the need to push the sleeves up partway through the run.

Running bra

It doesn't matter how big or small our boobs are, ladies – a high impact running bra is an essential investment to minimise bounce as much as is possible. Low and medium impact sports bras are fine for yoga, cycling and other non-boob-jiggling exercise; for running, we've got to strap the puppies down and nothing less than a high-impact sports bra will do.

In terms of sizing, again – it varies brand to brand and it is worthwhile going for a sports bra fitting in a shop if possible. I am able to buy my normal bra size and this is tight enough and doesn't restrict my breathing. Otherwise the regular bra sizing guidelines apply: wrinkles in the fabric of the cup indicate the bra cup is likely slightly too big, the underwire should sit just on our skin (not digging in) and also –

jump around a bit in the changing room while trying the bra on. If it rides up at all, it is likely too big around the rib cage.

A good sports bra is going to stop our boobs moving around too much when we run, which is essential in protecting the supporting ligaments and connective tissue, preventing any sagging in later life. Strapping down our Bristols is also going to help ensure that our running movement is as efficient as possible; having our boobs bouncing around means we're using muscles, and therefore energy, unnecessarily. This is quickly going to make us feel more tired but it is also a distraction and can be very draining the longer we run. Our boobs shouldn't be sore after a run and if we do experience any pain that wasn't there beforehand, it is time to invest in a new bra. Likewise if you are suffering any chafing, it is most likely that your bra needs retiring, either because you've lost some weight, or because the bra has lost its elasticity.

Personal go-to bra: the 'Ultimate Shock Absorber Run' (Extreme Impact) bra, available in sizes 30A up to 40HH. Other brands seem to go to 42L (UK sizes).

Running underwear

The obvious consideration here is to be aware of chafing if underwear is either too tight in places or too loose. For me, my regular, everyday knickers are perfectly good. Men – my research tells me that it is all down to personal preference, however per the sports bra advice for women and keeping our boobs in place with a decent bra, some support for the undercarriage is a worthwhile investment in the longer-term.

Running watch

A running sports watch is by no means essential but having a watch that gives us feedback about our run and how we are progressing is going to help keep us on track with building our running habit. Again – we don't have to spend a lot of money to buy a watch that does all of the things we need it to, plus there is a good market for refurbished, or second hand watches (because some people like to upgrade as soon as the new model comes out and will happily pass on their 'old' watch).

A basic 'GPS' watch will tell us how long we've been running and the distance covered. Using the 'Global Positioning System' allows us to more accurately track the distance we've covered compared to a step-counter and an estimated average stride length. It does however require us to wait for our watch to connect to the GPS before we start exercising (at time of writing, the GPS consists of a constellation of satellites flying at an altitude of approximately 20,200 km (12,550 miles) of which our watch needs to connect to four to determine our exact location). This GPS connection will mean we use our battery faster however, and the watch will need recharging every few days (although of course there are watches specifically designed for long battery life, even with GPS in constant use).

A slightly more advanced watch is also equipped with a wrist-based heart rate monitor, which is really useful for keeping track of how long we've spent in a 'high heart rate zone' (which is where we want our heart rate to be if we're building up fitness, and is also when we're burning the most fat. More on this in the chapter 'Running myths').

Most GPS watches can send the data via Bluetooth to an App on our phone, tablet or laptop, meaning that we're able to store all of our exercise data. This gives us the ability to track our activity week by week, check how many miles or kilometers we've run in the past month, see how our resting heart rate is improving with our fitness, or access pretty much any other data we might want.

These days the extra features available on a sports watch seem to be limitless (along with the price); pairing with wireless headphones and accessing our favourite music App, built in flashlight, location sharing, Ordnance Survey level detailed maps, weather reports; you name it. My go-to watch is a simple Garmin GPS Forerunner with a built in wrist-based heart rate monitor, and I use this with the Garmin Connect App (correct at the time of writing).

Running armband

Depending on whether you like to run with music or not, this may be a pouch for your phone, or if you're like me and prefer to listen to whatever is going on around me when I run, this is just a safe place to keep our door keys while we're out running. I see more and more people running with body 'pouches' or vests these days, which have multiple pockets and space for a water bottle too. It just depends how much stuff you have to carry (but again beware of the chafe if you have extra straps around your body).

Running rucksack

The step-up from the running pouch or vest, is a proper running rucksack. This is smaller, more lightweight and is tighter-fastening than a normal rucksack. The idea is that we put as little in there as is necessary but that the size makes these really handy if we're running to or from work and need to transport clothes or shoes.

The bag and the straps are shaped to be more comfortable as our arms are pumping back and forth, and a small clip at the front of the straps holds them closer together, helping to keep the backpack firmly in place and limiting the movement (saving our energy and our back and arms from any chafing).

Running in the winter, or in the dark

If the thought of wearing florescent clothing makes you think of a 1980's style roller-disco, I can reassure you that there are some decent options for florescent tops out there for our winter runs. In low light, make sure clothing has a couple of reflective strips too, which is going to help let drivers and cyclists know that we're there.

I've never liked the idea of wearing a head torch while running, but there is now a cross-body option too. These aren't expensive and are a must-have if running in the dark (both so we can see where we're going and also so others can see us).

Washing

Just as we need to wash ourselves as soon after we've finished exercising as is possible, our running clothes (socks, underwear, top and shorts) all need to go in a quick wash after our run too. A fast, cool wash is good enough (and washing with other clothes means that we're thinking about the environmental impact of our washing habits). Washing straight after exercise helps to get rid of the bacteria that make our clothes (and us) smelly.

That's our list of running equipment done.

Chapter Sixteen

Back to my routes – The Base Route

Our 'base route' and route planning

Another vital piece of preparation is our route planning. It is worth taking some time to plan a route because a good route can be the difference between being able to enjoy our run, or arriving home slightly traumatised by how busy the route was. If at all possible we want to avoid having to do several laps of a small course (this can get pretty boring after doing this a couple of times) and it is going to be even more beneficial for us if we're able to take in some nature as we go (extra stimulation for our nervous system). The basic idea is that our route is going to have a positive effect on our motivation to get out there and run.

We all need a 'base route', which is an easy route, close to home, and takes between twenty and thirty minutes to run. This is our go-to route when we're short on time and our only option to fit in a run is to head straight out of the door and start running. It doesn't matter how far our base route is, only that it takes us at least twenty minutes to complete when jogging or running.

There are various Apps and websites where we can search for 'running routes near me' but to plan our base route we can use any map and use our home as the start and end point.

Ideally our base route avoids busy roads as much as possible, and if there is an option to run to a park and include a lap of the park (or woods, or maybe even along the beach) this is good to avoid breathing in too many car fumes and is just going to be more enjoyable.

Having more than one route close to home means we can mix things up a bit, otherwise running somewhere with an ever-changing scenery will help to keep things interesting (again – running in nature means the route looks a bit different every time).

Knowing our route beforehand means we can relax and just be in the moment; after repeating the route a number of times we'll even stop having that "how far have I got left to go?" thought, which is never helpful on any run. Also on our longer runs it means that we don't have to stop every five minutes to check where we are and which direction we need to take.

> Tip for travelling: Don't let going on holiday or travelling with work disrupt your new running habit. Instead try and find a hotel in a runner friendly location, perhaps with a nice route along the coast, or for a city trip, close to a park. Even if you only manage one run while you're away this will have a significant impact on how likely it is that you continue with your running mission when you get home.

I always make room for my running gear in my bag when I travel; to have the option to go for an early morning run while I adjust to the time zone, or to run-off last night's meal, helps offset the negative elements of travel. I also find that going out for a run somewhere I'm staying for a few days helps me settle in more quickly. It's a great way to discover the hidden gems; the restaurants, juice bars, cafes, shops, museums, galleries, the bakery with the best croissants in town and just generally feel more at one with this new place.

Running on a treadmill

There is certainly a time and a place for running on a treadmill if we're unable to run outdoors for any reason. Perhaps during the winter time when it is dark outside, or if we're away from home and the easiest way to do our run is on the treadmill in the hotel, or perhaps if we're avoiding the heat of the midday sun? Treadmill running is different to running outdoors however, so if we're training for an event it is important to get our legs used to having to work a bit harder when unassisted by a moving belt on a running machine. That said, if we set the speed a little higher on a running machine, it is great for maintaining a faster pace for a longer period of time and pushing ourselves a bit more than we might if we're running outside. Personally I would avoid wearing the ultra-cushioned running shoes on a treadmill, which tend to have a little bit of bounce to them anyway; a double-bounce of the shoe and the machine could cause problems with knees, hips or to our back.

Chapter Seventeen

I'm me and you're you – Running style and technique

It upsets me when I hear that someone doesn't exercise because they are worried about running technique and what other people will think of them. It upsets me because anyone who goes out running should be thinking "I'm an absolute hero for doing this and for that reason I don't give a damn what anyone else thinks!" Certainly when I see anyone else out running, I think "good for you my friend; running is tough and it takes guts", and when I'm out running myself and I pass another runner, there is a mutual smile of acknowledgement of our efforts.

One of the most common concerns is that people are judging our style of running (our running action) and we're worried that we're 'not doing it right'. But it is right; just as the way you walk is right. The fact is that our body is built in a way individual to us; we will all walk slightly differently, and we will all run slightly differently too. Our body knows what it is doing and it knows what it needs to do to move us forwards in a walk, jog or run. If you begin with a walk, then speed up only very slightly into a really gentle jog, this is your start point with regards your own individual running style. This style is right - because it is how your body is naturally moving.

What about my arms? Most important is to try and keep our shoulders relaxed while running; if we hunch-up we're going to end up with a sore neck among other things. Otherwise our arms have the same role as when we walk, which is to provide stability as they counterbalance the movement of our legs. When we run, propelling ourselves forwards at a faster pace, the natural tendency is to have a bend in our elbows, this action of engaging the muscles across our upper body helps provide more power to each stride. If we begin to run faster, our arms will naturally pump more as they work with our legs to pick-up the speed. This pump action should be more of a forward and backward movement and without causing any twisting motion in our torso. A twisting upper body while running reduces our stability and increases the risk of injury but this can be easily fixed with some core strength exercises (see the chapter '...Avoiding injury').

Yes – professional athletes seem to glide along the track when they compete and if it wasn't for the grimace and the sweat, it looks almost effortless. But let's remember that a lot of these athletes would have been born with a physique that made them a natural born runner, which meant they were running competitively from a very young age. They have been honing their technique pretty much their whole life. This isn't the case for all athletes however; some would have had the natural talent but will have had to work on streamlining their movement so that they could compete at the highest level. Not to say that they weren't great and talented athletes before they started working on their arm movements or stride length, but that they realised some small tweaks could be the difference between coming in fourth place and winning Gold.

If we are looking to get to the very top of our running game and we're at the stage where knocking a few seconds off our 10K personal best is going to decide where on the podium we finish, this may be when we consult a running coach on our technique. It may be that with physio and a couple of months of consultation and re-training our body, they are able to help us to run more efficiently and crack that personal record we've been after. It will be tough however and require an ongoing effort to maintain this new style, which is no longer our body's natural movement. For that reason it could also increase the risk of injury, which is why we will need the help of a physiotherapist along the way. It can be done though and actually some people adapt their running style precisely because they have an old injury, or weakness in their body where they want to avoid placing too much strain. Perhaps by being re-trained to put the weight through a different area of their foot when they run, they don't have to give up on their fitness mission.

Assuming we're not a top athlete or someone wanting to breakthrough into being a professional, our running style is going to be absolutely fine for getting us out there and for getting fit. If we're doing our stretching post-run and our strengthening exercises between runs, we will address any areas of weakness as we go. We've just got to go with how we feel, don't overthink it (like we don't overthink how we walk) and definitely, definitely don't let what we imagine other people are thinking about us stop us from exploring how our body likes to move while we're running.

What about our breathing technique? I will begin again by saying that our natural breathing rhythm and getting the oxygen into our body and the carbon dioxide out, is going to happen exactly as our body dictates. Therefore we can try and keep our breathing as a steady in and out, but it will be difficult to control when we first begin to run. The fact of the matter is that when we start out, we're going to feel out of breath within about thirty seconds of running. This is normal and our lungs and heart will take some time to adjust to this new activity. So when we get out of breath, we slow down and walk for a minute or two, allowing our pulse rate to recover a bit before starting to slowly jog again. While we're walking, this is when we want to focus a bit more on trying to regulate our breathing, concentrating on breathing out as much as our body is forcing us to get more oxygen into our body. Just be careful not to hyperventilate by disrupting our natural breathing rhythm too much; we allow our body breathe in the air it needs and then we put a bit more effort into breathing out than we normally would. We also need to take notice of our posture while we're doing our recovery walk; if we slouch over we're going to restrict the amount of oxygen our body can inhale, slowing down the recuperation process. Instead – we create a long, straight line down the length of our back, keeping our head up, chest out and by putting our hands on our hips (or on our head) as we walk and recover our breath.

As covered in Part One, once we're more of a seasoned runner and we've been running a couple of times a week for five weeks or more, our breathing is going to get much easier. Our breathing muscles and our heart muscles are going to be stronger and more flexible, meaning we can push it for longer without this feeling of needing to gasp for breath at minute intervals during our run. It does take a bit of time but again – don't overthink breathing; our body is going to let us know if it needs more oxygen and it will adjust our rate of breathing accordingly, so just go with the flow and take a break and walk for a bit if we feel out of breath. If we're patient with our breathing and we persist with our new running habit, the health benefits are countless (as we have seen). We feel fitter, we feel stronger and our body and mind are thanking us; everyday activities are easier and quality of life exponentially better as our energy levels improve.

What about nose/nasal breathing while running (in through the nose, out through the mouth)? Personally I don't restrict my in-breath to my nose while I'm running; when I take in air it is coming in any which way it wants! This means I'm breathing in most of my oxygen through the conveniently gaping hole in my face while I'm running, with my nose providing a bit extra with each in-breath. This has always worked just fine for me, even during my younger days of competing. However – there are benefits to the slower breathing rhythm that nasal breathing enforces, especially if we're prone to anxiety. The steadier pace and the deeper breaths are going to keep our body and mind in a calmer state; this is only going to be good for our emotional wellbeing and our quality of sleep. But – I speak from experience when I say it will take practise to achieve this while running; I've never been able to get enough air in through my nose, even if I slow my pace right down. However – with the many reported benefits of nasal in-breaths, in my book this will go down as a personal choice!

To summarise my key points on running style:

1. Begin by walking at a normal pace; now start to jog very slowly. This is your running style and it is just fine as it is!

2. As you run a bit faster, this is also your running style and – it is just fine as it is

3. If you are just starting out on your running mission and you haven't exercised in a while, you are going to feel completely out of breath after about ten seconds of running. This is normal. Walk for a minute or so, being careful about your posture and allowing air into your lungs but also exaggerate your out-breaths (deep breathing will also help avoid getting a stitch). Allow your heart rate and your breathing to slow down and then go again

4. It will take five weeks, running at least twice a week but everything will get easier, including your breathing. Don't give up, I promise it is worth it!

5. Remember - anyone who tries to tell you that you can't, or that you shouldn't be running, is really only expressing their own frustrations about not being brave enough to put themselves out there and try something new and difficult. It is your unique body, it is your unique running style – don't keep it hidden away, show it off!

Chapter Eighteen

Fuelling the habit – Food and hydration

First of all we need to get over the belief (or temptation?) that because we're exercising we need to eat more. Assuming we're eating three 'normal sized' meals a day, this is plain wrong. In fact we can do full-on marathon training without needing to increase the quantity of food we're consuming. Carb loading? No – we do not need to 'load' with anything. Sure – we should tweak what we're eating to make sure we're getting enough protein for muscle repair after a session in the gym; just as we'll want to eat a few more carbs the evening before a big run to help power us to the finish. We do not need to increase portion size, or the frequency with which we eat however.

There is a lot of guidance online and in books about how much of each food type we should be eating on a daily basis. It does depend on age, sex, activity levels and consider any underlying health conditions but protein intake should be approximately 25% of our total daily calorie intake, carbs about 60%, leaving fats equating to around 15%. Working on the assumption that a woman needs approximately

1,600 calories on a non-exercise day, this breaks down to 400 calories through protein intake, 960 calories worth of carbs and fats of 240 calories. Similarly for a man on a non-exercise day, burning approximately 1,800 calories, the split between protein, carbohydrates and fats is 450, 1,080 and 270 calories respectively. Now if you look at the calorie count on the packaging of the food you buy and add the calories that you're drinking, you'll realise that without exercise there is a real risk of over-eating across breakfast, lunch and dinner. However - when we exercise two or three times a week, burning an additional 400 - 600 calories on those days, we can calculate that during the course of a week we will be burning as many calories as we're consuming; this is why we don't need to eat more on exercise days, because everything is balancing out across a seven day period. As a very simple guide to the quantity we should be eating each meal, the food on our plate doesn't need to amount to any more than roughly the size of the span of our hand (and not all piled up either!)

Eating a balanced diet is the key message to ensure that we're getting all of the food groups that we need to support higher intensity workouts. Unless we're burning an extra thousand calories during a workout, or we're running every single day, burning four hundred calories each run, we don't need to eat any more than we do on a normal day.

As our body is individual to us, there is no one defined diet that is going to work for everyone. It can take a simple bit of trial and error to find out how best to power our exercise, and also what works as a meal post-run. No one wants to wake up at 3am feeling hungry because they've not eaten enough protein to aid their muscle recovery after a tough exercise session!

Healthy carbohydrates are going to help fuel our running. Oats, sweet potatoes, beetroot, kidney beans and chickpeas are a few examples; regular potatoes and brown rice are great too; make sure to leave at least a couple of hours between eating these and going for a run. Pasta remains a great way to fuel ourselves for running. Eaten the night before a run, our body breaks down the carbohydrates into glucose providing us with the energy we need to complete our cardiorespiratory workout. However – pasta does gets mixed reviews and being carbohydrate-rich (highly calorific) it is one of the foods we should avoid eating too much of once we hit forty (watch out waistline!) If we are indulging, try not to overcook the pasta (aim for al dente), eat wholemeal pasta whenever possible (the fibre helps us to feel more full), avoid creamy sauces and don't eat too big a portion (there are only so many calories we can burn off, even during a really long run!).

Non-starchy vegetables contain slow release carbs: spinach, kale, tomatoes, broccoli, cauliflower and bell pepper are just some examples. Also for fruits: bananas, oranges and blueberries will give carb levels a boost.

Protein plays numerous crucial roles in our everyday functioning and must be a staple in our diet. We need protein to power the cells in our body and keep them healthy, meaning that optimal functioning of all of our bodily systems is dependent on our consuming the right amount, considering the amount of activity we do each day. This includes muscle development and maintenance and the health of our bones. In fact, whereas our meal might have a higher percentage of carbs the night before a run (and a slightly lower percentage of protein), we should eat a higher percentage of protein in our diet after exercise to help our muscles recover and to avoid feeling completely drained the day after a tough exercise session. Protein also has a satiating effect, which means it helps us to feel more full for longer after eating, helping to stave off the urge to snack between meals.

Protein is made-up from amino acids and because we don't store amino acids in our body, we need to consume a small amount every day. However we need to consider the 'protein package' when we consume protein, so while a steak is protein rich, it is also full of saturated fat (causing fatty deposits in blood vessels, hardening the arteries and increasing the risk of heart disease). Salmon however, while providing very slightly less protein than the steak, only contains approximately 20% of the amount of saturated fats (which the body can easily process). A cup of lentils on the other hand, will provide about half the amount of protein as a piece of salmon, is also packed with fibre and contains virtually no saturated fat. Getting our protein from beans, nuts, fish, pork or poultry, rather than red meat, or any processed meats is going to be better for our health in the long run.

Eggs are also a good source of protein, as are non-sweetened yoghurt, milk and cheese (in moderation). Even vegetables will provide us with some protein, particularly broccoli and Brussels sprouts. Consuming a variety of protein sources is beneficial in ensuring we're getting the complete range of essential amino acids we need for good cellular health, and therefore our overall well-being.

In terms of eating 'good fats' in our diet, avocadoes are great friends. Also almonds, cashew nuts, peanuts, sesame seeds and pumpkin seeds are good sources of monounsaturated fats. For our polyunsaturated fats, salmon, mackerel, sardines, flaxseed, chia seeds and walnuts are also going to provide us with essential omega-3 fatty acids (which our body can't produce on its own). Adding a small amount of good quality olive oil, dripped on vegetables, or over a salad is also a great way to make sure we're getting enough of this food group.

The jury is still out on how much salt we should eat in our diet but it is critical that we consume a small amount each day. Salt plays a role in electrolyte balance and is therefore essential for nerve impulse transmission, muscle function as well as regulating the distribution of water in and around our cells ensuring our optimal hydration. Too much salt will leave us feeling dehydrated however and more serious risks with consuming too much salt and an accumulation of this mineral in our body include hypertension and the negative impact this has on the health of our brain, heart and kidneys. That said – we shouldn't be afraid to season our meals with salt. As long as we're not consuming lots of ultra-processed foods containing high levels of added salt, we can certainly make sure our home-cooked meals taste good by adding a small amount of sea salt.

Talking of salt, there is more research around now that suggests eating fermented foods is a great way to balance our gut microbiota, which plays a crucial role in digestion, our immunity and overall health. As well as reducing any inflammation of our digestive tract and enhancing nutrient absorption, there is even emerging research suggesting a link between gut health and our mental health and well-being. Note that the fermentation process is different to the pickling process, with fermentation reliant on keeping the beneficial microbes alive in order to preserve the food, while pickling inhibits the growth of all bacteria to prevent spoilage. Examples of fermented foods include yoghurt, sauerkraut, kimchi, kefir, tempeh, miso and kombucha. There are lots of recipe books and information online about how to ferment at home. A starter kit includes salt, something to ferment (e.g. cabbage, cauliflower, beetroot), an airtight container and some pH papers to measure acidity.

What about sugar? We know that most foods with added sugar are not going to do us any good at all and will only ever serve that three-minute pleasure hit. Cake, biscuits, chocolate, sugary breakfast cereals, fizzy drinks, jam, sweets and sugar itself should all be kept to a minimum. Not only will our teeth thank us for this, but along with gluten, sugar is one of these things that are going to hit our waistline much harder after the age of forty than they ever did before. But the dangers of consuming too much sugar are much further reaching than just losing our teeth and struggling to fit into our jeans; the risk of type 2 diabetes also increases significantly. Possible health complications from high blood sugar levels and insulin resistance include cardiovascular and kidney disease, complications with our eyes and vision, numbness and pain in our legs and feet, skin diseases as well as there being evidence that type 2 diabetes increases the risk of developing Alzheimer's Disease. Sugar highs, and the lows that follow, are also going to mess with our mood and our energy levels, neither of which is helpful within our efforts to look after our mental health.

The easiest way for us to avoid eating these sugary enemies is simply not to buy them in the first place and to avoid ever having them in the house. For the extreme sugar cravings, try eating some dried fruit (raisin and nut mix) or buy a bar of pure chocolate, with an 80% cocoa content and just eat a small amount. An apple is also a good way to consume natural sugars because the fibre content helps with digestion and processing the sugar more effectively. If you don't like the idea of munching on an apple, try cutting it into quarters, remove the pips and core and eat it with a small bit of low-fat cheese; for some reason the apple seems to taste slightly different when consumed like this. Otherwise – we really need to try and limit the food and drink we consume that contains 'added sugar'. We can get all of the natural sugars that we need to function by eating a piece of fruit each day and consuming a diet rich in vegetables.

My personal go-to foods in preparation for a long run, or a marathon are wholemeal pasta the night before, topped with broccoli, tomatoes, chicken and a couple of spoonfuls of a good pesto. Just a regular sized cereal-bowl in quantity, containing one small chicken breast; this is plenty to power me through a marathon the next day. For breakfast on the day of the marathon, two slices of toast (having bought a fresh loaf of sourdough the day before) topped with marmalade for a quick sugar boost. And to reiterate: water, water, water; preferably drinking it in small amounts throughout the day before the run. If I'm going out for a long, steady run (anything more than an hour and a quarter), I'd take a half litre bottle of water with me to keep me hydrated until the end of the run. Before high-intensity training or a marathon, I drink a litre of water in the two-hour window beforehand and I will top-up through the session or on my way around the course.

Eating the right mix of protein, carbs and good fat, together with drinking enough water, is going to provide enough fuel without leaving us feeling lethargic after meals or having to worry about a growing waistline. And whether we're running the next day or not, we should always try and allow at least three hours between eating and going to bed. See Part Four for some pre and post-run meal ideas.

Bin the sin

Gluttony is listed as one of the seven deadly sins, yet somehow at some point in time, over-eating started being rewarded. Competitions to see who can eat the most, getting your meal for free if you can eat the giant sized plate of food, and the 'all you can eat' menu offered in restaurants. It is a crazy world when one person is eating enough in one sitting to feed five people and being made to feel that this is a good thing.

Portion size and second helpings are two of the major contributing factors to our overeating. The temptation to serve ourselves a full plate of food each evening, perhaps even piled up if we're feeling particularly hungry that evening; or we wolf down the first portion and then help ourselves to seconds. Both will lead to us taking on way more calories than we actually need and subsequently to our putting on weight.

In an ideal world, we'd chew each mouthful at least ten times while eating and we'd take twenty minutes or longer to finish our meal. It is only after twenty minutes, we start to feel full; our ghrelin level decreases, leptin levels increase, enhancing the feeling of fullness and making it much easier to say no to that second helping. In the real world, despite having spent anywhere up to an hour or more preparing food, we gulp it in down in a matter of minutes, barely giving the food we've eaten time to touch the sides and certainly not enough time for our body to register how much we've just eaten.

These are very simple reasons as to why we end up overeating and put more food into our body than it needs. What happens to the excess? Well – our body deals with it by storing it as fat. Over time, we put on weight. This is why, if we are to achieve good health, no matter what size, shape, weight or muscle make-up we are, our thirty minute sessions of exercise two or three times a week, must be complemented by a balanced diet, in sensible portion sizes, drinking plenty of water and avoiding second helpings.

Can I eat cake?

Personally I am an advocate for cutting down rather than cutting out completely because in the scheme of things, a little bit of what we fancy, balanced with regular exercise is the most realistic way of sustaining a healthy lifestyle on an ongoing basis. Plus I believe that once we've managed to cut-down on certain foods, it does become progressively easier to start to say "no" altogether on occasions where we would have previously caved-in to the temptation. It takes time to get here but persistent self-control does make us stronger each time it comes to saying "no thank you" as we lick our lips at the mere whiff of the freshly baked pastry. But I'm also well aware that for some people one bite can easily lead to ten and that in these cases avoiding certain foodstuffs completely is the only way to avoid the massive whack of calories and the guilt that comes with this.

With sugar I am really conscious about the effect this has on my body as a woman over forty and I really try and limit the frequency and the quantity I consume these days. However - put a piece of birthday cake in front of me, I will very likely accept "just a small slice please". But I would have the 'this is not healthy' alarm bells going off in my head as I said yes and I would certainly be thinking about when my next exercise session would be and when I would be burning these calories off. Yes – in an ideal world, I wouldn't eat the cake; in an ideal world my brain would be telling me "this is bad for you and therefore you're not going to enjoy this experience" much like it would if I was being offered a garden snail to eat. However my early experiences in life, eating a slice of delicious birthday cake, laden with unbelievable amounts of sugar (if you've ever baked a cake, you know what I'm talking about), then learning that if you combine cake with a cup of tea or coffee, you have this marvelous taste sensation of everything you know is bad for you but that provides thirty seconds of heavenly joy; it is proving difficult to shake this firmly embedded memory. But as the ideal world ultimate goal should be to wean ourselves off these bad foods and give our brain the time to forget that we enjoy a certain taste, the less often I consume cake, the more chance I have of achieving this goal (or at least to cut down to eating cake only a few times per year).

But exercise does open up the option for a guilt-free bit of what we fancy. If we're doing our two or three running sessions that week and otherwise eating a healthy diet, we can afford some small guilty pleasures while managing to balance the calories-in-calories-out equation. Maybe we can get to the point where half a slice satisfies the occasional craving too? Or maybe we limit ourselves to only ever eating one or two bad foodstuffs ever and cut out the rest? And with bad foodstuffs, don't feel bad about throwing it away when you've had enough. Obviously it is better not to buy it in the first place (you can't eat what you don't have) and in general food waste is a bad thing but it is better to put excess unhealthy food in the rubbish than into yourself!

Christmas? Yes – if our meal adds to the happiness of the occasion, we can give ourself the day, or couple of days of freedom to pile-up the plate a bit more! We just need to make sure that we get back on the healthy wagon again after those couple of days (or better still, get an early morning run in on Christmas Day and then enjoy your day knowing that you were burning your lunch off even before you started eating it!)

Why can't I just go on a diet (again)?

The problem with dieting (typically defined as maintaining a calorie deficit of between 500 and 1,000 calories per day, every day), or cutting out certain foods, is that this is really difficult to maintain over a long period of time, then when we revert back to our previous way of eating we lose any benefits we've managed to accumulate. Plus - cutting out certain food groups altogether may be counterproductive in the long run.

Remember the hunger hormone ghrelin, with one of its many functions being to signal when our stomach is empty and it is time to eat? Research that measures the different levels of ghrelin in people of different body weights, and in those who fast, seems to suggest that ghrelin is involved in the long-term regulation of body weight. This makes sense given that this hormone lets us know when it is time to eat, plays a role in stimulating our digestive system and how our body releases insulin and controls sugars within our body. But the evidence is that ghrelin also as helps to maintain healthy muscles, bones, metabolism, cardiovascular health and plays a role in mediating memory and stress. In fact research identifying the signaling pathways of the ghrelin system may even lead to new treatments for neurological diseases. In the scheme of achieving ongoing good health, we need to respect the ghrelin.

How do we ensure our body is producing the right level of ghrelin at the right time, and how do we maintain this healthy level? Well – here comes the argument against any fad diets, yo-yo dieting and carbohydrate free diets. These are all going to mess with our ghrelin levels, increasing production of our hunger hormone meaning any weight we've lost by cutting out carbs, or by crash dieting will quickly go back on once we return to eating our regular meals. Also cutting out certain food groups completely for a period of time will only confuse our body when we go back to eating those food types; our body isn't used to having to digest these foods and will have more difficulty processing the food. This in turn leaves us feeling tired, possibly even nauseous, and very likely with an uncomfortable feeling in our stomach for the rest of the day.

Instead, in order to manage ghrelin levels, we should eat a diet that includes healthy carbohydrates and lean proteins. Think whole grains, potatoes, vegetables, chicken, fish and pulses. And while we don't want to cut any food group out of our diet completely, it is good to have days where we eat fewer carbohydrates, and of course for meat-eaters, meat-free days are also going to be beneficial for our digestive systems. In fact it is a myth that we need to eat lots of red meat when we exercise regularly and push our body; we can get all of the iron and protein we need from other foods. It is also vital to limit ultra-processed foods, which typically contain ingredients that we don't use ourselves when cooking (for example 'hydrogenated oil' or 'anti-foaming agent'), especially foods high in sugar and E-numbers. Of course – sleep is also vital in maintaining healthy levels of ghrelin, as is staying hydrated by drinking plenty of water (five to six 300ml glasses per day).

What about fasting? The '16/8' fasting method is a relatively new concept, which involves not eating anything for sixteen hours and consuming all of the day's calories in an eight hour period (for example, between 11am and 7pm). It is gaining popularity, with reported benefits including weight management, improved insulin sensitivity, reduced blood pressure, reducing inflammation and if the early reports of cellular health are proved, could it even improve our longevity? Fasting may negatively affect our sex hormones however so may not be recommended if you're trying to get pregnant; it also takes careful planning to ensure you're still eating all of the vitamins, minerals and other nutrients our body needs to function properly. So yes – it is possible to do and some people seem to have this level of self-control, as well as a lifestyle that supports being able to fast for sixteen hours every day, 365 days per year. For the rest of us, who haven't yet trained ourselves to go without food for two-thirds of the day, or perhaps our body type or lifestyle doesn't suit this routine, we don't have to force our diets to this level to achieve optimal health. Yes – we need a lot of self-control once we're over the age of forty and it is going to be tough to say no to certain foods, or to resist having that second helping, but this does get easier and easier if we are looking after our body, exercising regularly and building new eating habits over time.

Water, water, water, water, water, water

In being healthy, water is our life-blood. Being well-hydrated means our red blood cells can replace themselves at the rate they need to so that we stay in good shape; and with approximately 60% of the human adult body composed of water it also helps to keep all other cells in our body nice and plump. In addition, being well-hydrated helps optimise our digestion, and it washes away toxins from our body.

In contrast, dehydration can manifest itself in many different ways, dry or cracked lips, a dry feeling at the back of the tongue, and most noticeably it can leave us feeling so tired and fatigued that we feel ready to go to bed by 7pm every day.

> Have you ever heard of ATP (adenosine triphosphate)? ATP is the primary energy source for our cells, enabling them to perform their role in the functioning of our body (across all of our bodily systems). Inadequate hydration can impair ATP production, thus contributing to our feeling mentally and physically fatigued and a general sense of exhaustion

If we're not getting enough water it adversely affects our blood pressure, which in turn is bad news for our organs, muscles and our cognitive function, leading to difficulty concentrating, headaches and irritability. Apart from dry lips, a good way to tell if we're dehydrated is by looking at the colour of our urine. Our first pee of the day will always be more dark and smell more pungent because it has been accumulating for several hours; if we're drinking enough water, our pee for the rest of the day should be almost transparent and (unless we've been eating asparagus) it shouldn't smell so potent either!

We should aim for at least one and half litres of water per day, or two litres if we've exercised. Beware that we don't want to drink too much water in one go as this will over-dilute the natural level of electrolytes in our body and can actually be harmful. So avoid drinking a whole litre in one go, and instead have approximately five or six medium sized glasses throughout the day. The same holds true during a long run; take many sips of water rather than guzzling down lots in one go. This does mean going to the bathroom more often during the day (as we cleanse our body) and may require either tactical drinking (such that we have a toilet nearby), or a tactical pee (if we're heading out and won't have access to a toilet for a period of time.) To avoid getting up during the night for a pee, we can try drinking our daily water requirement between the time we first wake-up, with our last liquid intake a couple of hours before going to bed.

Plain, ordinary water remains the best way to stay hydrated, whether it be hot, warm or at room temperature. If you're a coffee lover, the diuretic affect of caffeine means we will be going to the toilet more often. So while coffee may give us a short boost, we're also losing the liquid at a faster rate, limiting the hydrating effect of coffee. The same can be said for tea, which contains less caffeine (per 240ml cup: 40 – 70 milligrams versus 95 – 200 milligrams in coffee) but also won't have the desired effect on providing our body with the optimal hydration levels.

Sugary energy drinks are the real enemy here however, with the regularly induced spikes in blood sugar levels leading to inflammation, fatigue, hunger, cravings and ultimately, through prolonged consumption, increasing the risks of stroke, heart disease, liver disease and type-2 diabetes. And the problem with sugar-free energy drinks is that they are often loaded with caffeine and more often than not contain artificial sweeteners as well. Even those that claim to be healthy are said by the medical profession to have possible side-effects of nausea, bloating, adverse blood-pressure and hormone disruption. Some might say that if consumed in moderation (once per week) they won't do you any harm, but it is impossible to say that 'these are fine' when what is out there today is mostly just manufactured crap that is being sold to us as having certain post-exercise recovery benefits when in reality the harm of consuming these man-made products outweighs the benefits five-fold. It is so much better stick to water and if you really struggle drinking plain water, there are low-sugar, additive free electrolyte tablets on the market that can be added to water for a bit of flavour. But as with anything, even these should be consumed in moderation.

There are of course always exceptions to circumstance, and if we're running a marathon, training in the heat, or doing an activity where we're sweating a lot over a period of an hour or more, consuming an 'isotonic' (electrolyte) drink is going to help us push ourselves to the limit for longer. A decent electrolyte drink replaces the sugars and salt we lose as sweat while exercising over a longer period of time (maintaining a high heart rate for one hour plus) or when we're doing a particularly strenuous workout. Apart from during and after these particularly tough workouts we don't need to go anywhere near energy drinks and we definitely shouldn't be consuming these on a daily basis. And if you simply just don't like the idea of consuming these man-made drinks at all, if we are eating a balanced diet we can train our body to manage without consuming electrolyte drinks. The more regularly we train hard with only water to drink, the more our body will get use to managing without.

As a tip for running a marathon (and I'm aware that this goes against the "don't consume any crap" messaging in this book) is that I would only drink water on the way around the 26.2 miles but I would drink/eat (they tend to be quite thick) three or four energy gels along the route. These take five minutes or so to kick-in, but the kick is noticeable and for me, essential to get me over those inevitable heavy-legged moments. These gels are jam-packed with calories though and are really only necessary during a half-marathon, marathon or longer. And while everyone is different and will prefer a different way, or frequency of refueling, with the right diet and enough water, our body will have enough energy stores to get us through anything shorter than thirteen miles (twenty-one kilometers) without using these sugar-laden gels.

Chapter Nineteen

Building Fitness

There's this wonderful thing about getting fitter, aside from the fact we can feel really proud for having worked so hard to get to this point, we are also feeling much better in ourselves. Energy levels are high, sleep is undisturbed, perhaps we're even feeling a bit lighter in our step and just better equipped to deal with the day-to-day. This is going to have a knock-on effect to all other elements of our life and a snowball effect on our improving health.

Following the first five weeks of near-hell torture, then the next four weeks of steady improvement, running for a few minutes longer by the end of each week, by the time we get to week nine, we're running non-stop for thirty minutes.

This commitment we've made to ourselves, and the results we've seen, create a new awareness around other parts of our lives. We naturally become more aware of what we're eating: "Damn I'm feeling really good about myself right now, I'm going to say no to the second slice of birthday cake". Or "I want to go for a run after work, so I'm not going to have a chocolate bar at 4pm today because that will mess with my run". Or "I actually really want to eat oven-baked salmon and vegetables for dinner tonight. Eating a burger and chips means I won't see the full effect of my run on my body in the mirror tomorrow morning". This new awareness is a real thing and when embraced, we're going to see a double impact on our improving health.

The next obvious snowballing effect on our health is the fact that after nine weeks of running, our heart, lungs and muscles are getting stronger and fitter. Previously jogging for a minute would have caused a spike in our heart rate and our lungs would feel like they were about to burst out of our chest; now we're able to keep going, without stopping to walk, for thirty minutes. With our heart and lungs able to carry us for longer, the pressure now shifts to our muscles, which are also now being challenged to keep working for thirty minutes (instead of the two minutes we could manage when we first started out).

Whereas our muscles can manage a one-minute workout without really calling for any additional nutrients, by the time we are moving consistently and maintaining a high heart rate for anything more than twenty minutes, our muscles are screaming for more energy. It is at this twenty-minute tipping point that the fat our body is burning is accelerated, and if weight loss is the aim and we're watching our calorie intake, exercising regularly for more than twenty minutes at a time is when we will begin to notice the difference in our body shape.

During our run we will experience 'slumps' in our energy level, moments when we convince ourselves that we can't carry on and we need to stop. Most of the time however, if we slow down very slightly but carry on running, our energy levels will come back after a minute or so and we will be able to pick-up the pace again. This might only happen a couple of times during our run, or if we're running a marathon, no matter how much we've trained, we could experience this sensation as many as five or six times during the race! This might be because we've used up the energy from one source in our body and now it has to start providing fuel from one of our alternative energy stores meaning there is a small gap in the energy supply to our muscles. If we're able to continue running through this lull of energy provision and through the fatigue until we start to feel stronger again, this is a good sign that our body is doing what it needs to so that we can keep going. It is also a reassuring sign that we're burning more calories than those we had readily available. On other occasions however, if the feeling of fatigue is refusing to budge and our legs are getting heavier and heavier, even if we slow down to a jog, it could be that our body isn't up for it today and we are better off calling it a day. In this instance, eat a healthy protein-packed meal, some healthy carbs, drink plenty of water and get an early night.

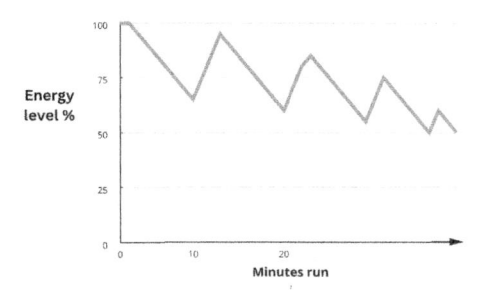

An example of how our energy levels shift during a run. It is normal to experience a period of low energy, when we convince ourselves we're going to need to stop. More often than not however we just need to slow down for a brief time, allowing our energy levels to rise again so we can continue on our mission

The benefits of pushing through the five-week pain barrier and persisting past week nine of this new running partnership keep on coming: depending on our level of fitness, it can take several minutes for our heart to come back to its resting rate after a run. This means that we continue to burn calories at a faster rate even as we stand in the shower after exercise. The accelerated replacement of cells in our body, as well as the muscle repair work that happens after a run are also going to keep our rate of calorie burning at an elevated level long after our run.

Have you heard the saying 'muscle burns more calories than fat'? It's true; because muscle consumes energy (calories) even at rest, when we start to build-up our muscles through repeated exercise, we're also speeding up our metabolic rate (the amount of energy our body burns to function when at rest). That said, and as covered in the chapter 'Running for weight loss', we should be aware about building up really big muscles in order to keep our weight under control. Muscle will degenerate pretty quickly if it isn't regularly being honed in the gym and the risk is that if we don't adjust our diet to account for the fact we don't need as many calories anymore, the benefits of the bodybuilding are quickly lost.

This is another reason why building enough muscle to support our body to run, plus complementing the running with Pilates and resistance training (using our own body weight to build strength) is the best, and most sustainable ways to boost our metabolism.

On an exercise day, not only will our 'active calories' burnt be approximately 200 calories for every twenty minutes of running we do, but our elevated heart rate immediately after exercise, plus the impact on our resting heart rate for the rest of the day means that, depending on how long we keep our heart rate raised during exercise, we will burn an additional 400 calories per day. This figure increases for every additional minute of exercise we do above the twenty minutes at approximately 10 calories per minute of exercise.

With the slow build in fitness levels until week five (35 days), followed by a reassuringly progressively easier four weeks to take us to week nine, it really is worthwhile fighting to get over the initial five week hump. By pushing past week nine and on to week thirteen, increasing our running efforts very slightly with each run, the benefits we're going to see and feel, mentally and physically, are going to be life-changing, making all of the pain of our efforts worthwhile.

Chapter Twenty

Dodging the running rut - Taking our training to the next level

There are a number of things happening in our body and mind as we become fitter and exercise becomes easier. For starters our body gets used to the movements we make when we run, our muscles, heart and lungs become much more efficient and there is less stress on our system as we go about living our life. This is all great news for our health, well-being and longevity. However with our heart now much fitter and able to handle a thirty minute jog no problem, if we then just keep repeating the same distance run, at the same pace week in, week out, our body will get stuck in a running rut .We are no longer pushing our body as hard as we were in our early running days, meaning we'll also see our weight plateau (at best). So having been a runner for at least four months by now and still experiencing many of the benefits that running gifts us, we will need to consciously push ourselves a bit more each week, or mix up our training to include some different intensity training sessions. There are multiple ways we can continue to push ourselves to the edge of our comfort zone:

Pacing

The easiest option to ensure that we continue to challenge our body and improve our fitness levels is for us to consciously make sure we're running at a very slightly faster pace when we go out for our run. We're not just maintaining cruise control level anymore, going through the motions at the same pace this run as the last run, and the run before that etc. but we're going to purposely increase the tempo of our legs. Even a small increase in our pace is going to make enough of a difference.

If we pay attention and listen to our body, we can feel when our heart rate is elevated and our breathing laboured (versus our breathing being 'comfortable'). If we're willing to recognise when we're not pushing ourselves to the point where we start to feel out of breath anymore (or if our watch is telling us that our heart rate is only ever reaching zone three now whereas previously a run got us into zone four and out of our aerobic comfort zone), this is when we should try and pick-up the pace. Ideally by the end of every run we should feel out of breath and that we couldn't run any further. This could be due to us running that bit faster, or extending the length of our run. If we need to plan a slightly longer route, take the time to do this upfront.

If we want to push ourselves even more, plan to build a couple of faster minutes into the run. Perhaps run at normal pace for ten minutes, then pick-up the pace slightly for two minutes, then normal pace for ten minutes, two minutes faster and finish the run at normal pace.

Mixing it up

Alternatively there are additional sessions we can add to our training schedule to ensure we continuously improve our fitness. 'Fartlek' is a training method developed in the late 1930s by Swedish Olympian Gösta Holmér. The literal translation is 'speed play' and the nature of it means this training can be done anywhere.

The concept involves alternating between short, fast paced bursts of running and our comfortable paced jog. This is tougher than it sounds and realistically we'll probably manage about twenty minutes to start with, a few seconds of speed, followed by a couple of minutes jogging. However we can build this up over time and once we're really fit, this interval training could be repeated over a total of forty-five minutes ('Super-fit' box – ticked!)

The fast-paced running in Fartlek is 'as fast as you can go' for approximately forty metres; the pace is then reduced to a jog for two or three minutes before repeating the fast-pace. The workout builds strength, and if we also increase the length of the speedy section, or the total length of running time, we'll quickly see an improvement in stamina as well. The better our stamina, the longer we can run; the longer we're able to run, the more calories we're going to burn, both while we're running, but also at our basal metabolic rate (at rest).

Because Fartlek running involves running at speed, we must warm-up properly before we begin, otherwise we risk injuring a muscle. So - a five minute jog beforehand, static stretching and then dynamic stretching, including some practice half-pace, then three quarter pace twenty metre runs. (Warm-up and stretching exercises are covered in detail in the chapter'...Avoiding injury').

Beach running on heavy, or unstable sand, and hill repetitions (run up the hill, jog back down, and repeat) are also great ways to build strength in our legs. These sessions quickly build fatigue in our leg muscles, and if we use them as part of our regular training, when it comes to our 'normal runs' we will be able to push it a bit faster, or a bit further. Doing either of these sessions for thirty minutes once a fortnight is definitely going to stop our fitness from plateauing.

If we're trying to make a quick difference to our fitness levels, Fartlek, beach or hill training are great ways to mix things up and quickly build strength. The watch-out if we are going to be doing any speedwork is that, having warmed our muscles up properly before we begin, we must gradually build-up our speed during the session. Following these sessions, we must also take the time to warm-down and also to stretch our muscles out again.

The intensity of speedwork will often leave our muscles feelings very tight; we're putting a high demand through the entire length of the muscle and activating our 'fast-twitch' muscle fibres. Our fast-twitch fibres have a lower concentration of blood vessels running through them (they're able to make their own quick source of energy); this is why we have to take the time to warm the muscle fibres up before exercise, as well as warm-down properly after exercise, pumping enough blood through so that the cells are receiving the energy they need to replenish ('repair') themselves.

In contrast, jogging relies first on our 'slow-twitch' muscle fibres, which not only have more blood vessels running through them but also contain more of the protein 'myoglobin', whose main function is to supply oxygen to the cells in our muscles. This richer supply of oxygen to our slow-twitch muscles, which are only able to carry a more limited force (or support a slower pace) versus our fast-twitch muscles, explains why we can sustain exercise for a longer period of time when jogging. While our slow-twitch muscles are more easily warmed up as we start jogging, they will still need to be warmed-down and stretched after running as well, pushing the blood (nutrients and oxygen) through the muscles, aiding the muscle repair.

High intensity interval training (HIIT) sessions will also help build muscle strength and endurance and put a different kind of stress on our cardiovascular system, ultimately meaning we can push our fitness levels up a notch. Explosive exercises such as push-ups, squats, kettle-bell swings, which use either our own body weight, or with an added weight (kettle bells, medicine balls, dumbbells), will work our muscles and push our heart rate up. This is not about heavy weights, but about faster movements with no or low weights. Anything more than a light weight is going to put too much pressure through certain muscles or joints and will cause an injury. Again – because movements are more explosive, a good warm-up is critical, including some slow tempo dynamic movements (easing ourselves into the full-on movements we'll be doing).

HIIT sessions are great to build core strength, which is going to support our running posture, as well as sustaining a high heart rate for a period of twenty to thirty minutes. HIIT sessions are best limited to one, possibly two per week however, otherwise we're not giving our muscles enough time to properly recover and we risk feeling drained for the rest of the week.

It can be daunting trying something new or different when we're exercising but by mixing up our training we'll quickly reap the benefits and notice the results in our performance. Plan these sessions into the week so that you know what you're doing on which days.

Another benefit of getting to this stage with our running is that once we've been running for a while, we don't have to start from square one every time we're forced to take time-out. This improved muscle memory is a big deal; we worked long and hard to get to this point; now, while the first run after a couple of weeks out of action feels tough, by the time we head out for our second run we'll feel like we're easing back to our regular pace. This is a big boost to motivation, so be sure to embrace it and persist after that first slightly rusty run that follows a break in our running habit.

We will all have different reasons for wanting to run, but if our aim is to continually improve our fitness, or to lose a certain amount of weight, we will need to keep track of our training and recognise if our running has become just a little bit too routine and easy. If we've been repeating the same run, at the same speed, our body will get to the stage where it isn't really being challenged anymore. It isn't that our body is losing fitness, and a routine run is still going to be raising our heart rate and giving our cardiovascular system a workout, but if we are able to push ourselves each run, increasing the pace, or perhaps the length of our run, we can avoid our fitness plateauing. Alternatively if we introduce a Fartlek, or a HIIT session once per week and make sure we're looking after our body; warming up, stretching and warming down before and after a more intense session (helping to avoid injury), we will also see our fitness snowballing. And not just our physical fitness but also our mental fitness; the time we have carved-out for ourselves to look after health, plus the investment we have made in our future self, will put us in a position to better cope with whatever life throws at us.

Chapter Twenty-One

No one needs to get hurt... Avoiding injury

It is really, really rubbish having to take an enforced break from running to recover from an injury when we've been putting in so much time and effort in steadily improving our fitness levels. Up until that point we'd been noticing the accumulation effect, watching all of our health metrics improve week by week. It is then doubly frustrating that instead of reaping all of the benefits of our weekly runs, we are having to spend this time doing physio exercises instead. However – if we look after our body and listen to what is going on with our body, it is possible to avoid ever having a time-out from running because of injury.

The sedentary lifestyle we've adopted brings with it many risks, including making it much more likely that we'll suffer from a muscle injury at some point, even while going about our day-to-day activities. Our muscles shorten when we don't regularly stretch them, meaning any sudden movement outside our shrunken comfort zone could easily end in a muscle strain.

The hours we spend sitting on our butt also mean that if we want to avoid injury while in pursuit of our running habit, we need to help our muscles transition from the crumpled state of the sitting position to springy, supple running motors. We do this by spending sufficient time warming up and warming down and gently easing our muscles into and out of exercise.

A frequent cause of muscular injuries these days is due precisely to the fact that as well as the natural age-related muscle loss, our muscles weaken to the point of the maximum exertion we put through them; if we then do something that's out of our routine suddenly we've pulled a muscle in our back, neck, leg, or shoulder.

Another common issue with improving our fitness while avoiding injury is muscle imbalance. As an example, when we run, our glutes (bum muscles) and our hamstrings must work in perfect harmony to ensure they take the right amount of force through each muscle such that no one muscle becomes overburdened. Any imbalance between the two muscles groups will eventually manifest itself as an injury. With the sedentary lifestyle, our glutes, which should be one of the strongest muscles in our body, actually weaken to the point where we become at high risk of overloading our hamstrings. Something has to take the strain when we run and because our glutes have become 'lazy', we risk overloading our hamstrings. Welcome knee pain, lower leg injury, or even hip pain, depending on how far the transference of workload has travelled! Keeping our glutes strong is paramount as we build up our running fitness and there are some simple exercises we can do to strengthen these muscles (as detailed later in this chapter).

Another injury risk materialises when we don't appreciate how important a strong upper body and core muscles are for running. Maintaining good strength in our arms, shoulders, across the length of our back, our chest, abdominals, obliques and rectus abdominis (abs) is going to support and stabilise us. The more stable we are when we run and the less our upper body is twisting from side to side as our arms pump back and forth, the better protected we are against jarring our back, or again – any imbalance through our hips, or forced over-compensation by muscles further down our legs. A strong upper body doesn't mean bulky muscle, but muscles that are strong enough to support our own body weight. This is again where Pilates is a great partner to running.

Muscle damage is generally caused when we suddenly put heavy strain on the muscle as a result of physical exertion, perhaps when the muscle is not warmed up properly, or if we twist it awkwardly. It can also be the result of a repetitive movement; eventually taking us out of our comfort zone, we can feel the muscle getting tired but we keep pushing harder anyway. The damage can cause a small amount of bleeding within the muscle itself, manifesting as tenderness and swelling. An ice pack can help reduce the immediate swelling and normally a short period of rest will allow the muscle to repair itself. If possible, it is worthwhile seeing a physiotherapist through the recovery period. A physio can assess the damage as well as use ultrasound or massage to ensure that there is no build-up of scar tissue as the muscle repairs itself (scar tissue is a tough, dense tissue and it can cause the muscle to lose some of its flexibility). Alternatively – grab some baby oil, or massage oil and give yourself a gentle massage for five minutes each day until the stiffness is gone. If after a period of rest the pain doesn't go away on its own, go and see a doctor to get a referral to the physio, or go and see the physiotherapist directly.

If we ever experience a sharp, stabbing pain in a muscle, bone, or joint while exercising, we need to stop what we're doing and observe if the pain goes away on its own after a couple of days. If it doesn't, again – now is the time to book an appointment with a physiotherapist, to rest and to let our body recover. A physio will be able to help identify if the injury is due to muscles imbalance or weakness and can then advise on strengthening exercises so that the same injury doesn't keep rearing its ugly head.

One thing we should always avoid with any running pains, or pain we experience during exercise is to numb it with painkillers or anti-inflammatory medication and then try and carry on as if nothing has happened. If we're experiencing pain in the same spot every time we run (or after running) then we should see a doctor or a physiotherapist for help and advice. Sometimes taking a paracetamol, or having a steroid injection will take the swelling down such that the pain goes away completely (if the pain was due to the swelling). However - pain is the body's response to injury and if we block out this signal to our brain without fixing the root cause of the issue, we risk doing even more damage, perhaps even permanent damage if we just carry on. We're certainly going to be in even more pain once the painkiller wears off! It is better to let the body do its own repair work, which it does by sending increased blood flow to the injury, with nutrients and oxygen aiding the repair and the waste products from the repair work being transported away from the area. But - we can complement the work our body is doing with some gentle massage, improving the blood flow and the delivery of nutrients to the injured area and whisking the away the waste, helping to prevent the build-up of scar tissue. Then we can work on strengthening any weaknesses at the root cause of the issue. And – very important for recovery: rest. After a few days the muscle will feel less stiff, our flexibility is improving again and we're feeling the stretchiness of our muscle return to normal. So yes, take ibuprofen to help reduce the swelling and the pain, but then rest and recover; don't just carry on running.

Injury Prevention

We can breakdown injury prevention into four subsets; the first is pre-run preparation, the second is what we do during our run, the third immediately after our run and the fourth considers what we do in-between our runs. In other words, 1) warming up properly before putting high strain on our muscles and 2) knowing how hard to push ourselves during our run, but just as importantly – 3) ensuring we stretch properly after exercising, draining our muscles of any excess lactate (lactic acid) that has accumulated during our workout, relieving muscle stiffness and reducing soreness the next day. Finally – but again vital in keeping ourselves off the physiotherapy table, is 4) to complement our running with body strength exercises, such a Pilates and resistance training.

1. Pre-run preparation

Build a training plan and start slowly

If we're just starting out with our new running ambition, or if it has been several months since we last ran, we must start slowly. Even if we feel great when we begin our jog, we need to remember that our leg muscles aren't used to our full body weight being transferred through each leg in turn as we propel our body forwards.

I recommend starting with a walk-jog running plan, such as the 'Absolute beginner', or the 'Couch to 5K' schedules described in Part Four (and if you'd like some additional motivation, join the '35 Day Running Challenge', with details also included in Part Four). Being patient with how quickly we can progress is going to give all of the muscles in our body (approximately 650 of them) the time to get used to this super tough exercise. Our skeletal and cardiac muscles, plus our lungs and our respiratory system are going to look after you, as long as you look after them by easing into your new exercise schedule.

By plotting our training schedule over nine weeks and giving ourselves this time, it provides each muscle with an opportunity to realise what is being demanded of it and slowly adjust. If we just throw ourselves straight in to a 10K run, including a sprint finish at the end because 'this run feels great!' this sudden exertion puts us at real risk of injury, or at the very least, inflammation of joints or muscles. Plus the aching the next day will be really painful, which could in itself be enough to put us off even pulling on our trainers again. Being patient and sticking to an introductory running schedule, then slowly increasing pace, or distance over time is going to help us avoid any injuries.

Warming up

As with any exercise, we're asking for trouble if we just throw ourselves in full-throttle in the first seconds. Our muscles are cold and neither our brain nor our senses have adjusted to action mode. If we are to avoid injury, it is important that we warm-up our muscles and wake-up our nervous system with some gentle rehearsal as to what's to come. The 'Couch to 5K' schedule includes a 'warm-up five minute brisk walk' at the start of every training session. However once we're past week five of training and we're really starting to notice our fitness levels improve, we can introduce a two or three-minute gentle jog instead of the five minutes of brisk walking. This initial warm-up at the start of our run is true even for the super-fit and we'll still want to run at a much more gentle pace for a couple of minutes, increasing our heart rate gradually as the blood flow increases and we begin to feel our muscles rediscover their springiness as our body warms up.

If we're going to be sprinting, or doing a fast training session or an organised race, our warm-up would include a five minute jog, ten minutes of static stretching and five minutes of dynamic stretching. This warms our muscles through and by imitating the movements we employ when sprinting, just at a slower pace, we limit the risk of injuring a muscle that hasn't been properly warmed up.

2. During our run

The most common mistake, which we all make at some point, is to push ourselves too fast, too soon. We might be out for a run and be feeling like we could run forever, so we push ourselves twice as far as we've ever run before. Or we've entered a race and we've not done enough preparation but we're determined to push ahead anyway. We might be running with a friend who challenges us to a final sprint to the end, despite not having run faster than a slow jog for the preceding forty minutes. Our body is strong, but once we're past our 'elastic' teenage years, we have to get used to the idea that our muscles need a little more respect and encouragement if we want to get the best out of them and not injure ourselves in the process. We need to be patient, sticking to our training plan and only increasing our pace, or the distance we're running very gradually. If we're feeling invincible during our run, resist the temptation to push-on, over and above what the training schedule dictates.

Pacing during a run

Unless we're doing a Fartlek, or an interval training session, where we're purposely mixing up our running pace, we should aim to keep the speed at which we run as steady as possible. This helps us to learn what pace works best for us, whether it be only slightly faster than our walking pace, or bounding along extending our stride length to almost full stretch. What we want to try and avoid is heading out too fast and then having to crawl the last bit home, exhausted and in pain.

Yes – we want to feel tired and out of breath at the end of a run, but if we're being patient and steadily building fitness, the idea isn't to kill ourselves each and every run (and running until we can't run any more isn't going to help our motivation to persevere with our running habit either). Instead – find your 'I could run forever at this pace' pace. This is a speed that has you breathing more deeply and frequently (as your heart rate increases and your lungs and respiratory system are stretching themselves to get more oxygen into your body) but not so completely out of breath that you couldn't have a bit of a chat with your running buddy along the way. This pace is going to be different for everyone, and is whatever feels comfortable (or just verging on the uncomfortable) for you.

In terms of likelihood of injuring ourselves during our run, there are two higher risk periods that we should be aware of and be more careful. The first, as already mentioned, is to take it very slowly when we set-off for our run; the first thirty metres or so should really be nothing more than a very slow jog. If we have been sitting all day long, we must give our muscles the opportunity to increase the blood flow through them and warm up a bit. We also need to be careful towards the end of our run, when we are starting to feel very fatigued. This is when we are at risk of our running style becoming a bit lazy; we might get more twisting movement in our upper body and we kick our legs out more than normal because we don't have the energy to lift our feet so far off the ground anymore. However - there is a significant decrease in this risk if we have strong core muscles providing stability to our body shape as we get more tired, otherwise it is another reason not to run to the point of exhaustion during our training runs.

As mentioned previously, unless we've been working on our sprinting skills, resist the sprint finish at the end of a training session too. Sprinting demands even more stretch of our muscles and puts even greater force through them. So however tempting that call of "race you to the front door" is at the end of the run, without our muscles being properly warmed up, it is an injury waiting to happen!

> Occasionally monitoring our breathing during a run can help to make sure we're not getting lazy with our out-breaths, which are just as important for getting enough oxygen into our body. I occasionally get stomach pains during my run, which in my opinion (having narrowed it down over time) is due to a lack of oxygen in/around my digestive system. What I've found works to get rid of the pain is to really focus on deep in-breaths and putting more effort into my exhalation as well. The pain doesn't go away immediately but it allows me to continue running and it does subside after five minutes or so and then I can run normally again.

3. Post run injury prevention

The cooldown jog

If we've got the time, taking two minutes at the end of our run to warm-down our muscles with a slow jog is always going to be beneficial. However if we've been on a steady-paced run it is very likely that the last couple of minutes were slightly slower anyway; in this case we can move straight on to our stretching exercises. For any speedwork sessions, or competitive races, where our pace was faster than normal, making time for a jog immediately afterwards will help our heart rate return to resting level more gradually as well as metabolise lactic acid at a faster rate, enhancing our recovery.

Stretching after a run

Stretching needs to be considered as an important part of our workout, and if we are to avoid injury and minimise aches and pains the day after a run, stretching must be factored in to our allotted exercise time.

Taking time to stretch and re-lengthen our muscles after our run ensures that the blood flowing through our capillaries reaches every last muscle fibre, aiding our recovery and helping to reduce muscle stiffness. Stretching also helps our body to process the bi-products of exercise (including lactate); transporting these away from the muscle so they can either be used elsewhere or be expelled from the body.

Stretching immediately after exercise, while our heart rate is still slightly raised and our blood pumping faster through our body makes clearing toxins and by-products easier on ourselves. Particularly after doing repetitive muscle movement, we need to stretch out all of the muscle fibres in our legs, across our back, core and shoulders. If we've had a tough run, there is no getting away from a degree of aching the next day, but we can limit the tightness in our muscles through regular stretching.

As a rule, I would always take eight minutes to stretch out my muscles immediately after my run. If I've run further, or faster than I have for a while, or if I'm just getting back into running after an enforced period out, I would also do some very gentle stretching just before going to bed (remembering that my muscles are cold and won't stretch as far as they do immediately post exercise). Also – just taking a few minutes the next day doing some very gentle leg and lower back stretches is going to ease muscular pain as our muscles repair and strengthen themselves. Keeping our muscles supple between runs will also protect us against an injury caused by a stiff muscle being called into sudden action, and it means that we won't be wincing when we start our next run.

What exactly do we mean by 'stretching'? Stretching after exercise is different to that first stretch we have in the morning, or after we've been sitting in the same position at our desk for too long, but they both serve the purpose of lengthening the muscles to their optimal resting length.

Running aside, we should all try and make stretching a daily habit because the benefits to the quality of our daily life are numerous. These include:

1. Our flexibility will improve over time, making every day tasks easier. Bending over to do up our shoe, squatting down to feed the cat, standing up and sitting down, will all be easier if our muscles start from a lengthened position

2. Avoiding injury: our 'softened' muscles, resulting from regular stretching, mean it is a lot less likely we ever feel, or hear, that dreaded 'pinging' sound of our muscle pulling or

tearing. Or even that stab of pain when we've stood up too quickly after sitting in the same position for too long and our muscles have seized-up

3. We'll improve the mobility of our joints. With more flexible muscles around our joints, our running (and walking) performance will quickly progress. Just think how much faster will you be able to cover five kilometers if each stride is just a few centimeters longer?

4. Strengthening our muscles and encouraging the nutrient rich blood flowing through them, will help to ensure good cellular and muscular strength. This also helps with muscle coordination so that even slightly tired muscles know what they need to do to help us get from A to B.

5. Mind-body time: stretching is also an opportunity to slow down for a few minutes and tune into our body, taking notice of any soreness, or aches post exercise, relaxing into the stretch and letting go of any stress

---

Stride lengthening is common practice among athletes, improving mobility around the hips, knee and ankle joints. Note however that adjusting our running style cannot (and shouldn't) be done overnight. Over time however, it is a simple way to knock a couple of seconds off personal best times!

There are different types of stretching: 'static stretching' involves holding one position for a number of seconds, whereas 'dynamic stretching' uses controlled movements to warm up our joints and muscles. Each serves a slightly different purpose but in both cases, our muscles need to be warmed-up first.

If I am going out for a jog or a gentle run, I will not static stretch beforehand but instead I will start my run slowly, allowing my muscles time to warm up over a period of a few minutes. I am then able to get into my stride as the run goes on, but I would never push it really hard during a run if I haven't done any stretching beforehand. It is only after I have finished my run that I do my static stretching. With my muscles still warm, I hold each stretch for 30 seconds (no bouncing). Stretching to the first point of tension, holding that position for 10 seconds, then pushing a tiny bit more into the stretch, hold for 10 and then a final push to see if I can get another millimeter or two and then hold for the final 10 seconds.

If I want to push myself, either during a race, or for a tough training session, (and definitely for any speedwork), my routine would be to start with a five minute jog and I would follow this with my static stretching routine. I would also add dynamic stretching to my warm-up. Dynamic stretching is a kind of rehearsal for what is to come for our muscles; mobilising as close as possible to the point they will be used during the run. This routine will ensure that my muscles and joints are ready to help propel me as fast as I can go without risking injury.

Static stretches

These are my go-to static stretches and reach all of my main running muscles (although you can find many more if you search online if you wish to increase your repertoire).

Static stretches are performed after our run, jog or walk-jog. Plus if we're competing or doing any speedwork, we can use these after a warm-up jog and before our dynamic stretching.

Static stretch 1: Top to toe stretch (full body stretch)

Standing up straight, rise-up onto your tip toes, raise your hands above your head and with your legs, body, back and arms in a straight line, reach your hands as high as you can, feeling that stretch along the full length of your body. Hold for 10 seconds.

Static stretch 2: Calf stretch (calf and into Achilles)

Find a wall, or something approximately the height of the bottom of your ribs that you can lean against. Stand so you're a forearms length away from the wall, hands flat against the wall with a ninety-degree angle in your elbows. Your body is in a straight line from head to ankle with no weight going through your arms at this stage. Now, keeping your body upright, left foot is flat on the ground but allow your left leg to bend slightly as you move your right foot behind you and place it flat on the ground so you can feel a really nice stretch at the bottom of your right calf muscle (right leg is straight in the final stretch position here). Hold for 30 seconds. Now find the 'neutral position' again (body in its natural standing position), legs together, body at forearm distance to the wall, hands flat on the wall at approximately the same height as you lower rib cage. Keeping both feet flat on the ground, now move the left foot straight back behind you. The right leg bends slightly and you can feel the stretch down the back of your lower left calf. Hold for 30 seconds. Note that you can move the position on the stretch down towards your Achilles by having a slight bend in both legs in the final stretch position.

Static stretch 3: Toe touch (glutes and back of the legs)

Start from a standing position, first reach your arms high above your head (giving your back a nice stretch before the bending movement), then - keeping your legs straight but without 'locking your knees' (i.e. keep your knee joint relaxed), bend down and reach your hands down as far towards your toes as you're able to. Feel that lovely stretch down the length of your hamstrings; hold for 10 seconds, then see if you can reach a bit further, and hold for 20 seconds. If you feel any tension in the joint of your knee itself, try bending your knees very slightly and holding this stretch.

Static stretch 4: Crossed leg toe touch (glutes and top of the hamstrings)

Still while reaching down towards your toes, cross your left leg over the front of your right leg (right leg is straight but without locking the knee). After holding for 30 seconds, switch legs. Again – we're trying to get as close to touching our toes as we're able to but with one leg crossed over the front of the other we're take the stretch deeper into the glute and the top of each hamstring.

Static stretch 5: Hamstring stretch

Start with your feet together, flat on the ground. Turn your right foot so that it is facing outwards at a 45 degree angle, now keeping your left leg straight and allowing a bend in your right leg, step your left leg forward and slightly out to the side, now turn your left foot out to a 45 degree angle. You will notice that your weight has shifted onto your right leg. Keeping both feet flat on the floor, put one hand on top of the other and slide both hands as far down your left leg as you can. Hold it there for 30 seconds (again - using the 10 and 20 second markers to push a bit further and hold) and you will feel a good stretch through your left hamstring. Now repeat on the other side.

Static stretch 6: Calf stretch (this follows on directly from the hamstring stretch)

While in the same position as you were for the hamstring stretch, keeping your heel on the ground, raise the toes of the front foot off the ground as far as you can get them. If you're able to, grab the toes of your front foot with both hands and hold this position for 30 seconds. If you can't reach that far, or only with one hand, just get both hands to reach as far as they can towards your upwardly flexed toes. Your back leg remains slightly bent, as before. Now switch sides.

Static stretch 7: Inner thigh and groin stretch (inner thigh, inside knee); hip mobilisation

Start from an upright position, hand on hips, feet facing forwards, just wider than shoulder width apart. Keeping your left leg straight, bend your right knee so it moves in-line with your right foot, until you feel a good stretch along the length of the inside of your left thigh. Hold for 30 seconds. Now come back up to the start position (feet facing forwards and slightly more than shoulder width apart), then slowly bend your left knee while keeping your right leg straight, until you feel the stretch along the inside of your right thigh. Hold for 30 seconds. Note that there are various adaptations of this stretch and the feet can be placed further apart while supporting the body by placing our hands on the ground in front of us. Both create a good stretch in the groin and inner thigh and it is down to personal preference and mobility which we opt for.

Static stretch 8: Quadricep stretch (full front of the thigh, muscles around the knee)

Standing up straight, feet together, keeping your body upright balance on your right leg while you bend your left leg back until you can grab your left foot with your left hand. Now, making sure that your knees are together, try and touch the heel of your left foot onto your left butt cheek (or as close as you're able to get it). All your weight is going through your right leg, which has a very slight bend at the knee (don't lock your right knee). If you need help balancing here, try focusing on one point directly in front of your eye line. Hold for 30 seconds, feeling a good stretch all the way up the front of your thigh, then repeat on the other side. Note that it is important that your knees are together while creating the stretch up your quadriceps; our knee joint supports the backwards and forwards movement of our femur (thigh bone) and tibia (shin bone) and if we start pulling our leg to one side while it is bent at the knee, there's a risk we'll pull something out of place.

Static stretch 9: Neck stretch

From a standing position, drop your right shoulder down (creating a bit of tension down the right side of your neck) and then with your left hand, reach behind your head and holding the right side of the back of your head, very, very slowly pull your head forward slightly and to the left. Feel the satisfying stretch down the right side of the back of your neck. Hold for ten seconds then switch sides.

Dynamic stretching

We need to include dynamic stretching in our warm-up routine if we're going to be doing any speedwork or pushing ourselves during a tough run and want to make sure our muscles and joints are ready for action. Once we've done our warm-up jog and our static stretching, we would spend another five minutes or so doing dynamic stretching. Simple exercises include torso twists, walking lunges, and a leg swing (to get some movement through our hips). If we want to go for the full monty, we can add 'high knees' (marching, lifting alternate knees up to the chest with the opposite arm moving in an exaggerated running movement so that our hand comes up level with our eye line), kick-backs (running on the spot, or slowly moving forwards, kicking the left heel back so that it touches the left buttock, then the right heel back to the right butt cheek, trying to keep a straight line down the front of the thigh so that the thighs remain perpendicular to the ground). If our muscles are feeling nicely warmed up by now, this can be rounded off with a couple of short, fast running bursts, ensuring our muscles know what is coming as the higher speeds we want to reach require additional lengthening of our muscles.

If we have been pushing ourselves during a run, it is also advisable to do a five-minute warm-down jog after the session and to finish off with our static stretching. This helps the body return to homeostasis, the heart steadily slowing to its resting rate, while pushing blood through the full length of our muscles and helping to clear away any superfluous by-products.

4. In-between runs

Complementary exercises

Body & mind, mind & body

While over time we are physically able to train ourselves to run every day, it is better for us if we give our body a day or two to recover between runs, particularly if we're just starting out, or if we've had some time out and are working on getting our fitness levels back up again. If we have the time however, doing some complementary exercise on the days we're not running, for example Pilates or yoga, is going to help muscle recovery, muscle strength, blood flow, coordination, and generally get our mind and body to full alertness if we are feeling a bit fatigued. Both are also great for stretching our muscles, regulating our breathing and concentration (being in the moment). These days professional athletes and sports people understand the benefits of strengthening their body through Pilates and many will have at least a couple of sessions each week.

Pilates and yoga work different muscles, including our core, in such a way that it complements our running and is going to help keep us injury free. I would recommend going to a few classes to start with, so that you have access to a teacher who can guide you through the basics. Once you know the moves however (and importantly – how to breathe through the movements), there are lots of Apps available with classes of all standards and different lengths too. Working out in our own is not as sociable as doing a class but it does save having to go to the gym at a specific time, for an hour-long class every time we want a Pilates or a yoga hit.

Pilates is a workout in itself and certainly not to be sniffed at! With the right teacher, an hour-long class will induce a good, healthy sweat as well as some pleasantly achy muscles, worked to the precise moment when fatigue sets-in. Also - it doesn't matter what level we're at: complete beginner, out of practice, forever intermediate, or strong enough to hold our body weight through one arm, in a class of mixed abilities the teacher will always welcome each of us to do as many repetitions as our body allows and push each movement just as far as we are comfortable. Without judgement, a good teacher acknowledges that our bodies are different and each one of us is doing the best we can for our body at that particular moment. The right teacher will also provide advice on how to tailor a movement so that it suits our own ability.

From my moderate experience the Pilates and yoga classes I've attended have a reasonable degree of crossover between the two. What I like about Pilates is that is focuses on building muscle strength to the optimal point to support our individual body weight. When we can hold the pose, or repeat the movement to the point of muscle fatigue, we know we are going to be a bit stronger for the next class. We're working all of our muscles in pairs and building equal strength. The exercise works all of the muscles through our body and also helps to quickly identify any weaknesses, but without putting such strain through them that we end up hurting ourselves. A few single legged squats and we'll soon know if our left side is weaker than our right!

There are many different types of yoga; the continuous movement of Vinyasa, will give us a good workout, Hatha is also going to help build strength and improve balance, or we can try Yin yoga for flexibility, boosting circulation and reducing tension.

Personally I love a good Pilates class (and recently tried a 'wall Pilates' class, which I assure you goes beyond the good ol' fashioned pre-skiing wall squat). I find that with my limited coordination skills, Pilates moves at a pace that allows me to focus on getting simple movements right so that I am working the right muscles in the right way and improving muscle strength. I find yoga classes are good for dynamic movement and giving my muscles a good stretch, and with the right teacher you can't lose either way. So find a gym or a Pilates or yoga studio nearby and just try a few different classes until you find what works best for you.

The power of resistance

Resistance training (also called strength, or weight training) is "the use of resistance to muscular contraction to build strength". The resistance can come from various sources, including dumbbells, medicine balls, kettle bells, resistance bands or our own body weight (for example press-ups and squats). The idea is that by subjecting our muscles to a level of resistance that is greater than they're used to, we stimulate the muscle fibres to adapt and become stronger over time. Resistance training is not about heavy weights; the benefits come simply by putting more weight through a muscle than we do going about our ordinary daily activities. We can start with light weights and very gradually increase the weight as we become stronger.

By specifically targeting the muscle groups that play a role in our running mechanics, we build strength, improve our stability and our endurance. Resistance training is also good for our bone density and is generally going to help us to continue doing all of the activities we enjoy doing into old age. As well as squats (working the muscles that we use to generate power during a run), we can try lunges (for improved stability), deadlifts (strong glutes help propel us forwards), step-ups (glute and hamstring strength, helping with stability again), calf-raises (strong calves help improve running efficiency), hip bridges, planks and the list goes on (see below for a selection of my favourites).

If we're attending a Pilates class once and week and making time to do a resistance training session within every seven-day period, the risk of ever injuring ourselves is significantly reduced. But what happens if we do experience some aches or pains while running? What are some easy exercises to build muscles strength when we recognise a weakness?

Glute weakness

The root cause of so many different injuries! Manifesting as sore or tight hamstrings, pain around the knee (including IT Band Syndrome), lower back pain, hip impingement, lower extremity alignment issues etc. etc. In summary – more than any other muscle in our body, our bum is deserving of regular attention.

I know from painful experience that taking the time to do specific glute exercises is a must for me. Diagnosed with the 'sitting disease' by my physio, I was prescribed with a host of bum strengthening exercises. There are many great (read: dull) exercises to work our glutes, and while they are rubbish to have to do, strong glutes are essential in avoiding injury. As well as improving our stability, glute strength makes a big difference in our running mechanics and therefore how quickly we feel fatigued. (Tip: listening to music, a podcast or audiobook while doing these exercises will help make them less boring).

Glute strengthening exercises

Bridge exercise: moderate difficulty:

Lie flat on your back, keeping your knees and feet together, bend your knees to an approx. forty-five degree angle, feet are flat on the floor. Arms are resting on the ground, tight against the side of the body with the palms of the hands facing downwards. Now - pushing down through your heels, raise your hips off the floor and push them up so that there is a straight line running from your shoulders, up through your hips and to your knees. With your upper back (between your shoulders) remaining flat on the floor, the effort should all be going through your bum muscles and you should feel the tension in your bum. Now, without moving any other part of your body, clench your butt and raise your left foot off the ground and make a straight line along your leg from your hip to your foot. Don't let your left hip drop towards the ground but keep your hips perfectly in line with one another (same distance from the ground). Now slowly put your left foot back flat on the ground. Now do the same with the right leg: clench buttocks, lift the right foot off the ground, creating a line from your hip to your foot, before slowly placing the right foot back on the ground. Repeat alternate legs until you've done ten on each leg, then slowly roll your hips back down onto the ground. With the clenching of the butt cheeks thrown in this is tougher than it sounds, but as your glutes become stronger, the repetitions can be increased up to fifteen per leg and eventually moving up to twenty per leg. Once you're at twenty per leg, keeping the rest of your body still and stable throughout, you have achieved a bum rating of 'strong'.

Single leg squats: moderate difficulty to tough:

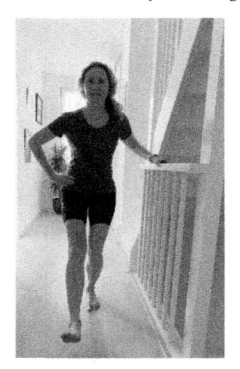

If you've not tried single leg squats before, I suggest easing yourself in and using some additional support to begin with. The back of a dining chair works well, alternatively something at approximately hip height that you can hold to as you squat. Start in an upright position, sideways on to the back of the chair with your feet together. Place the hand that is closest to the chair on top of the back of the chair and using the chair as a support, keeping your left leg straight, first lift your left foot off the ground, directly in front of you, until it is at an approximate 45 degree angle to your right leg (which is planted firmly on the ground, right foot also facing forwards). Now, keeping your back straight (without leaning forwards), bend your right knee such that your right butt cheek moves a couple of inches down towards your right ankle, then pushing through your right foot, push back up to a straight leg position. It is a simple up and down movement of the hips through the bending and straightening of the leg; try and keep everything else still so that you can move in a stable way through the squat. Watch out for one hip dropping lower than the other; try and keep both hips level and square to the ground. Repeat this ten times on each leg. You only need to do a shallow squat to get a good load going through the glute. As our glutes strengthen, we will be able to do this movement without support and we'll be able to get our butt cheek closer to our ankle, into a deeper squat. Once we can do the ten on each leg while maintaining complete control throughout, repetitions can be increased to fifteen per leg.

Swiss ball squat: moderate difficulty:

If you search online, there are plenty of glute strengthening exercises that we can do with a Swiss ball. A simple one is the Swiss ball squat: Standing with your back to a wall, standing close enough to the wall so that you can place the Swiss ball between the wall and the middle of your back and the ball stays in position. Now move your feet forward a couple of inches, so that they are very slightly in front of you; feet are facing forwards and are approximately hip distance apart. Keeping your chest up and your back in a straight line, keeping the tension on the ball, bend both knees at the same time and allow the ball to roll up towards your shoulders. Hips, back and shoulders move in a parallel line to the wall, first downwards and then push back up until your legs are almost straight again. Repeat this fifteen times. As the glutes strengthen, we can eventually squat so that our knees are at a ninety-degree angle.

Hip clams: easy:

Lie on your left side on the floor, with your head supported so that your neck is in a straight line with your spine (I use a rolled-up hand towel). Keeping your upper body in a straight line, bend your knees to a ninety-degree angle, legs and feet are together, right leg on top of left. Now clench your buttocks and keeping your feet touching together, slowly raise your right knee, creating a clam shape between your left leg on the ground and your right leg. Then slowly lower your right leg back on to your left. Repeat twelve times while lying on your left side and then flip on to the right side of your body and repeat twelve times with your left leg.

Glute stretch: moderate difficulty:

Lie on your back, knees together off the ground and bent at a ninety degree angle. Keep your spine in neutral (neck curve, upper and lower back curves all in their natural positions; head, shoulders and hips running in a straight line). Lift your left ankle and rest it against the top of your right leg, just above your right knee. Keeping your legs in this position, very gently raise your right foot off the ground a few inches, feeling the stretch deep in your left glute. Hold the stretch for ten seconds, release and then switch legs.

Knee strengthening exercises

In an ideal world we would be doing strengthening exercises for the muscles around our knees every single day. Vital to maintaining good mobility into old age, allowing us to continue to do the activities we enjoy but also the simple things in life, like standing up, getting out of bed and walking to see our friends. The good news is that there are lots of ways to keep these muscles strong (including the glute exercises above).

We need to focus on improving the stability, flexibility and the strength of the muscles surrounding the knee joint and we do this by targeting our quadriceps (front of the thigh), hamstrings (back of the thigh), glutes (as above), calf muscles, low-impact cardio (cross-training) and dynamic stretching. Here are just a few examples of exercises to strengthen our knee muscles:

Squats: easy to moderate difficulty:

The best way to master the technique of doing a squat is to use a chair or a bench to assist the movement. Start from a sitting position, now stand-up straight and make sure your feet are shoulder width apart. Now raise both arms so that they are directly out in front of you, engage your stomach muscles (try and suck your tummy in a little bit), then very simply push your hips back and sit back down on the chair. For the upward movement, arms are directly out in front of you, your back is in an upright position (no slouching) and by moving your arms and shoulders forwards slightly as you push up through your heels, return to the standing position. Apart from the curve in your lower back as you push off and return to the seated position, your back stays in a straight line. Engaging our stomach muscles is also going to help with the stability of our movements. Start with ten repetitions with the chair, have a two-minute break and then repeat for another ten. As we get stronger, we can move to squats without the aid of a chair. This is exactly the same movement, with the aim being that we get our thighs parallel to the ground. Note that our knees shouldn't go any further forwards than our toes.

Stationary lunges: moderate difficulty:

Start standing up straight, hands on hips, feet and knees together, stomach engaged. Keeping your shoulders back step your right foot flat on the ground approximately thirty centimetres in front of you and your left foot the same distance behind you; both feet are facing forwards. Now – as you bend both knees very slightly, the front foot flat on the ground and coming up onto the toes of your back foot, back stays straight, your body will naturally move downwards and take you into a lunge position. For the upwards movement, back stays straight, chest up and push back up through the front foot and the toes of your back foot. The front knee shouldn't go any further forward than your toes and while as a beginner we would start with only a very small up and down movement, as we build strength we can aim to get our front thigh parallel to the ground. Do ten repetitions on one side and repeat on the other side. As our stability improves, we can add some light weights to this movement; a dumbbell in each hand will add a little more resistance to the movement and build additional strength.

Step-ups: easy:

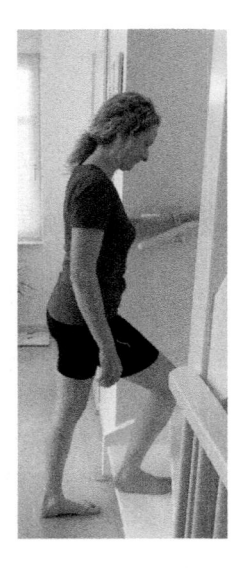

Using the bottom step of your staircase (or any flight of stairs), keeping your back straight, chest up; step your right foot up onto the step, then left foot up, right foot down, left foot down. Repeat twenty times. Want to make this a bit more taxing? Use the penultimate step of the staircase instead, stepping up two steps instead of one.

Assisted one-legged squats: easy to moderate difficulty:

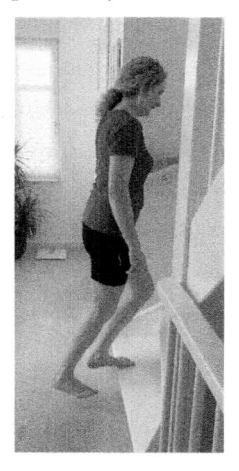

Again – using the bottom step of a flight of stairs, step both feet up onto the bottom step and holding the handrail, right foot stays flat on the bottom step and left foot is raised off the step behind you so that all of your weight in on your right foot. Keeping the rest of your body straight, slowly bend your right knee very slightly and then straighten your right leg again (left foot remains off the ground). Repeat this movement ten times and then switch legs.

Cross-training: moderate difficulty to tough: For knee strengthening, single leg squats are a good way to improve the muscles around our knees without the use of any equipment. However if we do have access to a gym, the cross trainer is a great, low-impact way to build up the muscles supporting our knee joints and work up a sweat at the same time. Turn up the resistance on the machine a few notches and don't use the moving arms of the machine, but keep your arms still (instead holding the static handles in front). Twenty to thirty minutes at a medium resistance is going to do wonders for our knees, and if we choose to push it a bit, we can easily get our heart rate up a couple of zones too (which is great for weight loss). Unless we have really strong muscles across our back, the moving arms can do more harm than good on a cross-trainer. If our body is twisting from side to side as our arms move backwards and forwards, this is asking for a back problem! It is better to do some light weights for our arms instead, and use the cross-trainer to focus on knee-strengthening and raising our heart rate.

Knee extensions: easy:

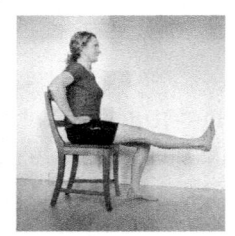

Sitting on an upright chair or stool with your feet flat on the ground and thighs parallel to the ground. Keeping your back straight and the rest of your body still, raise your right foot off the ground until you have a straight line along the length of your leg, then place your foot back on the ground. Repeat ten times then change legs. For additional resistance, use an elastic resistance band and tie one end to the bottom of the chair, and loop the other end so that it fits over your foot; at the right tension this will add to the work that your knee is having to do, adding more resistance and building more strength.

Ankle strengthening exercises

Standing heel raises: easy:

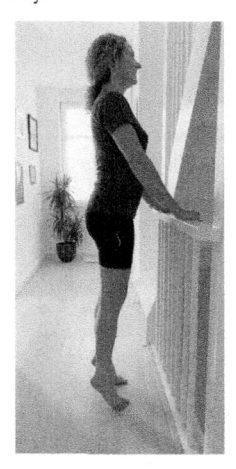

Standing in an upright position, using the back of a chair for stability, feet hip width apart and both facing forwards, push up onto your toes. Hold for five seconds, then lower you heels to the ground. Repeat ten times.

Single leg balance: easy:

Start standing upright, feet hip width apart, flat on the ground facing forwards. Keeping the rest of your body as still as possible, raise your right foot approximately one centimetre off the ground, hold the position for five seconds, put the foot back on the ground and repeat. Repeat this ten times on each foot.

Ankle rotations: easy: This is about keeping the flexibility in our ankles, which is equally important when it comes to avoiding ankle injuries. Sitting on an upright chair or stool with your feet flat on the ground, raise your right foot off the ground and keeping your ankle still, 'draw a circle' with your right toes, rotating your toes first clockwise for ten circles and then anti-clockwise for ten circles. Repeat with your left foot.

Core strengthening exercises

Strengthening our core muscles helps improve our overall stability, our balance and our posture, which will in turn reduce the risk of injury in all areas of our body. We have already covered Pilates and the benefits of doing a class a week to help improve our strength and stave off injuries, and there are lists of exercises online that we can do to work our core. I've included four simple exercises here, all of which will work our back as well as our abdominals so ensuring we maintain the balance between these two sets of muscle groups.

Half-plank: moderate difficulty:

Full plank on elbows. A half-plank, with knees on the ground is an easier option to begin with

Keeping your knees on the ground, move into a push-up position (as if you're about to do a half press-up), then lower your forearms so that they are flat on the ground. Engage your core (suck your tummy muscles in) and keeping the tension between your shoulders, maintain a straight line from your head through to your knees (this is easiest to check if you have a mirror sideways-on). Hold the position for thirty seconds, release down and then repeat. The duration of the hold can gradually be extended as you become stronger, alternatively you can move to a full-plank, starting from a press-up position with your body weight through your forearms and toes, rather than forearms and knees.

Table-top extensions: moderate difficulty:

Starting on all-fours (hands and knees), hands are shoulder width apart and placed directly under your shoulders; knees are the same distance apart as your arms and placed directly under your hips. Back is in a straight line between your shoulder blades and hips (check in a side-on mirror if possible) and your neck is in a straight line with your back (so you're looking at a spot on the ground very slightly in front of you). Engage your core so that you feel complete stability along your back and abdominals. Keeping your head, neck and the rest of your body still, slowly move your right arm up off the ground until it pointing directly out in front of you, then extend your left leg (opposite leg) out behind you so that your foot is pointing directly back behind you. Try not to let your hips or your shoulders drop, but maintain the line along your neck and spine and your core engaged. Just hold the position for a second, then return the hand and knee to the starting position. Repeat ten times on this side, then switch sides.

Swiss-ball plank and swiss-ball pike: tough:

With the swiss ball on the ground, kneel behind the ball and then slowly roll yourself over the top of the ball, first using your feet for stability, then by placing your hands on the ground in front of the ball. Continue this forward movement by placing your hands one in front of the other, until the ball is positioned under the tops of your legs. Feet are off the ground and legs are straight, creating a straight line down the length of your body. Keeping the tension in your abs so that your back doesn't arch, your arms are straight and at a ninety-degree angle with your body; hands are directly under shoulders (don't lock your elbows). Now to take this move to the next level, keeping the body in a straight line on the ball, parallel to the floor, move one hand in front of the other so that the ball moves down your legs and is now sitting underneath your shins. Abs tight, don't let your hips sag towards the floor. The next level of this exercise is a swiss-ball pike, where from the plank position on the ball and using your feet and legs you pull the ball back in towards you. Arms remain straight, top of the feet are on the top of the ball, now 'gripping' the top of the ball with your feet, pull the ball in towards you, knees bending underneath you. Abs are still tight, helping you to keep your back in a straight line from shoulders to hips. Planks can be held for thirty seconds, increasing up to a minute as your strength improves; the pike can be repeated ten times, increasing up to fifteen per set. This is going to give your shoulders a great workout as well as working through your core.

'Russian twist' (with or without a medicine ball): moderate difficulty:

Start sitting on the floor, with your legs straight out in front of you, heels on the ground and knees bent at a ninety degree angle. Put the palms of your hands together a couple of inches away from the front of your chest, as if you're praying (if you're using a medicine ball, hold the ball in front of you, level with your chest). Now tilt backwards very slightly, keeping your back in a straight line from your shoulders to your hips; at the same time your feet come a few inches off the floor, maintaining that ninety degree angle in your legs. Keeping your neck and your head facing forwards and the rest of your body still, with your palms still together move your hands towards the floor on your right-hand side, then in a kind of window-wiper movement, move your hands towards the floor on your left-hand side. If you are using a medicine ball, first move the ball and lightly touch it to the floor by your right-hand side (by your bum) and then the same on the left-hand side. You will feel a good twist across the oblique muscles down the side of the torso and maintaining the balance, with your feet off the ground is a great workout for the stomach muscles. Exhale as you twist and inhale as your hands move back to the centre of your chest. Try and twist tent times to each side (twenty in total) and steadily increase to thirty in total once your strength improves.

Arm strengthening exercises

The plank, table-top extensions and swiss-ball plank are all going to help with arm and shoulder strength. Even easier are using some weights for bicep and hammer curls, although this won't help much when it comes to having the mobility and strength in your shoulders when it comes to reaching for objects on high-up shelves. In an ideal world we'd all be doing shoulder presses everyday.

Bicep curls: easy:

Using light dumbbells (3-5kg in each hand), stand straight, feet shoulder-width apart, using an underhand grip on the dumbbell, arms long, hands are by your sides shoulder-width apart and with palms facing forwards. Keeping your upper arms stationary, elbow tight against the body, exhale and curl the dumbbells towards your shoulders, hold briefly before slowly lowering the dumbbells back down until your arms are almost straight down by your sides again (don't lock the elbows). Elbows stay close to your body at all times, keep your chest up, shoulders back and back straight. The movements are controlled up and down; don't just let your arms drop back down under the weight of the dumbbell. Repeat ten times.

Hammer curls: easy:

Hammer curls are almost the same as bicep curls except that instead of the palm of your hands facing forwards through the movements, now you hold the dumbbells with the palms of your hands facing each other. Standing straight, arms by the side of your body, a dumbbell in each hand with your palms facing your body. Keeping the upper arm still, elbows tightly against your sides, raise the weights towards your shoulders and hold briefly before slowly lowering the dumbbells to their start position. Repeat ten times.

Shoulder press: moderate:

Using light dumbbells (1kg in each hand is enough, 3kg is good, we can work our way up to 5kg in each hand). Stand straight, feet shoulder-width apart, holding a dumbbell in each hand, elbows are bent so the weights are at shoulder height. With your palms facing forwards, engage your core muscles (tighten the muscles across your back and the front of your body and slowly push the dumbbells upwards, extending your arms so that the weights are just above head-height. Hold the weights in this top position before very slowly lowering the dumbbells back to their start position, in-line with the tops of your shoulders. Note that the weights move straight up and straight down above your shoulders; at no point are they on-top of your head. Also - be careful not to lean back as you push upwards; the upper body stays still as the arms push upwards and are pulled downwards again. Repeat five times to begin with; increasing up to ten per set as your strength improves.

Half press-up: moderate:

Move into a push-up (press-up) position, keeping your knees on the floor, feet are flexed with toes lightly touching the ground as well. Knees are further back than your hips such that you've got a straight line running from your shoulders, hips and through to your knees. The position of your hands on the ground depends on how difficult you want the exercise to be; if your hands are directly below your shoulders the movement is much more difficult than if you put your hands a few inches wider on either side (hands are still in a line with your shoulders but wider apart). Engage your core muscles (suck your tummy muscles in) and keeping the straight line of your body from shoulders to knees, slowly lower your chest towards the ground just as far as feels comfortable (which may only be a couple of centimeters to begin with). For the upwards movement, keeping the straight line from shoulders to knees, push your chest back away from the ground again. The trick is to keep the straight line and not leave your bum sticking up in the air as you lower your chest down (a sideways-on mirror is great for checking your hips are also moving in a straight line with your upper body). Repeat five times to begin with, increasing up to ten per set as your strength improves.

Daily morning stretches – just because they feel good!

Cat-Cow stretch: easy:

On all fours, knees under hips, hands under shoulders so you're in a 'table-top' position. Now arch your back upwards as if you're a cat having a post-nap stretch, head tucks under, shoulders rounded, trying to create an upside-down U-shape in your back. Hold for a few seconds. Now, keeping knees and hands in the same position, we're going to recreate the cow stance, imagining that we have heavy udders forcing our back to arch in the reverse direction (a normal U-shape this time). Eyes look up to the sky as we arch our back, our abs are pulled in tight but we're allowing our belly to drop towards the ground. Hold for a few seconds and repeat the up-and-down arching of our back four or five times.

Child's pose: easy (this is a nice stretch!):

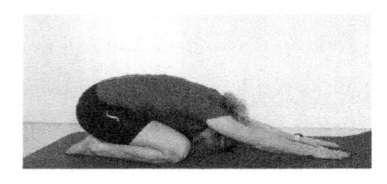

Start on all fours, now widen the space between your knees while at the same time bringing your feet together so that the tops of your feet are flat on the ground with your big toes touching each other. Keeping your arms stretched out directly in front, sit back onto your heels. Stretch your arms out further in front of you and your head tucks-down between your arms (you can rest the top of your forehead on the ground). Stay in this position for thirty seconds (or longer if you wish), breathing steadily and enjoying that lovely stretch down your back and across your hip muscles.

Note: for exercises that require you to be on your hands and knees, you'll either need a yoga mat, or to do these on a rug or thick carpet. Dumbbells can be substituted for cans of food, or any light weights that you can easily hold in the palms of your hands.

Alternative exercises – recovering from an injury

With only a pair of trainers and a running route as our prerequisites, running is the easiest way to get super fit and improve our health and the quality of our life. The lack of equipment, or time to get to and from a gym, plus the additional cost these entail is what makes running so accessible and means that everyone can enjoy running. This is also why it really sucks if we have to have an enforced break from running due to injury, illness, or other medical reasons. What do we do now? We need to do something to keep our mind and body in check whilst we're not able to run! Depending on our injury, or what the medical reason is for not running, I have always either moved to swimming (avoiding breast stroke if it is a knee issue), or the exercise bike or cross-trainer in the gym (without using the moving arms on the machine). Swimming is going to help keep our core in shape, as well as our back, shoulders, glutes and hamstrings; it is also a good workout for our cardiovascular system. A tough session on a cross-trainer (with the resistance level switched up) is again great for raising our heart rate, working our leg muscles and for getting a good sweat on. If we're being told that our legs need complete rest, then upper body resistance training at the gym, or with resistance bands at home, can be used to raise our heart rate and keep our body moving. Importantly - we also need to make time to do the physio exercises that will have us back running as soon as possible.

Massage?

If we're increasing the tempo of our running, or perhaps we're in training for a marathon and we're covering a greater number of miles each week, we will likely suffer from post-run muscle fatigue. Even if we're warming up, warming down and stretching, if we're consistently pushing our leg muscles to give us a bit more, we may find that a good deep tissue massage helps our body to recover a bit faster between runs.

Massage gets mixed reviews in terms of the benefits people feel and some of this will depend on the massage therapist. A good massage therapist may have studied the ancient art of massage across different cultures; perhaps as well as deep tissue, they offer Thai, Indian, or Chinese, each serving the needs of our body in a different way. And massage won't get rid of the muscle pain altogether but a good massage (plus drinking a pint of water afterwards) will help clear away the by-products of the repair work that our muscle cells perform post-run.

As an alternative, or to complement seeing a massage therapist we can invest in a foam-roller and use our body weight to help ease any post-run stiffness. Like a deep-tissue massage, I can't say that there is any pleasure in the experience (at all) but a foam roller isn't expensive to buy and it will help us to get deeper into the muscles than we would otherwise be able to on our own. Again – there are lots of videos online, depicting shoulder, glute, hamstring, quadriceps and calf massaging techniques (to name a few) as well as mobility exercises and stretches for our back.

Massage is also a great way to help our body recover from a muscle injury. Much like when we cut ourself and our body heals, when we injure a muscle, there is a build-up of scar tissue of sorts as our muscle works to repair itself. Scar tissue can affect the elasticity of our muscles, however a good massage therapist will be able to target the scar tissue and very gently break it down and send these old, broken cells on their way. The massage also helps to stimulate blood flow to the area, bringing oxygen and nutrients to the new muscle cells that are forming.

Acupuncture

It is worthwhile finding a really good acupuncturist in case we need to call on them for aches and pains or some other medical complaint we're having trouble shaking off. The underlying principle is based on the concept of Qi (pronounced "chee"), which is the energy that flows through pathways in our body known as meridians. According to Chinese medicine, if the flow of Qi is disrupted or imbalanced, it can lead to illness or pain. Similarly, if we have an injury, acupuncture is said to both influence the nervous system including helping with pain management but also to trigger the body's self-healing processes and restore the Qi around the place of the injury.

The benefits of this ancient medical practice are well documented and there is plenty of research that demonstrates the positive effects for various conditions, including chronic pain, migraines, osteoarthritis etc. From my personal experience in overcoming injury as quickly as possible, acupuncture can be seen as an additional tool to be used in conjunction with rest, gentle massage and easy movement of the injured site; what it isn't going to do is immediately return your injured muscle back to full-health on its own.

(Always check that the acupuncturist is properly qualified and licensed).

Our everyday shoes

Did you know that we have twenty-six bones in each of our feet? How about the fact that we have over a hundred muscles in our feet, making them one of the most intricately muscled parts of the body? The special arrangement of the bones, together with the numerous muscles, ligaments and tendons enables our feet to support our full body weight, providing stability when we move and helping us with our balance.

Many of us started being kinder to our feet during the pandemic and the realisation that our feet much prefer comfortable shoes rather than high heels, or stiff-soled Brogues. It isn't only our feet that benefit from a more flexible sole either; our calf muscles are less tight, having a knock-on effect on hamstrings, glutes and our back and shoulders.

Knowing that our feet are especially designed to be bendy and that only by allowing them to bend are we maintaining the strength in all of these muscles that support our weight, wearing the right shoes in our day-to-day life is going to help us be more stable on our feet as we age. I love my 'barefoot' shoes for walking; the thin sole took a bit of getting used to and I can feel that my muscles are being worked harder with the bigger range of movement, but now they're my go-to shoes about town.

Personally I don't wear barefoot shoes for running because I worry about not having enough cushioning on hard surfaces. However I know people who have, over time, trained themselves to run in barefoot shoes; perhaps coincidentally, they all have really strong calf muscles and I'm not sure which came first!

I can easily imagine a day when the advances in technology mean that we wear shoes manufactured for our unique foot shape. I say this purely because looking after our feet as we age is so vital in keeping us mobile and if we do want to be fitter than ever before in our eighties, what shoes we wear needs to be more of a consideration. And within this we need to be better at recycling our footwear, so when they are worn out, we would send them back to the manufacturer for recycling to ensure we're limiting the impact on the planet.

When is it time to see a physiotherapist?

If we have persistent pain in a joint or muscle every time we're running, or if our hamstring always feels really tight, even on the third day after going for a run (despite warming down and stretching properly), or if we feel a sharp pain in any of our joints when we're our running, don't ignore it. As well as helping to rehabilitate us after an injury, physiotherapists are trained to pick up on any weaknesses in our body that are impeding our ability to run without pain. Using a mixture of massage, ultrasound, and targeted exercises, the physio will be able to get our body back into balance such that the pain disappears. Then, with a degree of maintenance, which we can do ourselves once we know what the issue is, there is no reason we can't be running pain free on an ongoing basis.

To see a physiotherapist, you can either get a referral from your doctor, or if you don't want to wait, it is possible to pay to see someone on a per session basis.

Prevention is always going to be better than cure! We can give ourselves the best chance of avoiding injury by building up our exercise very slowly, stretching after exercise (and ideally briefly again before bed) and keeping those glutes, knees and ankles strong!

Rest days

Giving ourselves rest days (without exercise), getting to bed before

11pm every night (at least during the week but trying to be reasonably consistent at the weekends too), and a good night sleep are all going to help us avoid injury.

When we're tired our reactions slow, and our tired muscles can mean that our body doesn't react in the same way as when we're fully alert and on the ball. It can be as simple as rolling our ankle when we step off the pavement, or not fully concentrating on the path ahead and tripping over the root of a tree, or it could be more serious if we're not paying attention to the traffic as we cross the road outside our house.

We learn to listen to our body and it gets easier to figure out when we're so tired that we actually just need an early night, or whether a run is exactly what we need to clear our head and reenergise after a twelve hour work-day.

Unusually heavy-feeling legs while running are a sign of muscle fatigue and a good reason to slow things down for a few days. This is obviously quite common following a race, or a long-distance run and a day or two off, with some easy stretching (and eating a good mix of proteins and carbs) will soon have us back on track. If the heavy legs are accompanied by general fatigue and heaviness through the body, it probably means taking a week or so off completely. If the fatigue drags on for longer than two weeks, it would be advisable to see a doctor so they can do all the necessary checks that there isn't anything more serious going on.

A rest day can still include stretching if our muscles are stiff, or we want to get in some early preparation for our run the next day by loosening our muscles.

Food and water – as injury prevention and during recovery

You guessed it - fresh fruit and veg, beans, peas, lentils, nuts, seeds, fish, some dairy, and for meat-eaters, lean and non-processed meat. A diet consisting of these foodstuffs, while taking care that our portion size isn't too big is going to keep us super healthy. Avoiding ultra-processed foods, foods with E-numbers, flavourings, added sugar, high levels of salt, preservatives, or at least limiting these as much as possible, is also going to help keep our body in balance and recover from any injury faster.

Protein helps muscle repair; protein-rich foods include lentils, beans, grains, nuts, eggs, dairy food (in moderation), fresh fish and lean meat.

Fibre is vital for the health of our digestive system and helps to cleanse our body from the inside out. This includes fruit, veg, wholegrain cereals, nuts and seeds.

Complex carbohydrates ensure our cells have the energy they need to function and for repair when necessary. Our diet should include cereals, root veg, lentils and beans. Top this off with plenty of leafy green veg and other colourful fruit and veg, and we're doing really well. There are lots of recipes out there these days that mean eating healthily doesn't have to be boring, or take ages to prepare. Try and mix it up a bit too if possible; this helps to make sure we're getting access to a full range of vitamins and nutrients. Eating healthily does take planning and being organised with the shopping list, however these days AI tools can generate a 'balanced meal plan' for the week ahead and then translate this into a shopping list for us. Perhaps by the time you're reading this the supermarket will already be able to access the AI generated list and our shopping is being delivered the next day without us having to so much think about what we want to eat that week. In the meantime perhaps meal planning is another task for a Sunday evening? The meals themselves can be quick and easy to prepare and we can even cook in bulk and freeze food for later in the week.

And yes – water. Our 1.5 litres per day will help keep our muscles supple and avoid injury but also to help wash the toxins (by-products) away when we're recovering from injury. Room temperature rather than cold; warm or hot is also fine. Avoid sugary drinks, or energy drinks, which give a sudden spike in energy before quickly dropping away, leaving us feeling more tired than before, or craving another hit of energy drink. These will only wreak havoc with our liver as well as mess with our hormones and subsequently our sleep.

Chapter Twenty-Two

Safety first - Running safely

Running in the dark

We need to be able to see where we're going so that we don't injure ourselves, but just as importantly, people need to be able to see us when we're running. I recommend running under good street lighting if it is dark outside and at the very least wearing reflective strips, or clothing with reflective strips. For extra safety, we can wear a running chest light, which is going to shine a light on the path immediately in front of us, as well as letting other people know that we're there. There still needs to be some degree of street lighting on the route however, so if you live in the countryside being safe probably means either cycling, or driving, to somewhere it is safe to run at night, or running on a treadmill, or being really strict about protecting an hour earlier in the day when you can run while it is still light outside. Also think about whether running to or from work, or a part of the way is an option (with a bike, or public transport taking you the rest of the way).

Listening to music

I know that some people can't, and won't run without music. Being plugged into music rather than having our ears open for the sounds of passing cars etc. does mean having to pay extra attention when crossing roads, particularly towards the end of the run, when we're feeling a bit tired.

Share your route

Let people know where you run so that they are familiar with your different routes (with a running watch that connects to an App, you can also store your routes and share them across the App or online). Alternatively there are running Apps out there that allow you to share your real-time location with friends and family meaning they can see when you start and finish your run.

Women running solo

Don't run where you wouldn't feel safe walking on your own. If its dark, try and stick to a route where the street lighting is good or where there are other people around; if you're listening to music be extra vigilant and keep an eye on what's going on around you. If you're abroad and not sure how safe it is in the area you're staying, try and find a gym with a treadmill instead. In all my years of running and applying these simple rules, I struggle to think of any occasions that I've felt unsafe while out training on my own.

Running on narrow, windy roads

When there is no pavement or cycle path along a road and the road is single track, or with barely room for two-way traffic, the trick is to make it as easy as possible for drivers to see you as early on as possible. Obviously these roads are to be avoided in the dark, and there are some country roads where the locals drive so quickly that it isn't safe to run along these roads even in broad daylight. But if running along a quiet, windy road (with a low speed limit), try and make sure that you can quickly and easily be seen by both traffic approaching from behind you, as well as oncoming traffic.

The general rule is to run on the same side of the road as the oncoming traffic (so on the opposite side of the road than you would drive). However – if possible, we don't want to be running on that side of the road around a blind corner, where a car isn't able to see that we're there. Assuming there is no traffic coming from behind, we will need to switch sides of the road briefly so that we have a better view around the bend and drivers from both directions can see us.

Usually we can hear vehicles before we can see them on these roads, so we're able to quickly switch which side of the road we're running on so that we're on the opposite side of the road as the approaching vehicle. If there is a car coming from both directions at the same time, it is safest just to stop completely, standing on the outside of any bends in the road (so you can be seen from both directions) and stand as far into the side of the road as you're able to.

Running in the heat

During periods of hot weather, early morning tends to be the coolest time of the day; if you're able to, get your run in as early in the day as is possible. But regardless what time of day it is, running in the heat means we need to take it much easier, probably reducing our pace to around 75% our normal running speed. We'll also need to carry a bottle of water with us and stop in some shade if possible for a quick glug every now and then. If the sun is shining brightly too, wear a cap, sunglasses and be sure to smear some sun cream on any exposed skin.

Chapter Twenty-Three

Running myths

The myth about what it means to be healthy

The image that is presented to us by the media, social media and other advertising about what being fit and healthy looks like is often simply misleading. Perhaps this has improved somewhat during the past couple of years and we are slowly beginning to see more balanced, realistic images, however by and large we're still presented with a woman or man with barely any meat on their bones, a ripped stomach, muscular arms and a perfectly pert little bum. The idea that this body shape is the end result of being perfectly fit and healthy is not helpful. The chances are that the model didn't eat properly for days before the photo shoot (to ensure the right stomach definition in the photos), therefore didn't sleep properly either (eye make-up please!) and if is this behaviour was sustained for any period of time, what the model in question would actually represent is the very antithesis in what it means to be healthy!

To date, the images we see across the media rarely take into account the fact that we are all born with a different genetic make-up that means by the time we are twenty, more so when we're thirty and especially when we get to forty years old, our body is starting from a different body shape from the next person when we begin to exercise. This is why we have to get it out of our heads that being healthy means having a particular body shape, or having a particular level of body fat. Being healthy is in fact about how we are taking care of what is going on inside of our body and our mind, not how we look and how much we weigh. If we are raising our heart rate through regular exercise, eating the right amount of the right foods and enjoying good sleep as a result, then we're ticking all of the boxes that put us in the 'healthy human' category, no matter what weight we're starting from.

'Good health' as defined by the World Health Organisation is 'a state of complete physical, social, and mental well-being, and not merely the absence of disease or infirmity'. The definition recognises that optimal health is a holistic state of well-being, including: Mental & Emotional, Spiritual, Physical, Social, Medical and Nutritional. The emphasis is on the importance of a person's overall quality of life, encompassing physical health and mental and social well-being.

What should we be aiming for and what goals should we be setting ourselves along the way? As a beginner into exercise, the end game is to be doing two, preferably three, thirty-minute exercise sessions per week. Twenty minutes of the thirty with our heart rate beating at a faster rate, leaving three minutes to build up to that heart rate and seven minutes for stretching at the end. Add our strengthening exercises into the weekly mix (see the chapter '...Avoiding injury') and we're all set!

Maintaining a high heart rate for twenty minutes, with our heart beating twice to three times as fast as it does when we're at rest and doing this twice a week, is how we achieve 'good overall physical health'.

For those of us just starting out with exercise, we may find even a fast walk helps us achieve this higher heart rate. After a few weeks of doing this, with our fitness already improving, we will need to move to a walk-jog-walk routine to get our heart rate up to where it needs to be for twenty minutes. Eventually we will be jogging for the full twenty minutes to get our heart beating fast enough that we know we are pushing our body to a new level of fitness. Slowly but steadily our stamina is improving and we begin to notice that to achieve that same level of feeling out of breath during a run (with our heart beating at a high rate), we have to push ourselves that little bit more.

If you don't have a heart rate monitor (HRM) on your running watch, you can measure the number of beats per minute by placing two fingers on the underside of the top of your wrist, just below the thumb. Count the number of beats during a ten second time window and then multiply this number by six to calculate the beats per minute (BPM). A 'normal resting heart rate' varies from person to person and depends on fitness level, age, genetics and overall health (including medication). A healthy resting heart rate is usually anything up to 80 BPM; a resting heart rate above this suggests you probably lead quite a sedentary lifestyle. Because our heart rate is individual to us however it does make it difficult to say what is the 'right heart rate' for any one person and rather we have to measure trends and improvements in our own heart rate over time. This is easier to do with a watch with an inbuilt heart rate monitor and most of the newer watches will even tell us what heart rate 'zone' we're exercising at, with a zone representing a percentage of our maximum heart rate.

We calculate our maximum heart rate by using the equation:

Max heart rate (measured in beats per minute) = 220 minus our age

At age 45 for example, our max heart rate is 220 − 45 = 175 beats per minute; at age 70, our max heart rate is 150 bpm (220 - 70). This allows us to track what zone we're training in and helps us exercise at the right intensity to build stamina, target weight loss, or work on strengthening our cardiorespiratory systems.

When we're training in 'Zone 1', we're at approximately 50 - 60% of our maximum heart rate; it is a 'warm-up' (or warm-down) level of intensity. 'Zone 2' represents 'base fitness' and now we're at about 60 – 70% of our max heart rate; we can comfortably continue to chat while running at this pace. At 70 – 80% we're in 'Zone 3', our 'aerobic' zone and it becomes difficult to have a chat while running now. 'Zone 4' takes us up to 90% and moves us into 'Anaerobic Capacity'; this is when our body begins to rely on stored energy sources to fuel our workout; we can experience lactic acid build-up in our muscles, causing muscle fatigue and there is definitely no chatting now, our body needs to get as much oxygen as possible to our muscles so we can keep going. 'Zone 5' is the maximum threshold and is anything above 90% of our max heart rate; a sprinting pace or a pace which we're only able to maintain for a short period of time, we probably don't even have enough breath for a chat after we've finished our run at this intensity! So you can see that the speed at which we're running before we move from Zone 1 to Zone 2 and then Zone 3, is going to vary person to person. If we can get to at least Zone 3 during our run, just to the point where we don't have enough breath to speak to our running buddy anymore, this is when we will gradually start to see the improvements in our resting heart rate.

Tracking our heart rate over time is a great way to measure how our fitness is improving but also to help us trust in the process. On the days when our running mojo is low and it feels like we're not making any progress, we can take a look at how our resting heart rate is more efficient, with fewer beats required per minute than when we first started out on this fitness journey and now that we're five, ten, fifteen weeks in. We can use this improvement in our resting heart rate to help us keep the faith in what is happening in our body. We may not always be able to see the difference we're making reflected in a mirror but every time we exercise we're setting off a chain reaction of magical bodily processes which are going to help us live a better life, for longer.

I've been reading more about the 'zone 2' training recently, which as a longtime runner feels like a bit of a red herring to me. First up – training in a specific heart rate zone is a very new concept that has come about with the wearable heart rate monitors; we've been running for years pushing ourselves until the very easily measurable point of 'being our of breath'. Trying to train in a specific zone will likely distract from focusing on reaching an optimal level of total body fitness. Most of the runs I do take me into at least zone 4 and they always have done. Only when I'm doing a long training run, and by long I mean more than two hours, I will pace myself such that I happen to run at least some of this in zone 2 (otherwise I wouldn't be able to make it round the whole run). Without a doubt running at this slower pace helps build stamina and is an important part of training for a marathon. However for the first time I'm hearing more and more people talking about being worried that their heart rate is in zone 3 or 4 when in fact this is normal when we run. My advice – it is better to focus on enjoying our run, while of course, as always - listening to our body and taking it easier if it is telling us to slow down.

Another metric some watches will measure is 'VO2 max', or the maximum volume of oxygen used per minute per kilogram of body-weight. Or more simply put: how efficiently our body uses oxygen during physical activity. This is an indication of our cardiovascular fitness level and in summary, it should improve (increase) as we get fitter.

> We are getter fitter, which means our heart is growing stronger, our lungs are becoming more stretchy and as a result, our muscles are evolving, our blood vessels are widening, pumping all of the good stuff around our body and then super-detoxing our body of the stuff we don't need.

Since we are all different and all at different start points, there is no time limit on how long it will take to achieve being able to jog for twenty minutes with a raised heart rate. But if we just keep going at it, two to three times a week, we will feel it getting easier and importantly, we will be noticing the difference this new level of fitness is having on all other areas of our life.

What is also reassuring is that after approximately five weeks of this new routine (thirty five days) we will begin to experience a sort of snowball effect on our heath and fitness. Firstly we're going to be feeling stronger in our body; our heart is going to be a bit stronger, our legs and core muscles are able to carry us further, or faster than they could five weeks ago and we'll already be noticing that we now feel less out of breath when going for a walk, or climbing stairs. This feeling of progress is incredibly powerful in motivating us to want to make additional small tweaks in our lives, which is going to compound the speed with which we can reach our next goal. When we can feel, or clearly see the benefits of our hard work, it becomes much easier to start giving more focus to both what we eat, and really importantly, how much we are eating. This isn't about trying to stick to some fad diet, this is about eating a balanced diet each day, not overeating at meal times and creating good food habits on a week-by-week basis.

In summary, we do need to reassess what 'being healthy' actually means. Being skinny, or having a six-pack does not automatically equate to being healthy. Being healthy is being able to exercise for thirty minutes, two or three times a week, maintaining a high heart rate for twenty of those thirty minutes, with a few minutes warm-up and time spent stretching after the exercise. We complement this exercise with a good diet, eating a mix of food across the food groups, loads of leafy greens, colourful vegetables, whole grains, nuts, pulses, eggs, a bit of fruit each day and if possible, fish and lean meat a couple of times a week. As well as keeping us well-hydrated and all of our cells nice and plump, drinking water throughout the day is going to help us digest our food properly and keep everything moving through our body as it should.

'Running is bad' and other untruths

If you've tried running and been told that you shouldn't run for medical reasons, there is no arguing with that. However I often hear people explaining that the reason they won't try running is because they've read, or heard something that in actual fact simply isn't true. Some of the more common excuses I hear are as follows:

Running myth # 1: 'I will ruin my knees if I run'

Running is going to strengthen our quadriceps (front thigh muscles), calves and glutes, all of which help support and stabilise our knee joint and reduce the stress going through the joint itself. Not only this, but running improves the strength of the surrounding tendons and ligaments, as well as the density of all of our weight-bearing bones. The truth is that as long as we wear a pair of supportive running shoes and replace them often enough, our knees are going to be just fine (see the chapter 'The kit...' on how to select a decent pair of running shoes). In terms of replacing our sports shoes, if we're running a couple of times a week, a pair of trainers will last between nine and twelve months. If we're running more regularly than that, we will probably be looking to replace them every six to nine months. Other factors to consider when replacing shoes are the weather conditions we're running in and the running surface. If we're running in the rain a lot and our shoes are often wet or damp, or if we only ever run on hard pavements or roads, we will probably need to replace our running shoes every six months. It is also true that when we weigh more, we will wear our shoes down faster than when we've been able to lose a couple of pounds. But with running meaning we're managing our weight week-in, week-out, we're also going to be reducing the load on the knee joints. Ideally we want to be mixing up our runs so that we're not always running pavements but also in parks, or on grass, particularly if we're regularly running long distances.

Running myth # 2: 'Running causes arthritis and this will cause me problems into old age'

In terms of the arthritis argument, the fact is that approximately 50% of people aged 65 years or over report being diagnosed with arthritis by their doctor (I suspect there is also a good percentage of people who have some degree of arthritis but never visit the doctor to have it properly diagnosed). Anyway - whether we've run all of our life or not, once we hit our forties, we're losing more bone tissue than our body is creating and our bones very slowly weaken from that point on. The difference we can all make however is precisely by looking after our joints through regular exercise. Again - running will ensure that we have much stronger supporting ligaments and muscles around the joints, as well as muscles that support our stability in general, which will help to maintain good movement into old age. In support of this, according to OrthoInfo, a publication of the American Academy of Orthopedic surgeons, the degeneration of our musculoskeletal system is due more to disuse (inactivity) than to ageing itself. If we add the fact that exercise helps to maintain flexibility and muscles strength, as well as slow down the loss of muscle mass, all of the evidence suggests that we could run every week of our lives and well into old age without running having any adverse affect on our joints. Running will also help stave-off the age-related increase in body fat, which in itself can be a high-risk factor in osteoarthritis, but also produces proteins that can cause inflammation around our joints. As for running versus doing no exercise at all, running a couple of times a week is going to keep us fitter, healthier, more mobile and as a result - much happier, well into old age.

It is worth recognising the fact that of course everyone's body is different; some people may have had injuries that means their cartilage is already pretty wrecked, or arthritis has already restricted movement of the joints, such that at this point in time, running just isn't possible without causing a lot of pain and risking doing more damage. If brisk walking is an option, walking 10,000 steps a day may take a bit longer than a run and won't have all of the same benefits, but it is still going to make a massive difference in keeping health problems that come with old age at bay. Try adding a hill into the walk; this will raise the heart rate, helping to strengthen our cardiorespiratory systems and reach a different set of muscles than walking on flat ground does.

With research ongoing, until we can figure out how to stop, or reverse cartilage loss and how to maintain bone density and healthy joints as we age, it is sad to say that because of past injuries, or genetic disposition, there will always be a few people who are unable to enjoy the pleasures of running.

Running myth # 3: Running ages us

No, no, no, no, no. For all of the reasons above, and more. In fact running is going to help us to maintain our youthful looks for longer, and if we run regularly and consistently it is proven to reverse the ageing of blood vessels, improve heart health and reduce the risk of diabetes.

For the average adult, the ability to process oxygen declines by about 10% each decade after the age of twenty-five; this increases to 15% every ten years once we reach the age of fifty. While we don't notice it until after we reach our half-century, that feeling of being out of breath can be a direct result of our heart getting smaller and losing flexibility. By regularly raising our heart rate through running, we help maintain that flexibility, reducing risk of heart failure, and importantly, keeping our blood pumping more efficiently around our body.

This strong blood flow, being pushed from a healthy heart, through our healthy blood vessels all the way to the surface of our skin, helps maintain the elasticity of our skin; feeding our skin, while also helping remove toxins. Of course, this same strong blood flow is pumping to our brains, our organs, our muscles and as previously mentioned, is supporting strong bone density as well. So – far from ageing us, running will enable us to live our best, healthiest and most active life as we grow older.

One anti-ageing tip I will share however is that if we're going running in the sunshine, we do need to wear sun cream, a cap to keep the sun off our head and a pair of (non-fogging) sunglasses to protect our eyes. Having run in the sun, our body will also be calling out for us to drink an extra litre of water than we would on a non-exercise day.

Running myth # 4: I'm too old to start running now!

It is never too late to start running, and the benefits of taking up running, even later in life, are clearly evidenced in improved heart flexibility and more efficient processing of oxygen (with the knock-on impact of this positively affecting every area of life). If you're worried about jumping straight back into running, ask your doctor to check your heart rate and blood pressure and assuming they tell you that being more active is going to be good for you, just take it very easy to begin with. Start by introducing some brisk walking into a weekly routine, and when you feel ready try a 'walk-jog-walk-jog' session. Build up your running minutes only very gradually each week, listen carefully to any lingering complaints from your body and ease back if needs be. Regular strengthening and stretching exercises are particularly important and some very gentle muscle-lengthening after exercise is again key in our muscle maintenance and in minimising any post run aches and pains. See the Absolute Beginner training schedule in Part Four of this book to see how you can get going on the road to re-fitness.

Chapter Twenty-Four

Bringing it all together – The happier, healthier you

I was originally planning on having a section titled 'Making running fun' but thinking on this, I'm not sure I know of anyone who describes the running itself, as 'fun'? Yes – there are all of the physical, and the mental benefits that running provides us with, the happy hormones that pump through our body post run. Accessing that very brief moment of total bliss, a momentary feeling of complete clarity, a fleeting connection of our mind and body to something bigger than us. The great feeling of pride we feel for our dedication to getting fitter and healthier, of developing a new habit and sticking with it. Another plus point is the valuable opportunity to become a part of a running community; whether it be the local Saturday morning five kilometer Parkrun, joining a local running club, or taking part in other local events, the friendly camaraderie adding to the buzzy atmosphere.

As with trying anything new as an adult, admitting to ourself and to others that we're taking something seriously enough to try a group run on a weekend morning, or join a local running club, is a big step. It is a big, scary step. "What happens if everyone else is really good and I'm left trailing behind?" "How will I deal with being the new-person? And what if they try and make us do some weird kind of warm-up exercise to get to know one another beforehand?" (They won't). Yep – all the standard worst nightmare fears about feeling inadequate in comparison to other people, or uncomfortable when trying something new; all of the fears I still try and fight off whenever I try a new class at the gym, or enter a run having not put myself in a competitive situation for a while.

There is however a large, very friendly running community out there and if we're serious about keeping this running habit going then finding the right club or local running group to join locally is going to make a big difference to our chances of success. A quick search online to 'find running groups near me' can be a start point to find out what is happening when and where. If we're still in doubt as to whether the level of ability will be right for us, the running groups are usually also on social media and the organiser can be contacted directly to check in advance that we're not turning up to the 'The Mont Blanc Ultra Marathon death to the legs extreme hill-runner's club'.

Also – check out the Parkrun website to sign-up to a weekly Saturday morning five kilometer run near you. It happens every week at 9am, its completely free to take part, it doesn't matter if you're just starting out, trying to get fit again, or if you want to use it as a training session for a race you've got coming up. Some people walk the entire 5K, chatting all the way around, others will be using it as an opportunity to try and improve on their time from the previous week. The website will provide the information about your nearest Parkrun, where the meeting point is, how to get there (including transport links) and what facilities there are (toilet, changing, café etc.) When you sign-up you'll receive a barcode with your own membership number (take this with you when you run so that you get an official time at the end) and then just turn up at 8:50am (or earlier if you like a pre-run natter). Wear your running (or walking) shoes and just enjoy the run (or the walk and the chat...) What is great about Parkrun is that it is a community event and you will see the same faces week in, week out. It is the perfect opportunity to 'make running fun' (or – at least to get some fun out of running). Why not sign-up for your local Parkrun now and plan your Saturday morning routine so you can arrive there for a 9am morning walk or jog? (I note that at most Parkruns children over the age of four can register themselves, children under four years old can be pushed around in their buggy). What are you waiting for?

As well as Parkrun, there are plenty of other organised running events happening every weekend. There will generally be a small fee to take part, which helps cover the costs of running these organised events; perhaps roads need to be closed, or they need certain health and safety measures in place. You'll probably be given a bottle of water at the end, and sometimes the fee includes finisher's prizes too.

In fact these running events happen across the UK, Europe and beyond. What better excuse to visit new places with a group of your newfound running buddies than a Saturday or Sunday morning run around a foreign city, proceeded with a slightly decadent runner's meal the night before?

Once we've built running into a habit, entering an organised event and committing ourselves to the preparation we'll need to do upfront is a really good way to keep our training on track. Starting with a 5K run, perhaps building to a 10K and who knows, maybe eventually setting that half-marathon target? A half-marathon might feel like a world away, something only very fit people do, but I guarantee that unless you have a physical ailment to prevent you from covering the 13.1 miles, if you put your mind to it and do the training, this is absolutely achievable!

Try and avoid the mindset that says "I need to be fit before I enter a race"; how do you judge when you're fit enough? Also – entering the race first, giving ourself enough time to train, is going to provide that motivational boost we need to get our training on track!

The time we need to prepare ourselves depends on how fit we are when we start and the distance we're training for. A beginner wanting to do a 5K race will need nine weeks to prepare, whereas training for a marathon requires close to four months. But it means that we can start preparing today for a race we're going to do in a couple of months time.

You'll be amazed at how having other people running alongside us at an organised event can help push us on to the next level of fitness. In fact in these circumstances it is important to start the race at the pace at which we normally run and we don't get carried away by the crowd and start too quickly. Once we settle into a pace for the run, we will very often find that it is that bit faster than our 'I could run forever at this pace' pace, as we subconsciously (or consciously) compete with the people around us. As well as not starting too quickly, and being aware if we are running much faster than our regular pace, again – unless we've been practicing our speedwork, avoid the sprint finish. The twang of a tired muscle during the final forty metres of a 10K run as we try to overtake our friend who we can see twenty metres ahead of us is a very disappointing sound indeed.

Imagine though, a gentle jog through the British countryside, along the Great Wall of China, maybe the 'Rock 'N' Roll' Las Vegas half marathon, or perhaps Hawaii has always been on your bucketlist? There are so many running events being held everywhere, all of the time that the options are seemingly limitless! So in the vein of finding fun within our running, throwing in a holiday and meeting people who've travelled from around the world to be at an event, is a great way to spend a weekend (or week?).

Keeping track of our progress over time is going to help us to persevere with our new running habit. It can work as a great motivator to know how much time and effort we've put in since we completed our first run; the total distance we've covered, how our pace has improved, or how much longer we can maintain our heart rate in a moderate or high zone without stopping. Particularly in those moments when we're losing our running mojo and it feels like we're not getting any fitter and we're wondering if all this hard work we're putting in is worth it. To have these facts and figures at our fingertips gives us a picture of what we're capable of and everything we've achieved so far. This is really simple to do if we have a running watch that we can connect to an App or to our computer and view all of our historical data in one place. If our watch has a heart rate monitor we will be able to see how much our resting heart rate has improved since we did our first run, plus we can see that our recovery rate is better compared to when we first started out. Again – being able to measure this advancement in our fitness levels and health over time is going to help in the moments when we feel like we're starting from square one. Instead we can quickly see that we have a much better base fitness level than we did pre-habit.

If you don't have a running watch, or you can't connect your watch to an online data storage App, be sure to make a diary of how long you were running for on a given day and what distance you covered (e.g. two laps of the park). Having this log of all of your runs is again going to inspire you on the days when you are wondering if it is all worth the effort!

And make time to check-in with your latest running statistics on a weekly basis, even if it has been a 'bad' exercise week. Keep track of the ups and the downs from week to week, but notice how over a period of a month, or three, or six months, we are steadily improving over the longer-term. And even if we have to have some time out from running and our performance goes backwards slightly over a period of time, we can be proud of ourselves for getting out there and picking up the habit again. Yes - the first couple of runs after an enforced break are going to be tough; on the first run out we will probably feel like stopping half way round; plus we're going to ache the next day (which can be eased slightly with lots of stretching throughout the day). After those first couple of runs though, our muscle memory enters the situation, and when we return to running two to three times a week, we'll soon be back up to our prime fitness levels.

We may also want to keep a journal, or at least keep track of how we're feeling after each run and at the end of each week. Hopefully there is an obvious trend in how good we're feeling in ourselves and about the investment we're making in our health. Take note if you're feeling fitter, healthier or sleeping better. And while it is difficult to monitor the 'cleansing' processes within our body (which are being accelerated by the faster, stronger blood flow and everything our blood carries), we might notice that we feel more energised, or 'lighter' as our digestive system is kept in check by our new running habit. Each time our foot hits the ground during a run, the impact is literally helping to 'shake the shit' from our body; the raised body temperature a sign that we're sweating out toxins. The entries in our running diary hopefully start to read things like "I ran further than ever before without stopping today and I'm feeling super proud of myself", or "Daily energy levels running as high now as they were when I was at school!"

I also keep an eye on my weight (how my clothes are fitting me, rather than jumping on the scales) and I keep track of my mood, whether I'm feeling tired, how I'm sleeping, if my hormones are in-check (I track whether my cycle is regular and that my fertility hormones are doing what they should, when they should) and I notice what foods I eat. When I'm fit, I really do notice a knock-on effect across all other elements that we use to define being healthy. That isn't to say that I don't enjoy the pleasurable (short lasting) dopamine hit that follows eating a piece of chocolate every now and then, but because I'm more conscious of my weight, my sleep, my hormones, as well as the effort I'm putting in to keeping my health in check, I find that I don't want to undo all of the good work by over-indulging on foods that I know aren't good for me. I have also found that by going cold-turkey on certain food and drinks and cutting them out completely for a few months, when I reintroduce them into my diet the cravings are dramatically reduced and subsequently so is the amount of these foods that I consume.

Some days we are willing the motivation to run to come and slap us on the back and wish us well as we step outside to head off into the sunset for our run; but it is rarely that simple! I am fortunate enough to have reached the stage with my running where I still feel some resistance with getting out there and running (because it is going to be tough), however I value what running adds to my life so much and I know with 100% certainty that I'll feel better for having run (mind and body), I just do it. Then without over-thinking it, on goes my running gear, out the front door I go and then I find my legs just start moving. For those times when it is difficult to find the motivation, I'd advise trying not to dwell on the past runs you've done, perhaps worrying you were fitter before but instead focus on what you want to do for yourself today, on this new running adventure, now. You don't need to run for very long if you don't want to and it is better to jog and walk for ten minutes than to sit and torture yourself that you won't be able to run for thirty minutes at the same pace as last year. If you don't feel like going for your normal run then don't; go for ten, or twenty minutes instead; purposely run at a slower pace so that it feels more manageable. Or put your running shoes on and head out the door for a walk; perhaps you may even feel like jogging for fifty metres along the way.

Learn to love running in the rain (perhaps not torrential rain), and enjoy splashing through muddy puddles, just because we can. Try a new route and mix-up our routes each week; explore that park nearby that we've never been to before. Or find a bit of a mean hill and run up the hill and walk down ten times, raising the heart rate until we're feeling wonderfully out of breath. Or try running at a slower pace and then run further than we have done previously. Run until our face is bright red, knowing we're pushing our blood all the way to the end of our capillaries, feeding our skin cells with everything they need to stay healthy and plump. Run until we sweat, sweat and sweat some more. Sweat out all of the stuff we've put into our body that our body doesn't need, or want. Push ourselves just that little bit more each time; challenge our body to get a bit fitter each week and gently persuade it to become more efficient in all of our bodily processes, from hormone regulation, bone and muscle repair, through to heart and respiratory health.

I love feeling the strength in my body when I'm fit. I like knowing that I'm sweating toxins out of my body, I like knowing that I'm raising my heart rate and keeping my circulatory and respiratory systems in tip-top shape. I like knowing that I'm helping to regulate my hormones, I like knowing that a run will help reduce stress levels, that for me, a sort of 'meditation' and letting my mind wander where it needs to go. I like knowing that my running is helping to slow down the ageing process. All of this keeps me pulling on my running shoes, month after month, year after year, and pushing myself to maintain at least a good level of fitness. Of course there will be days when I'm just not feeling it and it will get to the end of the day and I've not gone out for a run; then I use that feeling of the missed opportunity to feel good about myself and of being nicely fatigued when I go to bed to spur me on and get out there the next day. I'm not exactly sure when the joy element happened, but I do love having running in my life. Not only is it one of life's pleasures, I genuinely feel a much happier person when I'm running regularly. Some days I can barely hold myself back from going for a run... Are you ready for that feeling too?

Part Four

Chapter Twenty-Five

Training schedules

There are plenty of websites and fitness Apps brimming with training schedules that cater for different abilities and covering all of the standard distances that we might want to try our hand at. Whether you haven't run since you were at school and you're just starting out building your running habit, or you're a seasoned runner looking to improve your 5K pace, there's a training schedule out there that is going to help steer us towards our goal.

The advice remains the same no matter which training schedule we're following, if we've been 'inactive' for a long period of time, or if we're looking to push our training to the next level: pushing too hard too soon will likely lead to injury, or burnout. So have patience and build-up slowly.

I've included some of the more common 'go-to' schedules on the following pages, as well as an Absolute Beginner schedule, for people who just want to be more active, without necessarily striving to complete a certain distance at the end. This simple programme is followed by a beginner's guide to getting started and working towards a 5K distance during the course of nine weeks. This includes the run-walk approach to building up our running fitness, allowing our body to adapt to activity in a safe way.

Once we've done our 5K we may set our sights on slowly building up to running a 10K. The third schedule I've included is an eight-week schedule for training for a 10K, which assumes a good level of fitness to start with. This could also be run as an eleven-week schedule to follow-on from the 5K training schedule. In this case simply repeat the 'Week one' schedule for training run one and training run two for the additional three weeks, but steadily increase the distance for training run three so that by week five, we're running four miles without stopping.

The Marathon training schedule is based on a 16-week preparation time and also assumes a good level of fitness. If you're starting from zero, this again could be increased to a 20-week schedule, follow the 'Week one' training run one and 2, then 'Week two' training run one and 2 and repeat each twice, building up to the training run three distance more slowly over the additional four weeks.

In case of the question "what pace does 'run' mean?" There is no one defined pace and this is completely individual to you. If for whatever reason running isn't an option for you, 'run' may actually translate to 'a brisk walk', or to someone who already plays sport every week and has a good level of base fitness, it may be the speed they run when tracking the ball back down a football pitch. To a beginner, it is going to be a walk-jog-walk-jog. Or - if we're able to raise our heart rate significantly simply by speed-walking for twenty minutes, we can repeat this three times a week for a couple of weeks until we feel ready to move to a jog-walk programme.

It is going to take determination, motivation and stamina to build a running habit, all three being transferable, life-empowering skills. I can promise that it feels really damn good when you've been at this for even a few months, let alone a year, or longer.

Looking for some extra motivation as you start-out on your running journey? Why not sign-up for the '35 Day Running Challenge'?

Visit: https://www.35dayrunningchallenge.com

Schedule one: Beginners Couch to 5K

Aim to run three times a week if possible. Always warm up with a five-minute brisk walk, or very easy jog. Stretch for seven minutes immediately after exercising as well as doing some very gentle stretching on rest days. Complement with Pilates and resistance training (strengthening exercises).

Week one: 5K
Warm-up: Walk at a fast pace for 5 minutes.
Training: Run for 60 seconds, then walk for 90 seconds. Repeat eight times (total training time: 20 minutes)
Warm-down: Static stretch for 7 minutes. Total workout time: 32 minutes
Repeat 3 times during the course of the week
Additional session: Pilates, yoga, or strength training (30 – 60 minutes)

Rest days: 7 minutes of very gentle stretching

Week two: 5K
Warm-up: Walk at a fast pace for 5 minutes.
Training: Run for 90 seconds, then walk for 2 minutes. Repeat six times (total training time: 21 minutes)
Warm-down: Static stretch for 7 minutes. Total workout time: 33 minutes
Repeat 3 times during the course of the week
Additional session: Pilates, yoga, or strength training (30 – 60 minutes)

Rest days: 7 minutes of very gentle stretching

Week three: 5K
Warm-up: Walk at a fast pace for 5 minutes.
Training: Run for 90 seconds, then walk for 90 seconds, run for 3 minutes, then walk for 3 minutes Repeat (total training time: 18 minutes)
Warm-down: Static stretch for 7 minutes. Total workout time: 30 minutes
Repeat 3 times during the course of the week
Additional session: Pilates, yoga, or strength training (30 – 60 minutes)

Rest days: 7 minutes of very gentle stretching

Week four: 5K
Warm-up: Walk at a fast pace for 5 minutes.
Training: Run for 3 minutes, then walk for 90 seconds, run for 5 minutes, then walk for 2.5 minutes Repeat (total training time: 24 minutes)
Warm-down: Static stretch for 7 minutes. Total workout time: 36 minutes
Repeat 3 times during the course of the week
Additional session: Pilates, yoga, or strength training (30 – 60 minutes)

Rest days: 7 minutes of very gentle stretching

Week five: 5K
Warm-up: Walk at a fast pace for 5 minutes.
Training run one: Run for 5 minutes, then walk for 3 minutes; repeat 3 times (total training time: 24 minutes)
Training run two: Run for 8 minutes, then walk for 5 minutes; repeat (total training time: 26 minutes)
Training run three: Run for 20 minutes (no walking)
Warm-down: Static stretch for 7 minutes
Additional session: Pilates, yoga, or strength training (30 – 60 minutes)

Rest days: 7 minutes of very gentle stretching

Week six: 5K

Warm-up: Walk at a fast pace for 5 minutes.

Training run one: Run for 5 minutes, then walk for 3 minutes, run for 8 minutes, walk for 3 minutes, run for 5 minutes (total training time: 24 minutes)

Training run two: Run for 10 minutes, then walk for 3 minutes, run for 10 minutes (total training time: 23 minutes)

Training run three: Run for 25 minutes (no walking)

Warm-down: Static stretch for 7 minutes

Additional session: Pilates, yoga, or strength training (30 – 60 minutes)

Rest days: 7 minutes of very gentle stretching

Week seven: 5K

Warm-up: Walk at a fast pace for 5 minutes.

Training: Run for 25 minutes (no walking)

Warm-down: Static stretch for 7 minutes

Repeat 3 times during the course of the week

Additional session: Pilates, yoga, or strength training (30 – 60 minutes)

Rest days: 7 minutes of very gentle stretching

Week eight: 5K

Warm-up: Walk at a fast pace for 5 minutes.

Training: Run for 28 minutes (no walking)

Warm-down: Static stretch for 7 minutes

Repeat 3 times during the course of the week

Additional session: Pilates, yoga, or strength training (30 – 60 minutes)

Rest days: 7 minutes of very gentle stretching

Week nine: 5K

Warm-up: Walk at a fast pace for 5 minutes.

Training run one & 2: Run for 30 minutes (no walking)

5K Race-day: Don't start too fast; remember the pace you've been training at

Warm-down: Static stretch for 7 minutes

Rest days: 7 minutes of very gentle stretching

Absolute Beginner: Let's get this show on the road

Want to ease yourself in to a regular routine? Or perhaps you're a little older but your doctor is still advising you to 'be active' and you're just starting out with this new fitness regime, the aim is to do some activity every single day, mixing up gentle stretches, walking, strength-work and some easy jogging. The schedule is designed for people who have lost trust that their body might ever be strong again, perhaps waiting instead 'for the next thing to go wrong', or just hoping to maintain enough strength to live a good life for as long as possible. The good news is – if you're still mobile, then you can still work out. If you're worried about exercising, please book an appointment with your doctor to have the basic checks done and to give you that final bit of confidence that you're not going to do yourself any harm by raising your heart rate while you build-up your strength again. You will build strength with every week of effort you put in. In fact after a few weeks of consistent exercise, the length of time you spend jogging can be steadily increased as you feel up to it. On the days when you're more easily out of breath, a fast walk will do just fine.

Make time to plan a route beforehand and if you're able to, find a park you can walk to and jog around. If you're running on pavement make sure your running shoes have decent cushioning through the sole. As with all these schedules, start very slowly, increase effort gradually and make time to do some stretching after each activity.

Week one: Absolute Beginner

Monday: Walk at normal pace for 30 minutes followed by gentle stretching

Tuesday: Walk for 10 minutes, slow jog for 15 seconds, walk for three minutes, jog for 15 seconds, walk for five minutes. Stretch

Wednesday: Glutes, arms and core strengthening exercises (follow the exercises in the chapter 'Avoiding injury', or for more variety search for videos online)

Thursday: Walk at normal pace for 30 minutes followed by gentle stretching

Friday: Walk for 10 minutes, slow jog for 15 seconds, walk for three minutes, jog for 15 seconds, walk for five minutes. Stretch

Saturday: Walk at a faster pace for twenty minutes

Sunday: Arms and core strengthening exercises (follow the exercises in the chapter 'Avoiding injury', or search for videos online), plus walk for 30 minutes. Stretch

Week two: Absolute Beginner

Monday: Walk at normal pace for 30 minutes followed by gentle stretching

Tuesday: Walk for 10 minutes, slow jog for 15 seconds, walk for three minutes, jog for 15 seconds, walk for five minutes. Stretch

Wednesday: Knee, ankle, arms and core strengthening exercises (follow the exercises in the chapter 'Avoiding injury', or search for videos online)

Thursday: Walk at normal pace for 30 minutes followed by gentle stretching

Friday: Walk for 10 minutes, slow jog for 15 seconds, walk for three minutes, jog for 15 seconds, walk for five minutes. Stretch

Saturday: Walk at a faster pace for twenty minutes

Sunday: Arms and core strengthening exercises (follow the exercises in the chapter 'Avoiding injury', or search for videos online), plus walk for 30 minutes. Stretch

Week three can be a repeat of week one; week four can be a repeat of week two.

Week five, six, seven and eight may involve more fast-walking and perhaps you jog for 20 seconds. Week nine and ten, perhaps a slight increase again. Importantly – keep up your stretching and your strengthening exercises. If you want to keep pushing on, how about working towards the Couch to 5K schedule?

Intermediate: Training for a 10K (assumes good base level of fitness)

Aim to run three times a week if possible. For the tempo runs (running at a very slightly faster pace than your comfortable 'steady pace') and interval training, always warm up and warm down with a 5 minute run at a more gentle pace. Both tempo runs and the fast runs in the interval training should very gradually become faster each week. If you don't have time for three runs in a week, prioritise the long run. If your leg muscles are particularly achy, the shorter run can be replaced with Pilates, yoga, cross-training or a core training session. Stretch for 7 minutes immediately after exercising as well as very gentle stretching on rest days. Complement with Pilates and resistance training (strengthening exercises).

Week one: 10K
Training run one: Run for 30 minutes, easy pace
Training run two: Jog for 5 minutes, 20 – 30 minutes tempo, jog for 5 minutes
Training run three: 3 mile run, easy pace
Additional session: Pilates, yoga, or strength training (30 – 60 minutes)
Warm-down: Static stretch for 7 minutes
Rest days: 7 minutes of very gentle stretching

Week two: 10K
Training run one: Run for 30 minutes, easy pace
Training run two: Jog for 5 minutes, 24 minutes interval training (3 minutes at a faster pace, 3 minutes jog; repeat 4 times), jog for 5 minutes
Training run three: 4 mile run, easy pace
Additional session: Pilates, yoga, or strength training (30 – 60 minutes)
Warm-down: Static stretch for 7 minutes
Rest days: 7 minutes of very gentle stretching

Week three: 10K
Training run one: Run for 30 minutes, easy pace
Training run two: Jog for 5 minutes, 30 minutes tempo, jog for 5 minutes
Training run three: 5 mile run, easy pace
Additional session: Pilates, yoga, or strength training (30 – 60 minutes)
Warm-down: Static stretch for 7 minutes
Rest days: 7 minutes of very gentle stretching

Week four: 10K
Training run one: Run for 30 minutes, easy pace
Training run two: Jog for 5 minutes, 30 minutes interval training (3 minutes at a faster pace, 3 minutes jog; repeat 5 times), jog for 5 minutes
Training run three: 6 mile run, easy pace
Additional session: Pilates, yoga, or strength training (30 – 60 minutes)
Warm-down: Static stretch for 7 minutes
Rest days: 7 minutes of very gentle stretching

Week five: 10K

Training run one: Run for 40 minutes, easy pace

Training run two: Jog for 5 minutes, 30 minutes tempo, jog for 5 minutes

Training run three: 6 mile run, easy pace

Additional session: Pilates, yoga, or strength training (30 – 60 minutes)

Warm-down: Static stretch for 7 minutes

Rest days: 7 minutes of very gentle stretching

Week six: 10K

Training run one: Run for 40 minutes, easy pace

Training run two: Jog for 5 minutes, 30 minutes interval training (3 minutes fast, 3 minutes jog; repeat 5 times), jog for 5 minutes

Training run three: 7 mile run, easy pace

Additional session: Pilates, yoga, or strength training (30 – 60 minutes)

Warm-down: Static stretch for 7 minutes

Rest days: 7 minutes of very gentle stretching

Week seven: 10K

Training run one: Run for 45 minutes, easy pace

Training run two: Jog for 5 minutes, 30 minutes tempo, jog for 5 minutes

Training run three: 7 mile run, easy pace

Additional session: Pilates, yoga, or strength training (30 – 60 minutes)

Warm-down: Static stretch for 7 minutes

Rest days: 7 minutes of very gentle stretching

Week eight: 10K

Training run one: Run for 45 minutes, easy pace

Training run two: Run for 20 minutes, easy pace

10K Race-day: Don't start to fast; remember the pace you've been training at

Additional session: Pilates, yoga, or strength training (30 – 60 minutes)

Warm-down: Static stretch for 7 minutes

Rest days: 7 minutes of very gentle stretching

Beginner: Training for a Marathon – I highly recommend the book "119 Days to go: How to train for and smash your first marathon", written by Chris Evans. This guide will take you day-by-day (including rest days) and you can keep a log of your progress as well.

Intermediate: Training for a Marathon (assumes starting from a good level of running fitness - able to run 10K)

This is a sixteen-week training schedule. If you're training for the marathon off the back of a good 10K time (less than an hour), you can probably get away with fourteen weeks of preparation. You don't need to run a full marathon distance as part of the training, however the closer you can get to twenty miles in the final week before tapering, the more confident you're going to feel on race-day and it is highly likely that you'll just enjoy the whole experience more as a result.

Aim to run three times a week if possible, add a session of Pilates and of resistance training. For the tempo runs (running at a faster pace) and interval training, always warm up and warm down with a 5 minutes run at a more gentle pace. Both tempo runs and the fast runs in the interval training should get very gradually faster each week. If you don't have time for three runs in a week, prioritise the long run. If your leg muscles are particularly achy, the tempo or interval training can be replaced with Pilates, yoga, a cross-training or a resistance session. Stretch for 7 minutes immediately after exercising as well as very gentle stretching on rest days. Complement with Pilates, yoga, or resistance (strength) training.

Week one: Marathon

Training run one: Run for 40 minutes, easy pace

Training run two: Jog for 5 minutes, run for 40 minutes at a faster pace, jog for 5 minutes

Training run three: 75 minutes, easy pace

Additional session: Pilates, yoga, or strength training (30 – 60 minutes)

Warm-down: Static stretch for 7 minutes

Rest days: 7 minutes of very gentle stretching

Week two: Marathon

Training run one: Run for 40 minutes, easy pace

Training run two: Jog for 5 minutes, 30 minutes interval training (4 minutes fast, 2 minutes jog; repeat 5 times), jog for 5 minutes

Training run three: 80 minutes, easy pace

Additional session: Pilates, yoga, or strength training (30 – 60 minutes)

Warm-down: Static stretch for 7 minutes

Rest days: 7 minutes of very gentle stretching

Week three: Marathon

Training run one: Run for 40 minutes, easy pace

Training run two: Jog for 5 minutes, run for 40 minutes at a faster pace, jog for 5 minutes

Training run three: 85 minutes, easy pace

Additional session: Pilates, yoga, or strength training (30 – 60 minutes)

Warm-down: Static stretch for 7 minutes

Rest days: 7 minutes of very gentle stretching

Week four: Marathon

Training run one: Run for 40 minutes, easy pace

Training run two: Jog for 5 minutes, 30 minutes interval training (4 minutes fast, 2 minutes jog; repeat 5 times), jog for 5 minutes

Training run three: 1.5 hours, easy pace

Additional session: Pilates, yoga, or strength training (30 – 60 minutes)

Warm-down: Static stretch for 7 minutes

Rest days: 7 minutes of very gentle stretching

Week five: Marathon
Training run one: Run for 40 minutes, easy pace
Training run two: Jog for 5 minutes, run for 45 minutes at a faster pace, jog for 5 minutes
Training run three: 1 hour 40 minutes, easy pace
Additional session: Pilates, yoga, or strength training (30 – 60 minutes)
Warm-down: Static stretch for 7 minutes
Rest days: 7 minutes of very gentle stretching

Week six: Marathon
Training run one: Run for 40 minutes, easy pace
Training run two: Jog for 5 minutes, 36 minutes interval training (4 minutes fast, 2 minutes jog; repeat 6 times), jog for 5 minutes
Training run three: 1 hour 50 minutes, easy pace
Additional session: Pilates, yoga, or strength training (30 – 60 minutes)
Warm-down: Static stretch for 7 minutes
Rest days: 7 minutes of very gentle stretching

Week seven: Marathon
Training run one: Run for 50 minutes, easy pace
Training run two: Jog for 5 minutes, run for 50 minutes at a faster pace, jog for 5 minutes
Training run three: 2 hours, easy pace
Additional session: Pilates, yoga, or strength training (30 – 60 minutes)
Warm-down: Static stretch for 7 minutes
Rest days: 7 minutes of very gentle stretching

Week eight: Marathon
Training run one: Run for 40 minutes, easy pace
Training run two: Run for 20 minutes, easy pace
Training run three: Half Marathon at race pace (try and find an organised event)
Additional session: Pilates, yoga, or strength training (30 – 60 minutes)
Warm-down: Static stretch for 7 minutes
Rest days: 7 minutes of very gentle stretching

Week nine: Marathon

Training run one: Run for 50 minutes, easy pace

Training run two: Jog for 5 minutes, run for 60 minutes at a faster pace, jog for 5 minutes

Training run three: 2 hours 30 minutes, easy pace

Additional session: Pilates, yoga, or strength training (30 – 60 minutes)

Warm-down: Static stretch for 7 minutes

Rest days: 7 minutes of very gentle stretching

Week ten: Marathon

Training run one: Run for 50 minutes, easy pace

Training run two: Jog for 5 minutes, 42 minutes interval training (4 minutes fast, 2 minutes jog; repeat 7 times), jog for 5 minutes

Training run three: 2 hours 45 minutes, easy pace

Additional session: Pilates, yoga, or strength training (30 – 60 minutes)

Warm-down: Static stretch for 7 minutes

Rest days: 7 minutes of very gentle stretching

Week eleven: Marathon

Training run one: Run for 50 minutes, easy pace

Training run two: Jog for 5 minutes, run for 65 minutes at a faster pace, jog for 5 minutes

Training run three: 2 hours 45 minutes, easy pace

Additional session: Pilates, yoga, or strength training (30 – 60 minutes)

Warm-down: Static stretch for 7 minutes

Rest days: 7 minutes of very gentle stretching

Week twelve: Marathon

Training run one: Run for 40 minutes, easy pace

Training run two: Run for 20 minutes, easy pace

Training run three: 20 mile run, race pace (try and find an organised event)

Additional session: Pilates, yoga, or strength training (30 – 60 minutes)

Warm-down: Static stretch for 7 minutes

Rest days: 7 minutes of very gentle stretching

Week thirteen: Marathon

Training run one: Run for 30 minutes, easy pace

Training run two: Jog for 5 minutes, run for 75 minutes at a faster pace, jog for 5 minutes

Training run three: 3 hours 15 minutes, easy pace

Additional session: Pilates, yoga, or strength training (30 – 60 minutes)

Warm-down: Static stretch for 7 minutes

Rest days: 7 minutes of very gentle stretching

Week fourteen: Marathon

Training run one: Run for 50 minutes, easy pace

Training run two: Jog for 5 minutes, 48 minutes interval training (4 minutes fast, 2 minutes jog; repeat 8 times), jog for 5 minutes

Training run three: 3 hours 15 minutes, easy pace

Additional session: Pilates, yoga, or strength training (30 – 60 minutes)

Warm-down: Static stretch for 7 minutes

Rest days: 7 minutes of very gentle stretching

Week fifteen: Marathon

Training run one: Run for 30 minutes, easy pace

Training run two: Jog for 5 minutes, run for 75 minutes at a faster pace, jog for 5 minutes

Training run three: 90 minutes, easy pace

Additional session: Pilates, yoga, or strength training (30 – 60 minutes)

Warm-down: Static stretch for 7 minutes

Rest days: 7 minutes of very gentle stretching

Week sixteen: Marathon

Training run one: Run for 50 minutes, easy pace

Training run two: Run for 30 minues, easy pace

Marathon Day: Smile, enjoy and know that you're well prepared (see Marathon race-day tips below!)

Warm-down: Static stretch for 7 minutes

Rest days: 7 minutes of very gentle stretching

Chapter Twenty-Six

Race-day preparation

Marathon race-day preparation and tips

1. Be sure to get your name printed on the vest or shirt you'll be wearing on race-day, or on your running number if this is an option. Having people cheer you on, shouting your name as you run past is excellent motivation and is going to help you through the toughest parts of your race

2. Training persistently over the weeks beforehand is tougher than the race itself! Be prepared for the week during your training when you start thinking that it is all too difficult and you're ready to give up. Instead give your body a couple of days rest; take a day or two off training, try and get to bed early and eat some good food. Remind yourself why you're taking on this massive challenge, stay focused on the end goal and make sure you have a couple of cheerleaders encouraging you through the most gruelling final weeks

3. You don't need to have run a full marathon in training be-

forehand however the closer you can get to twenty miles in your long run two weeks before race day, the more you're going to enjoy the race itself. Alternatively focus on running at a slower pace for as close to three hours as you're able to before the big day; this is also going to be a massive psychological boost on the day itself

4. Begin to taper your training two weeks before race-day; this gives the body time to recover from all of the hard work over the previous weeks and will help to ensure that we're in tip-top shape on the day itself. (This taper time is reflected in the training schedule above, reducing the duration and pace of our runs)

5. In an ideal world, we cut out all alcohol during our training period, however if the best option is to simply cut down, I'd advise not drinking the night before the weekly long run and totally abstaining during the week leading up to the marathon. Otherwise minimising alcohol consumption during the training period means our body can focus on getting fit

6. Do at least one long run in your full marathon kit beforehand so that you can check it is comfortable and isn't going to chafe. Be sure to apply the Vaseline, or plaster over any high-risk areas of the body on race-day (underarms and men – watch-out for nipple chafe as you begin to sweat!)

7. Do not wear any brand new clothing on marathon day, especially not new shoes. Everything should have been worn-in

(see above)

8. Practise with running gels and hydration during your training runs as well; which brand of gel you prefer (test the consistency, flavour, effect), how do you carry them (a pouch on your arm, a belt or body vest?), how often you want to aim to use them and how they work with your water intake (perhaps they take five minutes to kick-in, which might be useful information if you know you have an incline or hill halfway round)

9. Rest as much as possible in the final week before race-day and take it really easy the day before! If you need to pick up a race number, try and do it a couple of days beforehand rather than leave it to the day before. Anything you can do to avoid being on your feet too long the day before race-day is going to help. Avoid 'doing nothing' however as total inactivity may leave your legs stiff, or risk them seizing up. Gentle stretching is a good idea.

10. Take the time beforehand to calculate how long it is going to take you to get to the start of the race on race-day and then make sure you leave plenty of time to get there on the day itself. Check if there are different start zones, or start times and take into consideration that fact that you don't want to be rushing on the day itself. Depending on the weather, ideally you arrive so that you have about an hour to warm-up, go to the bathroom (twice)(including queuing time), drop your clothes off and get to the start line

11. Again – get to know what to eat, and how much to eat for dinner the evening before you do your weekly long run. Practise beforehand to figure out what works best for fuelling you through a long-distance race. The day before race-day, drink two litres of water, spread throughout the day; limit caffeine intake and eat a mix of carbohydrates, protein and 'good' fats. Perhaps a poached egg on toast for breakfast, tuna and avocado for lunch and pasta with chicken, broccoli, tomato and pesto for dinner. Don't eat more than you normally would and don't eat too late at night, otherwise you risk not sleeping or just feeling sluggish on the day of the race

12. Talking of sleep, try and get to bed early every night in the preceding week and get up early too. You might not have the best night sleep the night before race-day so you want something stored in your sleep bank; getting in the habit of waking up early will mean you're well prepared for the early start on race-day

13. Cut your toe nails the night before. You'll be feeling your feet in the final few miles of the race and the last thing you want is the discomfort of a nail rubbing against the end of your shoe

14. Make sure you have all of your clothes and shoes laid out ready the night before. Pack your gels, gel pouch, a snack (just in case), water, safety pins to pin your running number to your shirt, your running number (with emergency contact details written on the back), running watch, a fully charged

phone, a small amount of cash, or a card (just in case). If it is a sunny day, or is going to be sunny, be sure to slap on some sun cream and take your (running-tested) sunglasses; if it is a cold day take some old clothes with you

15. The idea behind the old clothes is that you use these to stay warm at the start line. You will be called to the start line before the race is due to begin and you may be waiting around several minutes before the race starts. Having some old clothes to keep you warm during that period, which can be discarded at the start of the race means you don't lose energy shivering away before you've even heard the start gun. These clothes are gathered up after the race and donated to charity or recycled

16. On the day itself, give yourself enough time to have breakfast before you have to leave the house. Breakfast might be two slices of toast with marmalade, eaten at least two hours before start time. Start to hydrate as soon as you wake up

17. Continue to hydrate until you've had 1.0 - 1.5 litres of water before the race. This probably means queuing for the toilet twice before start time (but going twice before the start means you can probably avoid using the portaloos on the way around the course)

18. If you're prone to the 'funny tummy' syndrome during a run, play around beforehand with what works best for you. Do you have your morning coffee and try and move things along, or do you avoid coffee completely for twenty-four

hours before a long run? By eating the right amount of fibre, protein, carbs and fats the night before and by avoiding an un-tested pre-race meal, this phenomenon can easily be avoided. Get your body into a good food and hydration routine before race-day; drinking two litres of water per day in the week leading up to the marathon and eating the right amount of fibre with each meal; this will help everything move through the pipes at a steady, consistent pace

19. Know where you need to drop your bag off and make sure it has your identifying number on (you might be given a sticker with the same number as your running number). Again – depending on the weather and whether you've got old clothes with you if it is cold, delay parting with your tracksuit (or whatever you're wearing over your running clothes) until the last minute possible (but don't miss the clothes van that transports the clothes to the finish line!)

20. Warm-up! Do a gentle jog for a few minutes, gently stretch out your muscles and do some easy dynamic movements

21. If you know what time you're aiming for, find your pacer at the start. Pacers are people who will run the 26.2 miles at a specified pace. They have big flags with the finishing time written on them so you can't miss them

22. Try and stay calm and don't let the nerves get to you. You've prepared yourself well, you know how far, and how long you can run for. Just try and keep to that pace while you're running

23. Don't start too quickly! It is very likely that you will get dragged off at a fast pace at the start, with everyone excited to get going. Yes – perhaps you can afford to run a little bit faster than your training pace, but don't get too carried away with how good you might be feeling with all those endorphins flying around at the start, and try and bring your pace back down after the first couple of miles

24. Remember that "pain is weakness leaving the body" (quote by Lieutenant General Lewis Burwell "Chesty" Puller). It will pass.

25. Enjoy the fruits of your labour; soak up the atmosphere and try and take it all in!

26. Have your medal engraved with your name, the date of the race and your finishing time. It doesn't cost much to have this done and it makes the medal all the more precious when you look back and remember your life-changing achievement.

Chapter Twenty-Seven

Meal ideas

Paying more attention to what we eat, and how much we eat is going to help us succeed with our fitness mission. By choosing healthy carbohydrates, lots of colourful veg, cutting back on red meat (getting our protein from alternative sources) and ensuring we drink plenty of water throughout the day, we're going to be feeling less fatigued, more energetic and stronger in our body. Naturally this then has a knock-on effect on the rest of our life, our stress levels drop and at the same time our sleep improves. Waking up each morning is a joy!

There are plenty of good recipe books, many of which break meals down into breakfast, lunch and dinner recipes. In this day of age there are also recipe books for people who do more sport, including athletes and runners. I'd recommended taking twenty minutes on a Sunday evening to go through the recipes for the week-ahead and make a shopping list, even placing your online grocery order if possible? There are some really delicious 'superfood' recipes these days meaning eating healthily doesn't mean eating flavourless, dull meals. These books teach simple things like cooking delicious Mexican food with fish instead of meat, replacing the sour cream with natural yoghurt and leaving out the cheese (not that we need to avoid sour cream or cheese, rather demonstrating that the healthier option can still be delicious). Wholewheat pasta meals with assorted delicious roasted vegetables. Think that eating salad is boring? Well now it doesn't have to be; somebody somewhere has written a recipe for a salad that you are going to love! And many of these recipes are even quicker to prepare than what you'll be cooking for yourself at the moment; yes – there might be more ingredients as we strive for that unforgettable flavour but some chefs can give you this within a thirty-minute, start-to-finish recipe.

Remembering that on a regular day we want approximately 25% of our daily calorie intake to be protein, carbs will make-up 60% and fats roughly 15%. The day before a long run we may find that eating a slightly higher percentage of our daily calories as carbs helps fuel us better and we reduce the amount of proteins very slightly. After exercise we may want to increase our protein intake very slightly to help with muscle repair, and we decrease the percentage of carb calories by the same amount; it really is a case of trial and error and finding out what works best for our own body. Otherwise the 25%/60%/15% split of protein, carbs and fats is a good guide to be working with.

The basic nutrition rules apply:

- Avoid fast food as much as possible, there is nothing good in there that is going to help our body prepare for, or recover from exercise.

- Limit ultra-processed foods as much as possible. This includes factory-made ready meals, chips, crisps, sweets and any other food we buy that contains ingredients that we ourselves don't use in our kitchen (for example, high-fructose corn oil, hydrogenated or intensified oils, hydrolysed proteins, flavours, flavour enhancers, colours, emulsifiers, emulsifying salts, sweeteners, thickeners, anti-foaming, bulking, carbonating, gelling or glazing agents).

- Eat plenty of fresh, brightly coloured vegetables, at least one piece of fruit per day, nuts, wholegrain rice, chickpeas, lentils, fish and for meat eaters, limit red meat and instead try and eat lean white meat.

- As a rough guide, eating fish twice per week, meat twice per week and going veggie for the other three main meals, will provide us with all the nutrients we need for our exercise and to ensure we feel energised around our exercise too.

Below are just a few meal ideas because I know it can be difficult to think of healthy recipes 'in the heat of the moment'. The full recipes can be found online.

Breakfast ideas

Eating a well-rounded breakfast, including carbs, proteins and fats, is going to help sustain our energy levels until lunchtime, meaning we can avoid the elevenses (mid-morning sugar-hit) completely! Protein and healthy fats are important for stabilising our blood sugar levels and in helping us feel fuller for longer. If we're planning on going for a morning run, after our breakfast has digested, porridge is a great option for pre-run fueling. Toast is a good option for many of us too, although watch-out for any possible digestion pains while running as bread can cause mild inflammation (personally I find toast quicker and easier to digest than bread).

> Muesli, with milk or yoghurt. Try adding some fruit (fresh or dried) or extra seeds and nuts
>
> Porridge. Add yoghurt, fruit, nuts, honey
>
> Eggs on toast: poached, scrambled, hard-boiled, omelette; option to add spinach or avocado
>
> Avocado on toast
>
> Potato cakes
>
> Wholemeal flour pancakes with fruit and natural yoghurt
>
> Homemade rice pudding (made the night before)

Lunch ideas

It is all too easy to just grab a sandwich for lunch but bread is one of the worst carbohydrates for inducing the post-lunch slump and too much bread in one go (even a small baguette) can leave us feeling lethargic and running will be the last thing we feel like doing later that day! Plus - if we're over forty years of age, bread is a nightmare when it comes to the battle against the belly fat, not helped by the fact that westerners tend to eat it everyday and the size of our sandwiches has super-sized.

If you eat bread everyday, try cutting it out completely for four weeks and see how much trimmer you are by the end!

Some research also suggests that how we have altered modern wheat over time may be linked to an increase in wheat intolerance and the digestive issues associated with the inflammation this causes. Plus with the latest available allergy testing, more people are finding out that it is the yeast in regular bread that is the issue, meaning an easy switch to sourdough or spelt bread can help alleviate inflammation (and the feeling of permanent fatigue this can induce). But the simple fact is that because it is convenient and it fills a hole, most of us just eat too much bread these days. As a woman over forty, I really try to limit my intake to weekends only; I find this makes a massive difference in keeping my waist measurements in the healthy range. Plus - there are some decent gluten-free wholegrain cracker-breads out there these days, which takes more preparation in the morning if we're taking lunch into work, but paired with cheese, boiled egg or houmous (or all three) is a much healthier option for us. Or make a simple egg noodle soup; add a vegetable bouillon block, some greens, some ginger and some seasoning and its ready in less than fifteen minutes.

If we're planning on running later that day, a wholemeal tuna pasta salad is a great lunch (perhaps leftovers from the night before?) Otherwise our lunch should provide a balanced mix of nutrients so that we're energised throughout the day. Think lean proteins, healthy fats and some vegetables.

- Sweet potato, chickpea and tomato soup
- Bean & vegetable soup
- Noodle soup with vegetables and optional tofu
- Soup with bread (tomato, courgette, leek & potato, vegetable, chicken, pho etc.)
- Chicken salad
- Prawn, or salmon salad
- Tuna salad with optional pasta
- Spinach salad
- Celery, apple and walnut salad
- Cheese, ham, egg and salad Ploughman's (wholegrain crackers replace the bread)
- Mackerel with salad
- Avocado and tuna with carrot or celery crudites
- Baked potato (small or medium sized) with a protein topping
- Bean & rice casserole
- Stuffed aubergine with a lean protein filling
- Quinoa and veggie bowl
- Wholegrain wrap with lean protein filling
- Omelette
- Jerk chicken with mango
- Veggie stirfry

Dinner ideas

Aside from the same message around eating a balanced meal, including lean protein, whole grains, vegetables and healthy fats, the important thing with dinner is to allow at least a couple of hours between eating and going to bed (preferably three hours). And – just because it is dinner, and for a lot of people 'the main meal of the day', it doesn't mean we have to stuff our face. If we get good at limiting our portion size for dinner and allow sufficient time for digestion, we're going to sleep much better; another great way to win the battle against the belly.

For me, if I'm doing a long run the next day, eating wholemeal pasta with protein, or sweet potatoes, chickpeas and veg sets me up really well. Otherwise I try and avoid eating pasta too frequently because it is highly calorific and being over the age of forty, if I'm not quickly burning it off, it goes straight to my waistline. If (like me) you find that eating certain types of pasta causes symptoms of mild inflammation, resulting in bloating and various other knock-on effects to our well-being, there are finally some decent gluten-free pastas on the market now too. If there is no long run to look forwards to tomorrow, dinner is back to balancing the 25%/60%/15% protein, carbs and healthy fats.

- Chickpea and spinach curry
- Vegetable stir-fry with tofu
- Veggie and bean chilli
- Potato-based pizza
- Sweet potato and peanut curry, with wholegrain rice
- Spinach, sweet potato and lentil dahl
- Stuffed peppers with a lean protein filling
- Roasted vegetables (sweet potato, beetroot, pumpkin, squash, bell pepper) and goat's cheese
- Oven baked salmon, spinach and potatoes
- Salmon with sweet potato and asparagus
- Grilled fish and potato salad
- Fish pie
- Prawn linguine (try using spiralised courgette instead of pasta)
- Seared tuna steak with veg or salad
- Turkey breast with veg and wholegrain rice
- Roast chicken with veg
- Grilled pork chops with veg
- Lean beef, or turkey tacos
- Corn tortillas or tacos, with chicken, guacamole and tomato salsa
- Casserole
- Cumin chicken curry
- Chilli con carne with wholegrain rice

Snacks

Because sometimes we just need a snack to see us through...

> Nuts
> Seeds
> Dates
> Figs
> Savoury popcorn (preferably homemade)
> Raw carrots (or other chopped vegetables)
> Celery with peanut butter (the 'no added sugar' variety)
> A boiled egg
> Banana
> Apple ('an apple a day keeps the doctor away')
> Satsuma, mandarin, clementine

Drinks:

> Water: room temperature
>
> Teas: fresh ginger, mint, lemon, fennel, rooibos, chamomile, black
>
> Fresh juices: carrot, apple, ginger, orange, beetroot, broccoli, pineapple, sweet potato, celery etc. Try and include more veg than fruit
>
> Smoothies: berries, banana, avocado (mix with some fresh juice)

Chapter Twenty-Eight

Are you with me?

Running, especially running outdoors, really is the best all-mind and body exercise we can do. Working all of our muscles to various degrees, stimulating our digestive system, nervous, skeletal, endocrine, cardiovascular, respiratory and even our lymph and immune systems. The repeated, automatic movement also provides us with headspace and time-out to let our mind wander where it needs to go. We must listen to our body as we start out; taking it easy to begin with, being patient with our running schedule, even if we feel we could do more. Eat well, have rest days and always run safely.

When our fitness levels are such that we feel like we're cruising at times, and we know that when we're going through a tough phase, if we just keep putting one foot in front of the other, we'll come out the other side and reach cruise control again. These moments of cruising and the warm hit of dopamine these provide, are one of the things that keep us coming back for more. But - running is tough. Even for the super fit, there will be moments during a run when our body feels a bit like it is being weighed down, like a small child pulling on it's parent's arm when it doesn't want to walk anymore, our legs can feel heavy, or our upper body stiff and restrictive. We're trying to boost our body into action and our body is saying "I don't want this today". If we're eating a healthy, balanced diet alongside our training, most of the time we can run through the aches and stiffness, loosening up after five minutes of jogging and we can then settle into our normal pace. In fact unless the aching is accompanied by a sharp, shooting pain through a joint, or very localised muscle pain which doesn't improve as our muscles warm up (in which case we should book to see a physiotherapist), or unless we have burnt ourselves out and the fatigue means our legs aren't doing what our brain is telling them to do anymore (in which case we need complete rest), then we can tell ourselves that "this is good pain".

There will be days when we just don't feel like going out for a run. Some days we just won't be in the right headspace to consider trying to persuade ourselves that we do actually want to go out for a run, and we can give ourselves those days and do something else that nurtures our soul instead. However more often than not on these days, if we think about the knock-on effect of going for a run on our mind and body, we can use this as motivation to put our running kit on, get out the front door and get our run done. Our motivator might not be weight loss but perhaps simply clearing our head, knowing we will sleep better that night, or triggering our endocrine system to help keep hormones in check. We can also help ourselves form our running habit by adding a social element, joining a running club, or taking part in a local Parkrun. Keeping track of our progress, both the ups and the downs can also be used as a motivator as we note how we're steadily improving over time. Once running is a habit, it will be easier to persuade ourselves to get out for our regular run, as well as if we're returning to running after some time out. If we miss a run, we try and go out the next day instead. We don't let one, or two missed runs put us off our mission!

Enjoy running in all weather; don't be afraid of a bit of rain. Try something new to keep things interesting, a new route, some hill running; and enter a race once you've been running for a few months. Completing a race, which is perhaps something you may have never imagined possible, will feel really good and extremely satisfying!

It will be tough when first creating this new running habit, if we persist with it however, we will achieve a level of fitness where we're able to find pleasure in every run (almost every run...) Whether it be enjoying the nature around us, or the buzz of a run in a busy metropolis, or just lapping up the knowledge that we're doing this for our future self. Our tomorrow self, our two-weeks time self, our next year self, our eighty year old self. We reach a point where we have both the short-term pleasure of a run as well as knowing we're doing what we can today to help try and ensure our longer-term happiness.

Every single time we get out there for a run, no matter how long or short, how fast or slow, we can feel really, really proud of ourself.

Keen to get started and looking for some extra motivation? Why not sign-up for the '35 Day Running Challenge'?

Visit: https://www.35dayrunningchallenge.com

One last thing before you jump into the notes and references: please can I ask you to leave a review for this book on the site from which you purchased it? Whether you loved it, or you think it is missing something; perhaps you have feedback for me about any information I have included in the book, or errors I might have made and missed along the way. Your feedback is invaluable; thank you!

Notes and references

Introduction

bone - which ounce for ounce are stronger than steel: OK - so the idea that bones are stronger than steel should be understood as a metaphorical statement rather than a precise scientific fact; comparing bones directly to steel can be misleading. The strength of our bones varies depending on the type of bone and the location in our body, and bone is a complex living tissue whereas steel is a rigid material. This statement probably refers to the fact that our femur, the largest bone in the human body can support the weight of a person's body several times over, which if we were to look at a very specific amount of this bone versus the same weight in a certain kind of steel, the bone would be stronger. In short, our bones are extraordinarily strong and the composition of our bones is fascinating. It is within our power to maintain the strength of our bones into old age; exercise is the best way to ensure we are putting 'moderate strain' (both magnitude and frequency) through our bones to support good bone health (https://www.ncbi.nlm.nih.gov/pmc/articles/PMC5601257/)

The decision to stand up: the initial decision is made in the brain's cognitive centre, the prefrontal cortex. Once the decision is made, the motor cortex gets involved, quickly planning the sequence of muscle movements required for standing. The motor cortex sends signals to the spinal cord and the neurons in our spinal cord are responsible for controlling muscle contractions, in this case primarily in our leg and core muscles. Balance and coordination are coordinated by the cerebellum and other regions of the brain and there is a feedback loop from our muscles, joints and skin informing our brain about any corrections needed to ensure we're balanced. Standing up is a combination of conscious decision-making and subconscious motor control. Don't go over-thinking though…

Our body gets on with what it needs to do: the ability to perform tasks without consciously thinking about them is a result of the brain's efficiency in automating routine actions. For example when we repeatedly perform a task or activity, this strengthens neural connections associated with this activity and the more we practice, the more efficient these connections become. The basal ganglia is a cluster of nuclei deep within our brain and helps to initiate and regulate learned motor patterns so we can perform tasks without conscious effort. When a task becomes automatic, our brain moves this to our subconscious, allowing us to do two (or more) things at once (for example, having a conversation while walking). Because our body sends feedback to our brain, our brain can then fine-tune our actions as necessary (for example stepping up onto the kerb (U.S. curb) to prevent us tripping over it). Automating routine tasks by practicing and repeating them means we have more cognitive energy left to expend on complex, novel challenges.

With a little bit more maintenance each week, we can live a significantly happier, healthier life, and for longer: there is a substantial body of scientific evidence that suggests that taking care of our well-being can lead to a longer and healthier life. The assumption here is that if we are healthier, we are also happier because we don't have to deal with the issues around poor health. 'Maintenance' includes eating a balanced and nutritious diet, taking regular exercise, getting adequate sleep, managing stress and maintaining social connections; all things I cover within this book. However it must be noted that individual circumstances and genetics also play a role in health outcomes.

See also: Furrer R, Hawley JA, Handschin C. The molecular athlete: exercise physiology from mechanisms to medals. Physiol Rev. 2023 Jul 1;103(3):1693-1787. doi: 10.1152/physrev.00017.2022. Epub 2023 Jan 5. PMID: 36603158; PMCID: PMC10110736.

A little bit of time invested in looking after ourselves today is going to help make our future life more satisfying, with continued independence into old age: there are various factors that can lead to a loss of independence as we age. Age-related health conditions include osteoporosis, mobility impairments (for example, muscle atrophy, or muscle loss), diabetes, heart disease, depression and anxiety are examples where exercise has been proven to help counter the age-related decline. The assumption here is that we are more satisfied with life if we are able to maintain independence as we age and we don't have to rely on others just to go about our daily tasks.

Part One

Why do I hate exercise?

Mrs Pepperpot is a fictional character in a series of children's books created by the Norwegian author Alf Prøysen. I loved these stories and went through a stage of repeatedly borrowing the same Mrs Pepperpot books from the library every few weeks. I was young at the time.

Why running?

Your body, while perhaps a little creakier these days, is still perfectly capable of making a gradual switch from its usual walking pace to a jog: building muscle and bone strength as we age is not only possible but also highly beneficial for maintaining overall health and mobility. The speed at which we are able to build strength will depend on multiple factors, including previous activity levels, health issues, weaknesses from old injuries, age etc. For some the transition from walking to jogging will be more gradual. For older adults, working with a qualified fitness trainer or physical therapist will help to ensure you work within a safe and effective exercise programme that is tailored to your needs.

you can even reverse some of the ageing that your body is experiencing: exercise improves heart and lung health, is good for the brain, bones, muscles (therefore, stability) and mood. It has been proven time and again that exercise improves the overall health of our blood vessels, making them more flexible and better able to dilate or constrict as needed; this is vital for a healthy blood pressure and blood flow. Exercise also has anti-inflammatory effects, reducing the risk of damage to our blood vessel walls due to plaque, which accumulates in arteries as a result of conditions related to chronic inflammation. Exercise helps with managing weight, reducing the load on blood vessels, particularly in the cardiovascular system and on the heart. To top it off, regular physical activity helps to regulate blood sugar levels, reducing the risk of insulin resistance and type 2 diabetes.

providing we ease into our running and don't push it too hard, too fast, the benefits for both the body and the mind are unequalled: there are always discussions about which is the most effective way to spend our exercise time: running, swimming, cycling, rowing, resistance training, Pilates? There are obvious benefits to doing any of the above and if we had the time to do a bit of all of these each week we'd be in bloody great nick (assuming we weren't gorging ourself with fast-food in between). This isn't realistic for most people however and we need to select what works best for us. The simple way to look at the overall effectiveness on our good health can be measured by the number of different muscles we use when we run, the requirement of the nervous system to be fully alert (not so much when running on a treadmill), the load we put through our lower limbs (keeping our bones healthy) and the effect running has on our breathing because of this work our body is having to do (good for the heart, the flow of blood around our body and deep-breathing is good for our nervous system). As a beginner into any sporting activity, running is going to work more of your body in a twenty or thirty minute period.

Newton's second law of motion: states that the acceleration of an object is directly proportional to the net force applied to it and inversely proportional to its mass. Mathematically it is expressed as F = ma (F = force, m = mass of the object and a = the acceleration of the object). The law describes the relationship between the force, mass and acceleration of an object (in this case the object is us). When we run, we are raising our entire body weight off the ground as we accelerate to move faster (increased mass and increased acceleration). This requires us to put a lot more force through our legs (and body) to create this forward motion compared to when we walk (and of course versus when we are still). This higher level of force requires more energy, energy is calories, so we use (burn) more calories.

One of the reasons running will make us fitter, stronger and ultimately healthier, is that is really is working every bit of our body: there are very few muscles that remain totally passive during running, particularly as our fitness improves and speed increases and we call on what might be considered normally 'passive muscles' to help with additional stability as we move faster. Ideally our facial muscles remain relaxed, hands and fingers too and we're not particularly calling on the forearm muscles either. Otherwise a good running posture, supporting the efficient use of energy and of breathing is also going to call on neck, chest and upper back muscles. And yes - there is no force going through the bones in our arms (hence the need to complement running with resistance training) but when we raise our heart rate sufficiently, our blood is being pumped with force to all of our extremities (including our arms and fingers).

Part Two

Run for your life! Why our bodily systems LOVE running

But I manage perfectly fine without exercise…

How would you feel if you slept well every night, clocking up your seven or eight solid hours sleep: during deep sleep, our body undergoes physical restoration, including processing emotions and cleansing toxins from the brain. While we slumber our energy is focused on tissue and muscle repair as well as boosting our immune system. Hormone production is better regulated when we're not tired, particularly when it comes to our stress hormones and those related to appetite (therefore helping with weight management). We're more alert and better able to deal with daily tasks after a good nights sleep, which helps doubly with our emotional well-being, for which good sleep is vital.

See also: National Sleep Foundation (www.thensf.org)

How about being able to climb several flights of stairs in one go, without getting out of breath when you got to the top: regular cardiovascular exercise (exercise that gets our blood pumping and forces us to breathe deeper as our body demands more oxygen) can help to improve heart and lung capacity. This makes it less likely that we feel out of breath during activity, including climbing stairs. Improving the strength of the muscles in our legs will also make climbing stairs easier and feel less tiring.

See also: Agarwal SK. Cardiovascular benefits of exercise. Int J Gen Med. 2012;5:541-5. doi: 10.2147/IJGM.S30113. Epub 2012 Jun 22. PMID: 22807642; PMCID: PMC3396114.

What about knowing you are slowly down the ageing process of your muscles and bones: we naturally lose muscle strength as we age (a condition known as sarcopenia) however exercise helps to preserve (and even increase) muscle mass. Weight-bearing exercise, such as running, helps to maintain bone density.

See also: Bilski J, Pierzchalski P, Szczepanik M, Bonior J, Zoladz JA. Multifactorial Mechanism of Sarcopenia and Sarcopenic Obesity. Role of Physical Exercise, Microbiota and Myokines. Cells. 2022 Jan 4;11(1):160. doi: 10.3390/cells11010160. PMID: 35011721; PMCID: PMC8750433.

Trying to get pregnant? The acceleration of oxygen rich blow-flow induced by exercise is going to help thicken the uterine lining: by regulating hormonal balance and enhancing blood flow, exercise can indirectly contribute to improving uterine health. A healthy lifestyle, including exercise, will positively impact overall reproductive health. It should be noted that excessive exercise, or training at an intense level (pushing ourselves to the point of exhaustion) can be detrimental to our reproductive health.

See also: Orio F, Muscogiuri G, Ascione A, Marciano F, Volpe A, La Sala G, Savastano S, Colao A, Palomba S. Effects of physical exercise on the female reproductive system. Minerva Endocrinol. 2013 Sep;38(3):305-19. PMID: 24126551.

See also: Ribeiro MM, Andrade A, Nunes I. Physical exercise in pregnancy: benefits, risks and prescription. J Perinat Med. 2021 Sep 6;50(1):4-17. doi: 10.1515/jpm-2021-0315. PMID: 34478617.

Brain, spinal cord, nerves and neurons – Our nervous system

Our wondrous brain, the most complex of all of our organs: some would go as far to say that our brain is one of the most complex biological structures in the known universe. Composed of around 86 billion neurons, each of which forms part of a vast network and communicate with each other through the estimated trillions of synapses within the different regions of the brain. The functions of the brain include cognition, memory, emotions, perception, consciousness (a subject of ongoing philosophical and scientific research), as well as the regulation of various bodily functions.

See also: Caire MJ, Reddy V, Varacallo M. Physiology, Synapse. 2023 Mar 27. In: StatPearls [Internet]. Treasure Island (FL): StatPearls Publishing; 2023 Jan–. PMID: 30252303.

Our central nervous system, working together with our interconnected peripheral nervous system and automatic nervous system, controls and coordinates all of our body's activities:

The body receives external stimuli via sensory organs (eyes, ears, skin etc.) as well as information about what is going on inside our body (for example, changes in our blood pressure). This information is translated into electrical pulses and transmitted to the brain, which then decides on the appropriate response. Once this decision is made, the brain sends messages out to the appropriate part of the body to react. For reflex responses, requiring urgent action, the brain is by-passed and the spinal cord or brainstem generates the reaction (for example, pulling our hand away if we touch something really hot).

See also: Waxenbaum JA, Reddy V, Varacallo M. Anatomy, Autonomic Nervous System. 2023 Jul 24. In: StatPearls [Internet]. Treasure Island (FL): StatPearls Publishing; 2023 Jan–. PMID: 30969667.

See also: Marzvanyan A, Alhawaj AF. Physiology, Sensory Receptors. 2023 Aug 14. In: StatPearls [Internet]. Treasure Island (FL): StatPearls Publishing; 2023 Jan–. PMID: 30969683.

The brain can also be mapped according to which part of our body it is receiving information from: with the advancements in neuroimaging techniques like fMRI (Functional Magnetic Resonance Imaging) and PET (Positron Emission Tomography), scientists are able to observe brain activity in real-time so we can see which part (or parts) of the brain are reacting to certain stimuli. For example, which parts reacts to sight, sound, smell, or which area of the brain reacts when we need to make a decision, or if we're trying to remember something. It is hoped that advancements in brain mapping will help to identify treatments for brain disorders.

See also: Siddiqi SH, Kording KP, Parvizi J, Fox MD. Causal mapping of human brain function. Nat Rev Neurosci. 2022 Jun;23(6):361-375. doi: 10.1038/s41583-022-00583-8. Epub 2022 Apr 20. PMID: 35444305; PMCID: PMC9387758.

Through repetition and consistency our 'muscle memory' for a given activity becomes stronger, meaning that each time we run it becomes easier to do and recovery is also more efficient:

muscle memory is defined as: "the ability to move a part of your body without thinking about it, learned by repeating the movement many times" (https://dictionary.cambridge.org/dictionary). Our **Putamen** is a structure within the basal ganglia, which is a group of nuclei deep within the brain. The basal ganglia play a significant role in motor control, habit formation and movement regulation (as well as other brain activities). As our actions become habitual, the action shifts from being consciously processed to automatic.

See also: Gardner B, Lally P, Wardle J. Making health habitual: the psychology of 'habit-formation' and general practice. Br J Gen Pract. 2012 Dec;62(605):664-6. doi: 10.3399/bjgp12X659466. PMID: 23211256; PMCID: PMC3505409.

(The brain) requires a constant, good flow of blood and food (glucose) so that it can operate at 100% all of the time...Our brain forms only 2% of our bodyweight, but consumes approximately 20% of the body's oxygen: See: Mergenthaler P, Lindauer U, Dienel GA, Meisel A. Sugar for the brain: the role of glucose in physiological and pathological brain function. Trends Neurosci. 2013 Oct;36(10):587-97. doi: 10.1016/j.tins.2013.07.001. Epub 2013 Aug 20. PMID: 23968694; PMCID: PMC3900881.

a good run will also get our blood pumping at a much faster pace than it does when we're sitting down: Our heart rate can double, or even triple when we exercise with our VO2 max (milliliters of oxygen consumed in a minute per kilogram of body weight (mL/kg/min)) increasing several times over. All that extra oxygen, inhaled deep into the lungs and whizzed around the body is really going to remind us that we're alive!

See also: Joyner MJ, Casey DP. Regulation of increased blood flow (hyperemia) to muscles during exercise: a hierarchy of competing physiological needs. Physiol Rev. 2015 Apr;95(2):549-601. doi: 10.1152/physrev.00035.2013. PMID: 25834232; PMCID: PMC4551211.

Be Alert!

our nervous system, alive with non-stop electronic pulses, runs through the entirety of our body, sending and receiving messages about what is going on both inside our body but also about everything that is happening externally too: Our nervous system includes the brain, spinal cord, cranial nerves, spinal nerves, ganglia, 'fight or flight' system, 'rest or digest' system, as well as our enteric nervous system, which manages the functions of the gastrointestinal tract.

See also: National Institutes of Health (US); Biological Sciences Curriculum Study. NIH Curriculum Supplement Series [Internet]. Bethesda (MD): National Institutes of Health (US); 2007. Information about the Brain. Available from: https://www.ncbi.nlm.nih.gov/books/NBK20367/

The more we train our brain by exposing it to all of this sensory information...this is going to improve our alertness in every day life: consistently giving our brain new information to process can boost alertness and overall brain health. Knowing what we now know about the brain and how different areas of the brain react to different stimuli, it makes sense that by feeding our brain with and assortment of sensory information (sight, sound, touch, smell and taste) that we keep our brain fit and improve alertness.

See also: https://www.brainhq.com/world-class-science/the-proven-benefits-of-brainhq/

we know that feeding our brain with sensory information helps in the fight against cognitive diseases as we age: Alzheimer's, Parkinson's, dementia, mild cognitive impairment, Huntington's disease (a genetic disorder) are a few of the diseases that we are at a higher risk of developing as we age. There is still a lot of research into why some people develop these diseases, while other people will not. What has been proven is that regular medical check-ups, a healthy lifestyle and staying mentally and socially active can help to manage, or even mitigate the effects of many of these conditions.

See also: https://www.nia.nih.gov/health/infographics/making-healthy-lifestyle-choices-may-reduce-your-risk-dementia

See also: https://www.nih.gov/news-events/news-releases/combination-healthy-lifestyle-traits-may-substantially-reduce-alzheimers

As with our brain, the rest of our nervous system must have a good supply of oxygen and nutrient rich blood feeding it and keeping it in good working order: We know that the brain consumes approximately 20% of the body's total energy expenditure when at rest and that the high energy demand is primarily due to the continuous activity of its billions of neurons and supporting cells. With the rest of the nervous system also regularly being called upon to provide information and feedback to the brain, the nervous system also needs to be provided with the energy to do this. This energy (glucose), together with the required oxygen, is carried in our blood and delivered to the active cells.

Regular aerobic exercise has been proven to improve cognitive function and it is believed that this is due to the increased blood flow.

See also: Mergenthaler P, Lindauer U, Dienel GA, Meisel A. Sugar for the brain: the role of glucose in physiological and pathological brain function. Trends Neurosci. 2013 Oct;36(10):587-97. doi: 10.1016/j.tins.2013.07.001. Epub 2013 Aug 20. PMID: 23968694; PMCID: PMC3900881.

See also: Joyner MJ, Casey DP. Regulation of increased blood flow (hyperemia) to muscles during exercise: a hierarchy of competing physiological needs. Physiol Rev. 2015 Apr;95(2):549-601. doi: 10.1152/physrev.00035.2013. PMID: 25834232; PMCID: PMC4551211.

Our nervous system: what happens when things go wrong?

Exercise is the most effective way to keep our blood pressure under control:
See:

https://www.bloodpressureuk.org/your-blood-pressure/how-to-lower-your-blood-pressure/healthy-living/exercise-physical-activity/

Regular exercise plays a significant role in brain health:
See: https://www.health.harvard.edu/mind-and-mood/exercise-can-boost-your-memory-and-thinking-skills

See also: Mandolesi L, Polverino A, Montuori S, Foti F, Ferraioli G, Sorrentino P, Sorrentino G. Effects of Physical Exercise on Cognitive Functioning and Wellbeing: Biological and Psychological Benefits. Front Psychol. 2018 Apr 27;9:509. doi: 10.3389/fpsyg.2018.00509. PMID: 29755380; PMCID: PMC5934999.

Current research suggests that chronic migraines are also linked to the brain and a disturbance in the activity of brain chemicals. It is thought that the brain rewiring causing the disturbance happens over time, with stress being a major contributing factor: the exact cause of migraines is still being researched but there are triggers that contribute to the onset of an attack. It is believed that electrical activity in the brain leads to blood vessel constriction, followed by dilation and the release of inflammatory substances causing pain. The trigger can vary greatly from one person to the next: eating certain foods (especially ingredients in ultra-processed foods), skipping meals altogether, tiredness, irregular sleep as well as stress and anxiety can all induce an attack. Identifying and avoiding personal triggers can help to manage migraines.

Of those who suffer chronic migraines, the vast majority are women (with some stats suggesting this could be as high as 85%). There is currently no cure to prevent the debilitating attacks and exercise and reduction in stress are currently the only known treatments.

See also: Sutherland HG, Albury CL, Griffiths LR. Advances in genetics of migraine. J Headache Pain. 2019 Jun

21;20(1):72. doi: 10.1186/s10194-019-1017-9. PMID: 31226929; PMCID: PMC6734342.

I heart you lungs

Every single cell of our body relies on the steady circulation of life-giving blood; providing oxygen and nutrients, and removing carbon dioxide and waste products from those same cells:
See: Pittman RN. Regulation of Tissue Oxygenation. San Rafael (CA): Morgan & Claypool Life Sciences; 2011. Chapter 2, The Circulatory System and Oxygen Transport. Available from: https://www.ncbi.nlm.nih.gov/books/NBK54112/

every heartbeat, approximately 100,000 times every day: if an average heart beats 70 times per minute, that's 4,200 times over 60 minutes (one hour), which over 24 hours equates to 100,800 times every day.
See also: https://www.bhf.org.uk/informationsupport/how-a-healthy-heart-works

The network of arteries, veins and capillaries in our body extends for more than 100,000 km, or 60,000 miles, meaning...we could wrap it around the Earth two and a half times: the earth has a circumference of approximately 40,000 km (25,000 miles).
See also:
https://www.blood.co.uk/news-and-campaigns/the-donor/latest-stories/functions-of-blood-transport-around-the-body

coronary heart disease (and) is caused by plaque buildup in the walls of the arteries:
See: https://www.blood.co.uk/news-and-campaigns/the-donor/latest-stories/functions-of-blood-transport-around-the-body
See: https://www.nhlbi.nih.gov/health/coronary-heart-disease

by reducing the amount of bad fat and bad cholesterol we consume, we also reduce our risk of heart disease:
See: https://www.bhf.org.uk/informationsupport/support/healthy-living/healthy-eating

exercise plays many roles in both helping our body process any cholesterol and fats we're eating today but also in ridding our body of excess cholesterol that has already accumulated over the years:
See:
https://www.nhlbi.nih.gov/files/docs/public/heart/chol_tlc.pdf

exercising until we've worked up a good sweat is a good sign that the battle against the bad stuff is in full swing: sweat primarily regulates our body temperature (through evaporation). Composed of water, electrolytes (salts), urea and uric acid, lactic acid (especially during physical exercise), glucose (again increases with exercise), proteins and peptides, lipids, dermcidin, hormones and metabolic by-products, it is an effective way to rid the body of waste products.

See: Baker LB. Physiology of sweat gland function: The roles of sweating and sweat composition in human health. Temperature

(Austin). 2019 Jul 17;6(3):211-259. doi: 10.1080/23328940.2019.1632145. PMID: 31608304; PMCID: PMC6773238.

See also: Mahlouji M, Alizadeh Vaghasloo M, Dadmehr M, Rezaeizadeh H, Nazem E, Tajadini H. Sweating as a Preventive Care and Treatment Strategy in Traditional Persian Medicine. Galen Med J. 2020 Dec 25;9:e2003. doi: 10.31661/gmj.v9i0.2003. PMID: 34466623; PMCID: PMC8343902.

elevating our heart rate for a period of at least twenty minutes...is going to help keep our arteries clean and both our arteries and our heart healthy and strong:

See: Nystoriak MA, Bhatnagar A. Cardiovascular Effects and Benefits of Exercise. Front Cardiovasc Med. 2018 Sep 28;5:135. doi: 10.3389/fcvm.2018.00135. PMID: 30324108; PMCID: PMC6172294.

See also: Moholdt T, Lavie CJ, Nauman J. Sustained Physical Activity, Not Weight Loss, Associated With Improved Survival in Coronary Heart Disease. J Am Coll Cardiol. 2018 Mar 13;71(10):1094-1101. doi: 10.1016/j.jacc.2018.01.011. Erratum in: J Am Coll Cardiol. 2018 Apr 3;71(13):1499. PMID: 29519349.

it is still very much within our power to make it (our heart) stronger and fitter:

See: https://www.hopkinsmedicine.org/health/wellness-and-prevention/3-kinds-of-exercise-that-boost-heart-health

Over to you O2

Where would we be without oxygen? Well - very simple we wouldn't. Essential for life: our brain is particularly sensitive to oxygen deprivation and can become damaged after only four minutes if the supply to the brain is cut-off. We need oxygen for ATP (adenosine triphosphate) generation, which is the primary energy source for our cells and without which everything stops. Also for oxidation of fats and alcohols, with the liver using oxygen to metabolise toxic substances.

See also: Manoj KM, Gideon DA, Jaeken L. Why do cells need oxygen? Insights from mitochondrial composition and function. Cell Biol Int. 2022 Mar;46(3):344-358. doi: 10.1002/cbin.11746. Epub 2021 Dec 28. PMID: 34918410.

it is our diaphragm, a large dome-shaped muscle which sits at the base of our chest, working together with the muscles that sit between each rib (our intercostal muscles), which form the body's main breathing muscle: our nervous system (specifically the phrenic nerve) controls the rhythmic contractions and relaxation of our diaphragm, depending on how much oxygen our body needs with each breath. When relaxed our diaphragm is naturally dome-shaped, when we breathe in however the dome flattens, increasing the capacity of our chest, allowing the air in (with the air forced into our lungs due to the difference in pressure inside our chest versus outside our body). Keeping our diaphragm strong through regular exercise can help to stave off age-related respiratory complications. Our intercostal muscles elevate the ribs when we inhale, allowing the increase in volume of our chest.

See also: Fogarty MJ, Mantilla CB, Sieck GC. Breathing: Motor Control of Diaphragm Muscle. Physiology (Bethesda). 2018 Mar 1;33(2):113-126. doi: 10.1152/physiol.00002.2018. PMID: 29412056; PMCID: PMC5899234.

When we exercise however, we shift to what is known as 'forceful inhalation': now we're maximising the volume of air (and the amount of oxygen) we can take into the lungs with each breath. We're use more muscles here too: the sternocleidomastoid (a muscle in our neck) elevates the sternum, the scalene muscles (again in our neck) lift the upper ribs and the pectoralis minor (a muscle in our chest) assists in raising the ribs. During active, forced exhalation (following forced inhalation) our muscles may play a role in depressing the ribs, helping to force out the additional air.

See also: Washino S, Mankyu H, Kanehisa H, Mayfield DL, Cresswell AG, Yoshitake Y. Effects of inspiratory muscle strength and inspiratory resistance on neck inspiratory muscle activation during controlled inspirations. Exp Physiol. 2019 Apr;104(4):556-567. doi: 10.1113/EP087247. Epub 2019 Feb 28. PMID: 30714220.

the total air exchange can be twenty times more when exercising than when at rest: when at rest, air exchange is approximately half a litre in and out with each breath, 12 - 17 times per minute; equating to around 6 - 9 litres per minute. When we exercise, we can suck in an extra 2 litres of air with each breath (air exchange of 4 litres per each breath in and out) and the rate at which we breathe can increase up to

51 breaths per minute (34 - 39 more breaths per minute than when at rest). This equates to between 136 and 156 litres more air being exchanged every minute when we're exercising compared to when at rest. That's oxygen in, carbon dioxide out but importantly pushing our blood and lymph faster around our body in the process.

See also: Tiller NB, Campbell IG, Romer LM. Mechanical-ventilatory responses to peak and ventilation-matched upper- versus lower-body exercise in normal subjects. Exp Physiol. 2019 Jun;104(6):920-931. doi: 10.1113/EP087648. Epub 2019 Apr 15. PMID: 30919515; PMCID: PMC6594000.

See also: Stickland MK, Lindinger MI, Olfert IM, Heigenhauser GJ, Hopkins SR. Pulmonary gas exchange and acid-base balance during exercise. Compr Physiol. 2013 Apr;3(2):693-739. doi: 10.1002/cphy.c110048. PMID: 23720327; PMCID: PMC8315793.

through regular exercise and pushing our breathing to the point of exertion, we can strengthen these critical (respiratory) muscles and make them more flexible:

See also: Aliverti A. The respiratory muscles during exercise. Breathe (Sheff). 2016 Jun;12(2):165-8. doi: 10.1183/20734735.008 116. PMID: 27408635; PMCID: PMC4933622.

Deep, or forced breathing has also been proven to be good for our nervous system...as well as improving how different areas of the brain communicate with one another:

See also: Boyadzhieva A, Kayhan E. Keeping the Breath in Mind: Respiration, Neural Oscillations, and the Free Energy Principle. Front

Neurosci. 2021 Jun 29;15:647579. doi: 10.3389/fnins.2021.647579. PMID: 34267621; PMCID: PMC8275985.

See also: Russo MA, Santarelli DM, O'Rourke D. The physiological effects of slow breathing in the healthy human. Breathe (Sheff). 2017 Dec;13(4):298-309. doi: 10.1183/20734735.009817. PMID: 29209423; PMCID: PMC5709795.

Through exercise we are training these (breathing) muscles to be more flexible; allowing more air in with each breath, our respiratory system becoming more efficient, so enabling us to be more active without getting out of breath:

See also: Your lungs and exercise. Breathe (Sheff). 2016 Mar;12(1):97-100. doi: 10.1183/20734735.ELF121. PMID: 27066145; PMCID: PMC4818249.

the improved efficiency (of our cardiorespiratory system) as we get fitter (even) means our rate of breathing slows down when we are resting:

See also: Cheng JC, Chiu CY, Su TJ. Training and Evaluation of Human Cardiorespiratory Endurance Based on a Fuzzy Algorithm. Int J Environ Res Public Health. 2019 Jul 5;16(13):2390. doi: 10.3390/ijerph16132390. PMID: 31284468; PMCID: PMC6651740.

our blood is richer in oxygen and therefore in a resting state our heart doesn't have to work so hard just to keep us alive:

See also: de Carvalho Souza Vieira M, Boing L, Leitão AE, Vieira G, Coutinho de Azevedo Guimarães A. Effect of physical exercise on the cardiorespiratory fitness of men-A systematic review and meta-analysis. Maturitas. 2018 Sep;115:23-30. doi: 10.1016/j.maturitas.2018.0 6.006. Epub 2018 Jun 12. PMID: 30049343.

The perfect partnership

Good lung and heart health are vital if we want a long and active life and with our respiratory system and cardiovascular system working in synergy to provide oxygen to each individual cell in our body, we must look after both:

See also: https://www.nhlbi.nih.gov/health/lungs/respiratory-system

If we let either weaken (heart and lungs), the other will also weaken faster as we age:

See also: https://www.webmd.com/lung/heart-conditions-cause-breathing-problems

This (keeping our lungs healthy) will help maintain the strength of our lungs and the muscles in our chest: when we breathe deeply, we're using more muscles in our neck and chest than simply our diaphragm and intercostal muscles. By maintaining, or enlarging, our lung capacity through exercise, we ensure we're able to keep practising deep, deep breathing well into old age. If we don't ever stretch our lungs, they will continue to weaken and could even lead to respiratory illnesses in old age. It is advised that we should all take several deep breaths each morning immediately after brushing our teeth.

See also: Sharma G, Goodwin J. Effect of aging on respiratory system physiology and immunology. Clin Interv Aging. 2006;1(3):253-60. doi: 10.2147/ciia.2006.1.3.253. PMID: 18046878; PMCID: PMC2695176.

Everything will be easier as we age: if we maintain the capacity of our lungs and within that, the strength of the muscles we use to breath, we can avoid getting out of breath as we go about our daily lives. Deep breathing, and especially forced inhalation (and exhalation) resulting from cardiovascular and resistance training will help preserve (and build) the strength of these vital muscles.

lower blood pressure means no heart palpitations after a small amount of activity, it is easier to relax, easier to get to sleep, and we can sleep more deeply:
See also: https://www.health.harvard.edu/diseases-and-conditions/trouble-falling-asleep-linked-to-high-blood-pressure

There is also the 'muscle memory' element to consider; once we have noticed that our resting heart rate has slowed down as a result of our improved fitness, our muscles will be at the stage where they are better able to maintain their strength: if we've been exercising at a frequency and consistency that our heart rate is now lower than it was when we first started on our fitness mission, this implies that our muscles will also be stronger. It is a two-way relationship as well: stronger, more efficient muscles as a result of exercise means our heart doesn't have to work as hard as it would do if our muscles aren't used to exercising.

See: https://www.health.harvard.edu/exercise-and-fitness/staying-in-shape-a-case-of-use-it-or-lose-it

Feeding the mind, body and soul - Our digestive system

a hormone called Ghrelin, also known as the 'hunger hormone'...although it has many other vital functions within our body:

See also: Davis TR, Pierce MR, Novak SX, Hougland JL. Ghrelin octanoylation by ghrelin O-acyltransferase: protein acylation impacting metabolic and neuroendocrine signalling. Open Biol. 2021 Jul;11(7):210080. doi: 10.1098/rsob.210080. Epub 2021 Jul 28. PMID: 34315274; PMCID: PMC8316800.

We might even experience 'hunger pangs', a grumbling stomach, and the sight of food may even make us dribble a bit as our saliva glands kick into action:

See: https://health.clevelandclinic.org/hunger-pangs

See also: Rogers PJ, Hill AJ. Breakdown of dietary restraint following mere exposure to food stimuli: interrelationships between restraint, hunger, salivation, and food intake. Addict Behav. 1989;14(4):387-97. doi: 10.1016/0306-4603(89)90026-9. PMID: 2782122.

all of the nutrients from the digestible food can be absorbed into the blood and lymph:

See: https://www.niddk.nih.gov/health-information/digestive-diseases/digestive-system-how-it-works

fibre gives these muscles (in our digestive system) a good workout and is therefore essential to our diet:

See: https://www.nutrition.org.uk/healthy-sustainable-diets/starchy-foods-sugar-and-fibre/fibre

See also: https://www.hsph.harvard.edu/nutritionsource/carbohydrates/fiber

This isn't where our digestive processes stop however; our liver is also involved, as is our gall bladder, and our pancreas:

See: https://my.clevelandclinic.org/health/body/7041-digestive-system

When we exercise, our body needs more nutrients. Our muscles need more energy, our brain is more stimulated...all of this burns through considerably more calories than sitting on the sofa does... In fact we continue to burn through these energy stores in our cells even after exercise; as our muscles cool down we are still burning calories at a faster rate than normal:

See: Mul JD, Stanford KI, Hirshman MF, Goodyear LJ. Exercise and Regulation of Carbohydrate Metabolism. Prog Mol Biol Transl Sci. 2015;135:17-37. doi: 10.1016/bs.pmbts.2015.07.020. Epub 2015 Aug 20. PMID: 26477909; PMCID: PMC4727532.

Metabolic process: "Metabolism refers to the chemical (metabolic) processes that take place as your body converts foods and drinks into energy". See: https://my.clevelandclinic.org/health/body/21893-metabolism

See also: Judge A, Dodd MS. Metabolism. Essays Biochem. 2020 Oct 8;64(4):607-647. doi: 10.1042/EBC20190041. PMID: 32830223; PMCID: PMC7545035.

the list of functions our liver plays...is a long one:

See: Kalra A, Yetiskul E, Wehrle CJ, et al. Physiology, Liver. [Updated 2023 May 1]. In: StatPearls [Internet]. Treasure Island (FL): StatPearls Publishing; 2023 Jan-. Available from: https://www.ncbi.nlm.nih.gov/books/NBK535438/#

hepatic portal circulation: As well as our liver receiving oxygen-rich blood from the hepatic artery, the 'hepatic portal circulation', a complex network of veins servicing our digestive system, also delivers oxygen-poor, nutrient-rich blood from the digestive tract via the hepatic portal vein. The blood flowing into the liver from this localised circulation can be cleansed of toxins as well as our liver monitoring and regulating what else is being carried in this blood (including "endocrine homeostasis") before it returns to the heart.

"The liver is the only organ reported to have regional blood flow monitored by the autonomic nervous system". See: Lautt WW. Hepatic Circulation: Physiology and Pathophysiology. San Rafael (CA): Morgan & Claypool Life Sciences; 2009. Available from: https://www.ncbi.nlm.nih.gov/books/NBK53073/#

See also: Harkins JM, Ahmad B. Anatomy, Abdomen and Pelvis, Portal Venous System (Hepatic Portal System) [Updated 2023 Aug 8]. In: StatPearls [Internet]. Treasure Island (FL): StatPearls Publishing; 2023 Jan-. Available from: https://www.ncbi.nlm.nih.gov/books/NBK554589/

the often underrated liver...is vital in deciding what happens to our food once it has been digested:

See: Wang S, Miller SR, Ober EA, Sadler KC. Making It New Again: Insight Into Liver Development, Regeneration, and Disease From Zebrafish Research. Curr Top Dev Biol. 2017;124:161-195. doi: 10.1016/bs.ctdb.2016.11.012. Epub 2017 Jan 17. PMID: 28335859; PMCID: PMC6450094.

So the weight-loss equation of 'calories burned being greater than calories consumed' is indeed confirmed: Calories burned is greater than calories consumed leads to weight loss: while this statement is true in so much that if we haven't consumed as many calories as our body has used, we will begin to deplete glycogen stores, which in turn leads to weight loss, it is oversimplified. For starters, if we're eating so few calories that our body goes into 'starvation mode' this can affect our hormones, which in turn can then actually lead to weight gain when we start eating 'normally' again (see reference to **Leptin** below). It is also worth noting that how we consume these calories (what we're eating) is also going to have an effect on weight-loss. If we consume all of our daily calories by eating an enormous bowl of pasta with a creamy sauce on top, we're going to be eating way more carbs in one sitting than we need. This together with the lack of fibre means our body will probably be telling us we're hungry again within a matter of hours, and this is where the risk of then over-eating come in (consuming more calories).

See: Hoie LH, Bruusgaard D, Thom E. Reduction of body mass and change in body composition on a very low calorie diet. Int J Obes

Relat Metab Disord. 1993 Jan;17(1):17-20. Erratum in: Int J Obes 1993 Jun;17(6):365. PMID: 8383636.

See also: Kreitzman SN, Coxon AY, Szaz KF. Glycogen storage: illusions of easy weight loss, excessive weight regain, and distortions in estimates of body composition. Am J Clin Nutr. 1992 Jul;56(1 Suppl):292S-293S. doi: 10.1093/ajcn/56.1.292S. PMID: 1615908.

This assumes no underlying medical conditions impacting the rate of weight loss: genetics play a role in fat storage, both how much and where on the body. Additionally, medical conditions such as polycystic ovary syndrome (PCOS), or Cushing's syndrome (prolonged elevated levels of the hormone cortisol), as well as thyroid issues (to name a few) can also lead to weight gain.

See also:

https://www.niddk.nih.gov/health-information/weight-management/adult-overweight-obesity/factors-affecting-weight-health

Lovin' the Leptin

eating more slowly gives our body the opportunity to let us know that we're full...If we eat too quickly, we can easily over-eat before our body has the chance to send the 'stop' signal:

https://www.health.harvard.edu/blog/why-eating-slowly-may-help-you-feel-full-faster-20101019605

There is still a lot of research being done on Leptin and the role it plays in our bodily functions but when respected, it is definitely our friend...when leptin becomes less efficient in our

body, it can play a role in weight-gain, mood swings and brain fog...The amount of leptin in our blood is directly proportional to the amount of fat in our body and the best way to keep our leptin levels in check is through exercise and eating a healthy, balanced diet...the way leptin works in our body means that dieting can actually make our body think it is starving and a feeling of intense hunger is stimulated:

See: Park HK, Ahima RS. Physiology of leptin: energy homeostasis, neuroendocrine function and metabolism. Metabolism. 2015 Jan;64(1):24-34. doi: 10.1016/j.metabol.2014.08.004. Epub 2014 Aug 15. PMID: 25199978; PMCID: PMC4267898.

Staving off the Lymphatic system lymp

The lesser-known lymphatics system consists of vessels ('veins'), nodes, ducts, patches, as well as our spleen, tonsils and thymus. It is vital in maintaining our health and well-being:

See: Null M, Arbor TC, Agarwal M. Anatomy, Lymphatic System. [Updated 2023 Mar 6]. In: StatPearls [Internet]. Treasure Island (FL): StatPearls Publishing; 2023 Jan-. Available from: https://www.ncbi.nlm.nih.gov/books/NBK513247/

Our lymphatic system...also helps maintain fluid balance in the body, preventing the buildup of excess fluids that could lead to tissue swelling (edema):

See: Lent-Schochet D, Jialal I. Physiology, Edema. [Updated 2023 May 1]. In: StatPearls [Internet]. Treasure Island (FL): StatPearls

Publishing; 2023 Jan-. Available from: https://www.ncbi.nlm.nih.gov/books/NBK537065/

On a separate note, 'Lymphedema' is swelling in the limbs due to the accumulation of lymph. There is currently no known treatment. 'Lipidema' can present the same symptoms however it is a distinct disease and the cause is even less well understood. Both are much more prevalent in women than in men.

See also: Duhon BH, Phan TT, Taylor SL, Crescenzi RL, Rutkowski JM. Current Mechanistic Understandings of Lymphedema and Lipedema: Tales of Fluid, Fat, and Fibrosis. Int J Mol Sci. 2022 Jun 14;23(12):6621. doi: 10.3390/ijms23126621. PMID: 35743063; PMCID: PMC9223758.

See also: Sørlie V, De Soysa AK, Hyldmo ÅA, Retterstøl K, Martins C, Nymo S. Effect of a ketogenic diet on pain and quality of life in patients with lipedema: The LIPODIET pilot study. Obes Sci Pract. 2022 Apr 21;8(4):483-493. doi: 10.1002/osp4.580. PMID: 35949278; PMCID: PMC9358738.

See also: Trincot CE, Caron KM. Lymphatic Function and Dysfunction in the Context of Sex Differences. ACS Pharmacol Transl Sci. 2019 Sep 9;2(5):311-324. doi: 10.1021/acsptsci.9b00051. PMID: 32259065; PMCID: PMC7089000.

In the average resting person, the flow may be as little as 125ml per hour, or an estimated four litres per day. However - when we exercise the, the flow of lymph is elevated several times over:

See: https://en.wikipedia.org/wiki/Lymph

See also: https://www.frontiersin.org/articles/10.3389/fcvm.2023.1094805/full

You'd be nothing without me - Skeleton & muscle

Did you know that as an adult we have 206 bones in our body:
See: Cowan PT, Kahai P. Anatomy, Bones. [Updated 2022 Jul 25]. In: StatPearls [Internet]. Treasure Island (FL): StatPearls Publishing; 2023 Jan-. Available from: https://www.ncbi.nlm.nih.gov/books/NBK537199/

once we're in our twenties our skeleton is constantly breaking down and renewing itself, with most of the adult skeleton replaced every ten years:
See: Office of the Surgeon General (US). Bone Health and Osteoporosis: A Report of the Surgeon General. Rockville (MD): Office of the Surgeon General (US); 2004. 2, The Basics of Bone in Health and Disease. Available from: https://www.ncbi.nlm.nih.gov/books/NBK45504/#

one of the most vital roles of our skeleton is the fact that in our long bones we have spongy bone marrow tissue containing stem cells, which produce our blood cells; red, white and platelets:
See: Cooper B. The origins of bone marrow as the seedbed of our blood: from antiquity to the time of Osler. Proc (Bayl Univ Med Cent). 2011 Apr;24(2):115-8. doi: 10.1080/08998280.2011.11928697. PMID: 21566758; PMCID: PMC3069519.

by the time we hit forty we slowly begin to lose bone mass...vi-

tamin D is vital for keeping our bones strong, exercise is also critically important in maintaining a strong skeletal system into old age:

See: Benjamin RM. Bone health: preventing osteoporosis. Public Health Rep. 2010 May-Jun;125(3):368-70. doi: 10.1177/00333549 1012500302. PMID: 20433030; PMCID: PMC2848259.

running actually helps stave off osteoporosis in later life:

See: Benedetti MG, Furlini G, Zati A, Letizia Mauro G. The Effectiveness of Physical Exercise on Bone Density in Osteoporotic Patients. Biomed Res Int. 2018 Dec 23;2018:4840531. doi: 10.1155 /2018/4840531. PMID: 30671455; PMCID: PMC6323511.

Wolff's Law: named after the German anatomist and surgeon Julius Wolff, the principle states that the architecture of a bone is determined by the mechanical stresses placed upon it and that the bone will adapt over time to withstand those stresses. In very simple terms this means that our bones react to the amount of force (or weight) we put through them and as a result they are able to grow stronger over time (or retain their strength as we maintain our exercise). Wolff's Law also recognises that if bones are not regularly stressed, for example due to prolonged bed rest, or a sedentary lifestyle, our bones tend to lose strength and mass. What is recognised across the fields of orthopedics, physical therapy and sports medicine is the importance of physical activity for maintaining bone health.

decreasing oestrogen levels mean women are more prone to osteoporosis:

See: Ji MX, Yu Q. Primary osteoporosis in postmenopausal women. Chronic Dis Transl Med. 2015 Mar 21;1(1):9-13. doi: 10.10 16/j.cdtm.2015.02.006. PMID: 29062981; PMCID: PMC5643776.

men will experience a decline in testosterone levels, which can also lead to loss of bone mineral density and weakened, fragile bones:

See: https://www.nhs.uk/conditions/osteoporosis/causes/

Running, coupled with diet including plenty of calcium, vitamin D, magnesium, vitamin K and protein, can help maintain good bone mass as we age:

See: Papadopoulou SK, Papadimitriou K, Voulgaridou G, Georgaki E, Tsotidou E, Zantidou O, Papandreou D. Exercise and Nutrition Impact on Osteoporosis and Sarcopenia-The Incidence of Osteosarcopenia: A Narrative Review. Nutrients. 2021 Dec 16;13(12):4499. doi: 10.3390/nu13124499. PMID: 34960050; PMCID: PMC8705961.

Having optimal bone health as we get older is going to help reduce the risk of age-related bone loss and any annoying fractures:

See: Santos L, Elliott-Sale KJ, Sale C. Exercise and bone health across the lifespan. Biogerontology. 2017 Dec;18(6):931-946. doi: 10.1007/s10522-017-9732-6. Epub 2017 Oct 20. PMID: 29052784; PMCID: PMC5684300.

Amazingly our body has more than 300 different joints, most of which are freely moving synovial joints:

See: https://my.clevelandclinic.org/health/body/25137-joints

See also: Juneja P, Munjal A, Hubbard JB. Anatomy, Joints. [Updated 2023 Apr 1]. In: StatPearls [Internet]. Treasure Island (FL): StatPearls Publishing; 2023 Jan-. Available from: https://www.ncbi.nlm.nih.gov/books/NBK507893/

whether we exercise or not, our knee cartilage naturally becomes thinner as we age:

See: Hudelmaier M, Glaser C, Englmeier KH, Reiser M, Putz R, Eckstein F. Correlation of knee-joint cartilage morphology with muscle cross-sectional areas vs. anthropometric variables. Anat Rec A Discov Mol Cell Evol Biol. 2003 Feb;270(2):175-84. doi: 10.1002/ar.a.10001. PMID: 12524692.

See also: Li Y, Wei X, Zhou J, Wei L. The age-related changes in cartilage and osteoarthritis. Biomed Res Int. 2013;2013:916530. doi: 10.1155/2013/916530. Epub 2013 Jul 22. PMID: 23971049; PMCID: PMC3736507.

See also: Eckstein F, Hudelmaier M, Putz R. The effects of exercise on human articular cartilage. J Anat. 2006 Apr;208(4):491-512. doi: 10.1111/j.1469-7580.2006.00546.x. PMID: 16637874; PMCID: PMC2100201.

However the joints that we use while running, in particular the knee, are stabilised by external ligaments and supported by the surrounding muscles:

See: Abulhasan JF, Grey MJ. Anatomy and Physiology of Knee Stability. *Journal of Functional Morphology and Kinesiology*. 2017; 2(4):34. https://doi.org/10.3390/jfmk2040034

if we wear the right footwear, running is more likely to help delay osteoarthritis than be the cause of it:

See: https://www.health.harvard.edu/staying-healthy/exercise-rx-for-overcoming-osteoarthritis

See also:

https://www.arthritis.org/health-wellness/healthy-living/physical-activity/other-activities/tips-for-running-safely-with-arthritis

See also: Kunz, M., Williams, A., McKenzie, C., Burstein, D. and Eckstein, F., 2005. No prolonged deformation of knee joint cartilage after the Boston marathon. *Osteoarthritis Cartilage*, *13*(Suppl 1), p.S124.

With this degenerative joint disease (osteoarthritis) affecting many people after the age of sixty to some degree or another, we are less likely to suffer pain in our joints if we're active and keeping fit:

See also: Williams PT. Effects of running and walking on osteoarthritis and hip replacement risk. Med Sci Sports Exerc. 2013 Jul;45(7):1292-7. doi: 10.1249/MSS.0b013e3182885f26. PMID: 23377837; PMCID: PMC3756679.

While cartilage can help to promote the healing of bones, it has a limited ability to repair itself. Research is ongoing as to how to re-grow cartilage in the joints:

See: https://med.stanford.edu/news/all-news/2020/08/Researchers-find-method-to-regrow-cartilage-in-the-joints.html

See also: Householder NA, Raghuram A, Agyare K, Thipaphay S, Zumwalt M. A Review of Recent Innovations in Cartilage Regeneration Strategies for the Treatment of Primary Osteoarthritis of the Knee: Intra-articular Injections. Orthop J Sports Med. 2023 Apr 27;11(4):23259671231155950. doi: 10.1177/23259671231155950. PMID: 37138944; PMCID: PMC10150434.

The hustle with our muscle

Our skeletal system would be useless without our muscle tissue:

See: DiGirolamo DJ, Kiel DP, Esser KA. Bone and skeletal muscle: neighbors with close ties. J Bone Miner Res. 2013 Jul;28(7):1509-18. doi: 10.1002/jbmr.1969. PMID: 23630111; PMCID: PMC4892934.

Our muscular system does so much more than just help us move around:

See: https://www.niams.nih.gov/health-topics/kids/healthy-muscles

See also: Song Q, Zhang X, Mao M, Sun W, Zhang C, Chen Y, Li L. Relationship of proprioception, cutaneous sensitivity, and muscle strength with the balance control among older adults. J Sport Health Sci. 2021 Sep;10(5):585-593. doi: 10.1016/j.jshs.2021.07.005. Epub 2021 Jul 20. PMID: 34293496; PMCID: PMC8500852.

How do we keep our muscles strong and healthy? Through regular use and training:

https://www.nia.nih.gov/health/four-types-exercise-can-improve-your-health-and-physical-ability

whole teams of muscles are engaged to achieve the precise movement in a given direction:

See: Liu MQ, Anderson FC, Schwartz MH, Delp SL. Muscle contributions to support and progression over a range of walking speeds. J Biomech. 2008 Nov 14;41(15):3243-52. doi: 10.1016/j.jbiomech.2008.07.031. Epub 2008 Sep 25. PMID: 18822415; PMCID: PMC4423744.

proprioception: This is the fascinating ability of our body to sense its own position, motion and equilibrium and is how we're able to coordinate our movements in relation to our surroundings, while maintaining balance and agility.

Note: "In 1906, the English neurophysiologist Sir Charles Sherrington coined "proprioception", from a combination of the Latin "proprius" (one's own) and "perception", to give a term for the sensory information derived from (neural) receptors embedded in joints, muscles and tendons that enable a person to know where parts of the body are located at any time. He referred to proprioception as "the perception of joint and body movement as well as position of the body, or body segments, in space". See: Han J, Waddington G, Adams R, Anson J, Liu Y. Assessing proprioception: A critical review of methods. J Sport Health Sci. 2016 Mar;5(1):80-90. doi: 10.1016/j.jshs.2014.10.004. Epub 2015 Feb 3. PMID: 30356896; PMCID: PMC6191985.

kinesthesia: "Some researchers define proprioception as joint position sense only, and kinaesthesia as the conscious awareness of joint motion; while others consider that kinaesthesia is one of the submodalities of proprioception, and that proprioception as a construct contains both joint position sense and the sensation of joint movement (kinaesthesia)"...it has been argued that it is appropriate to interpret "proprioception" and "kinaesthesis (kinaesthesia)" as being synonymous". See again: Han J, Waddington G, Adams R, Anson J, Liu Y. Assessing proprioception: A critical review of methods. J Sport Health Sci. 2016 Mar;5(1):80-90. doi: 10.1016/j.jshs.2014.10.004 . Epub 2015 Feb 3. PMID: 30356896; PMCID: PMC6191985.

the 'sitting disease': with the evolution of the workplace (from farming to manufacturing and now to information-gatherers) and the advancements in transportation and technology, our lives have become more and more sedentary over the years. As of 2020 it was estimated that "a third of the global population aged 15 and older engages in insufficient physical activities". Living a sedentary lifestyle affects how much energy we use (our metabolic rate slows down), decreases cardiac output (leading to heart problems), increases our risk of cancer and metabolic diseases (for example, diabetes), as well as for musculoskeletal diseases, depression and cognitive impairment.

See: Park JH, Moon JH, Kim HJ, Kong MH, Oh YH. Sedentary Lifestyle: Overview of Updated Evidence of Potential Health Risks. Korean J Fam Med. 2020 Nov;41(6):365-373. doi: 10.4082/kjfm.20.0165. Epub 2020 Nov 19. PMID: 33242381; PMCID: PMC7700832.

See also: Furrer R, Hawley JA, Handschin C. The molecular athlete: exercise physiology from mechanisms to medals. Physiol Rev. 2023 Jul 1;103(3):1693-1787. doi: 10.1152/physrev.00017.2022. Epub 2023 Jan 5. PMID: 36603158; PMCID: PMC10110736.

Given what our body and our muscles are capable of and how quickly we can build strength with just a little concentrated effort:

See: Jiang CH, Ranganathan VK, Siemionow V, Yue GH. The level of effort, rather than muscle exercise intensity determines strength gain following a six-week training. Life Sci. 2017 Jun 1;178:30-34. doi: 10.1016/j.lfs.2017.04.003. Epub 2017 Apr 13. PMID: 28412240; PMCID: PMC6067674.

or have the strength to lift an object from a shelf above our head: use it or lose it! How often do you lift your arms above your head as you go about your daily life? How often would you hold a light weight in each of your hands as you lift your arms above your head? The fact is that this very simple movement is something we do less and less as we age. No wonder when it comes to lifting items from shelves when our years are somewhat advanced that we lack the strength (and confidence) to do this ourselves. Thankfully these muscles in our arms and shoulders can easily be strengthened, even using very light weights once a day for a couple of minutes is going to help. This can also help to stave off the curvature some people experience in the top of their back as they age (Hyperkyphosis), for which one of the known causes is muscle weakness. The reduced mobility is again a menace for allowing us to reach our arms above our head as we age.

See: Katzman WB, Wanek L, Shepherd JA, Sellmeyer DE. Age-related hyperkyphosis: its causes, consequences, and management. J Orthop Sports Phys Ther. 2010 Jun;40(6):352-60. doi: 10.2519/jospt.2010.3099. PMID: 20511692; PMCID: PMC2907357.

No wonder either that we're quickly put off the idea of exercise when even walking for an hour leaves us feeling tired and our legs complaining for three days afterwards: we know that by repeating the same actions every day our body adapts, slowly learning these actions so that the effort we need to exert decreases over time. If we walk for 10 minutes every day, in no time at all, 10 minutes feel like nothing. If we haven't walked for an hour for many years and then we do so, our body isn't used to the repeated action for such a long period of time and it becomes tired. We can understand that our muscles start to feel tired; they can manage 10 minutes but are having to call on extra energy reserves to have enough strength to walk the additional 50 minutes. But it isn't just our muscles on their own, not surprisingly our nervous system plays a big role in how tired we feel too. The messages being sent from the muscles to the brain and then back out to the muscles again via our 'motor units', which are systematically recruited and 'derecruited' as we exercise. The firing of these messages also slows down as we become tired which then affects the messages our muscles are receiving and how our muscles behave as we become more tired. The good news is - as we repeat the one-hour walk more regularly, our body will adjust and we become fitter and stronger, with our nervous system also able to continue to react to the messages from our muscles without becoming fatigued. As for the muscles, delayed onset muscle soreness (DOMS), this is the discomfort that sets in about 24 - 48 hours after unaccustomed or strenuous exercise. It is muscle tenderness and stiffness, rather than acute or sharp pain. It is nothing to worry about and some gentle stretching, self-massage, foam-rolling and walking is all going to help ease the aches while the muscles rebuild their energy levels and 'repair' themselves. An acute or sharp pain could be a more serious injury and will need complete rest and if it persists, will benefit from physiotherapy.

See: Taylor JL, Amann M, Duchateau J, Meeusen R, Rice CL. Neural Contributions to Muscle Fatigue: From the Brain to the Muscle and Back Again. Med Sci Sports Exerc. 2016 Nov;48(11):2294-2306. doi: 10.1249/MSS.0000000000000923. PMID: 27003703; PMCID: PMC5033663.

Regulate! - Our endocrine system

our hormones (as) chemical messengers:
See: https://www.endocrine.org/patient-engagement/endocrine-library/hormones-and-endocrine-function

(our endocrine system) is responsible for regulating the hormone levels in our body:
See: Hiller-Sturmhöfel S, Bartke A. The endocrine system: an overview. Alcohol Health Res World. 1998;22(3):153-64. PMID: 15706790; PMCID: PMC6761896.

the massive importance of hormonal balance on our overall well-being, and how both internal and external factors are at play with our hormones still isn't getting the attention it de-

serves: imbalances in the hormonal system can lead to all kinds of medical conditions and diseases and while many can now be treated, many are still a mystery and sufferers are left without answers. Diabetes, thyroid and adrenal disorders, imbalances affecting fertility and reproductive health, growth disorders, osteoporosis, menopause-related symptoms, metabolic syndrome, mental health issues and many more conditions caused due to the fact that our body isn't sending, or receiving, the right chemical messages. While genes may play a part, lifestyle choices and external factors can also contribute. With environmental factors affecting the balance of hormones, including endocrine disruptor chemicals (EDCs) such as plastics, pesticides, household products are known to impact circadian rhythm, the thyroid, fertility and cause cancer. It is acknowledged that there is more research to be done

See also: Kalra S, Kapoor N. Environmental Endocrinology: An Expanding Horizon. [Updated 2021 Mar 14]. In: Feingold KR, Anawalt B, Blackman MR, et al., editors. Endotext [Internet]. South Dartmouth (MA): MDText.com, Inc.; 2000-. Available from: https://www.ncbi.nlm.nih.gov/books/NBK568568/

See also: Bova TL, Chiavaccini L, Cline GF, Hart CG, Matheny K, Muth AM, Voelz BE, Kesler D, Memili E. Environmental stressors influencing hormones and systems physiology in cattle. Reprod Biol Endocrinol. 2014 Jul 4;12:58. doi: 10.1186/1477-7827-12-58. PMID: 24996419; PMCID: PMC4094414.

melatonin regulates our sleep:

See: Minich DM, Henning M, Darley C, Fahoum M, Schuler CB, Frame J. Is Melatonin the "Next Vitamin D"?: A Review of Emerging Science, Clinical Uses, Safety, and Dietary Supplements. Nutrients. 2022 Sep 22;14(19):3934. doi: 10.3390/nu14193934. PMID: 36235587; PMCID: PMC9571539.

oestrogen and progesterone, regulating our menstrual cycle and supporting pregnancy:

See: Reed BG, Carr BR. The Normal Menstrual Cycle and the Control of Ovulation. [Updated 2018 Aug 5]. In: Feingold KR, Anawalt B, Blackman MR, et al., editors. Endotext [Internet]. South Dartmouth (MA): MDText.com, Inc.; 2000-. Available from: https://www.ncbi.nlm.nih.gov/books/NBK279054/

See also: Kumar P, Magon N. Hormones in pregnancy. Niger Med J. 2012 Oct;53(4):179-83. doi: 10.4103/0300-1652.107549. PMID: 23661874; PMCID: PMC3640235.

See: Cable JK, Grider MH. Physiology, Progesterone. [Updated 2023 May 1]. In: StatPearls [Internet]. Treasure Island (FL): StatPearls Publishing; 2023 Jan-. Available from: https://www.ncbi.nlm.nih.gov/books/NBK558960/

oestrogen is also important for bone strength:

See: Parker SE, Troisi R, Wise LA, Palmer JR, Titus-Ernstoff L, Strohsnitter WC, Hatch EE. Menarche, menopause, years of menstruation, and the incidence of osteoporosis: the influence of prenatal exposure to diethylstilbestrol. J Clin Endocrinol Metab. 2014 Feb;99(2):594-601. doi: 10.1210/jc.2013-2954. Epub 2013 Nov 18. PMID: 24248183; PMCID: PMC3913806.

Our stomach secretes hormones that digest our food:

See: Parikh A, Thevenin C. Physiology, Gastrointestinal Hormonal Control. [Updated 2023 May 1]. In: StatPearls [Internet]. Treasure Island (FL): StatPearls Publishing; 2023 Jan-. Available from: https://www.ncbi.nlm.nih.gov/books/NBK537284/

our kidneys secrete a hormone that helps produce red blood cells in our bone marrow:

See: https://www.niddk.nih.gov/news/media-library/17455

our adrenal glands regulate metabolism as well as producing adrenaline...The pancreas regulates blood sugar levels and also makes sure our cells have the energy they need. The list (of the role our endocrine system plays) goes on:

See: Hiller-Sturmhöfel S, Bartke A. The endocrine system: an overview. Alcohol Health Res World. 1998;22(3):153-64. PMID: 15706790; PMCID: PMC6761896.

exercise also stimulates the production of certain hormones: growth hormone, testosterone, prolactin and cortisol levels rise, as does LH (luteinising hormone) (following recovery). Levels of FSH (follicle stimulating hormone) and TSH (thyroid stimulating hormone) remained unchanged. Note that cortisol is essential for our body to function, however sustained high levels can lead to problems, including weakening our immune system.

See: Gawel MJ, Park DM, Alaghband-Zadeh J, Rose FC. Exercise and hormonal secretion. Postgrad Med J. 1979 Jun;55(644):373-6. doi: 10.1136/pgmj.55.644.373. PMID: 482180; PMCID: PMC2425585.

See also: Thau L, Gandhi J, Sharma S. Physiology, Cortisol. [Updated 2022 Aug 29]. In: StatPearls [Internet]. Treasure Island (FL): StatPearls Publishing; 2023 Jan-. Available from: https://www.ncbi.nlm.nih.gov/books/NBK538239/

prolactin, which plays a role in our reproductive functions, immune system, glucose homeostasis, insulin secretion, as well as behavioural responses:

See: Freeman ME, Kanyicska B, Lerant A, Nagy G. Prolactin: structure, function, and regulation of secretion. Physiol Rev. 2000 Oct;80(4):1523-631. doi: 10.1152/physrev.2000.80.4.1523. PMID: 11015620.

Exercise can help reduce stress levels:

See: https://www.frontiersin.org/articles/10.3389/fphys.2014.00161/full Childs E, de Wit H. Regular exercise is associated with emotional resilience to acute stress in healthy adults. Front Physiol. 2014 May 1;5:161. doi: 10.3389/fphys.2014.00161. PMID: 24822048; PMCID: PMC4013452.

the small spike in cortisol released while exercising has been proven to suppress the cortisol response to every day stresses ('fight or flight' response), so promoting 'stress resilience':

See: https://www.sciencedirect.com/science/article/pii/S0306453021002109 Caplin A, Chen FS, Beauchamp MR, Puterman E. The effects of exercise intensity on the cortisol response to a subsequent acute psychosocial stressor. Psychoneuroendocrinology. 2021 Sep;131:105336. doi: 10.1016/j.psyneuen.2021.105336. Epub 2021

Jun 18. PMID: 34175558.

exercise can help regulate and improve thyroid function and how our body uses energy:

See: Shahid MA, Ashraf MA, Sharma S. Physiology, Thyroid Hormone. 2023 Jun 5. In: StatPearls [Internet]. Treasure Island (FL): StatPearls Publishing; 2023 Jan–. PMID: 29763182.

See also: Klasson CL, Sadhir S, Pontzer H. Daily physical activity is negatively associated with thyroid hormone levels, inflammation, and immune system markers among men and women in the NHANES dataset. PLoS One. 2022 Jul 6;17(7):e0270221. doi: 10.1371/journal.pone.0270221. PMID: 35793317; PMCID: PMC9258892.

these (endorphins, serotonin and dopamine) help induce a sense of well-being and reduce the risk of depression and other mood disorders:

See: Dfarhud D, Malmir M, Khanahmadi M. Happiness & Health: The Biological Factors- Systematic Review Article. Iran J Public Health. 2014 Nov;43(11):1468-77. PMID: 26060713; PMCID: PMC4449495.

Running for weight loss

running is a great way to lose weight:

See: Williams PT. Greater weight loss from running than walking during a 6.2-yr prospective follow-up. Med Sci Sports Exerc. 2013 Apr;45(4):706-13. doi: 10.1249/MSS.0b013e31827b0d0a. PMID: 23190592; PMCID: PMC4067491.

As human beings, it is well documented that our relationship with food has changed over time; what we eat, how often we eat and most of all, how much we eat:

See: Mingay E, Hart M, Yoong S, Hure A. Why We Eat the Way We Do: A Call to Consider Food Culture in Public Health Initiatives. Int J Environ Res Public Health. 2021 Nov 15;18(22):11967. doi: 10.3390/ijerph182211967. PMID: 34831723; PMCID: PMC8623951.

If we didn't eat and our body wasn't getting the energy that it needs, we'd waste away and eventually we'd die:

See: Kottusch P, Tillmann M, Püschel K. Oberlebenszeit bei Nahrungs- und Flüssigkeitskarenz [Survival time without food and drink]. Arch Kriminol. 2009 Nov-Dec;224(5-6):184-91. German. PMID: 20069776.

we have this complex experience of flavour:

See: https://www.nature.com/articles/486S6a

in a world where 'man-made' ultra-processed foods are often cheaper than fresh fruit and veg:

See: https://www.cambridge.org/core/journals/public-health-nutrition/article/ultraprocessed-foods-what-they-are-and-how-to-identify-them/

eating junk food, we are putting our long-term health at risk:

See: Monteiro CA, Levy RB, Claro RM, de Castro IR, Cannon G. Increasing consumption of ultra-processed foods and likely impact on human health: evidence from Brazil. Public Health Nutr. 2011 Jan;14(1):5-13. doi: 10.1017/S1368980010003241. PMID: 21211100.

Ultra-processed foods with high levels of added sugar, salt, fat content and E-numbers...are the real danger foods:

See: Aceves-Martins M, Bates RL, Craig LCA, Chalmers N, Horgan G, Boskamp B, de Roos B. Nutritional Quality, Environmental Impact and Cost of Ultra-Processed Foods: A UK Food-Based Analysis. Int J Environ Res Public Health. 2022 Mar 8;19(6):3191. doi: 10.3390/ijerph19063191. PMID: 35328877; PMCID: PMC8948822.

E-numbers to make the flavour more appealing: if what you're eating contains E-numbers between E600 and E699 then it contains flavouring, or flavour enhancers. The more responsible producers are using natural flavours in our food and drink rather than artificial flavouring. Some people are extra sensitive to artificial flavours and some will even be intolerant. The side-effects of monosodium glutamate (MSG, or E621) have been known to include palpitations, dizziness, headaches (and migraine like headaches), pains in the neck and arms as well as difficultly sleeping.

See: Kayode OT, Bello JA, Oguntola JA, Kayode AAA, Olukoya DK. The interplay between monosodium glutamate (MSG) consumption and metabolic disorders. Heliyon. 2023 Sep 9;9(9):e19675. doi: 10.1016/j.heliyon.2023.e19675. PMID: 37809920; PMCID: PMC10558944.

these have been specifically made to trigger an addiction by way of dopamine release in our brains:
See: Baik JH. Dopamine signaling in food addiction: role of dopamine D2 receptors. BMB Rep. 2013 Nov;46(11):519-26. doi: 10.5483/bmbrep.2013.46.11.207. PMID: 24238362; PMCID: PMC4133846.

over time we can train ourselves to avoid certain foods and to appreciate other (hopefully healthier) flavours more:
See: Boesveldt S, de Graaf K. The Differential Role of Smell and Taste For Eating Behavior. Perception. 2017 Mar-Apr;46(3-4):307-319. doi: 10.1177/0301006616685576. Epub 2017 Jan 6. PMID: 28056650.

Getting through the initial cravings in the first fortnight...realistically it probably takes about a year for our taste buds to forget the pleasure of a give flavour: the year-long time frame is going to depend on many factors, including genetic factors such as how likely we are to become addicted, or are we someone who can easily give something up because we know its not good for us. And there will be foods or drinks that have become engrained in our 'pleasure' memory banks, habits we've formed that are really difficult to break free from. In some cases initially giving up may not be difficult, but abstaining over a long period of time is really tough to do because we have good memories associated with the pleasure. It may not even be the taste we crave by now but the desire to recreate this moment of pleasure, or even of happiness from our past. Having convinced ourselves that this was wholly dependent on our consuming the given food or drink, and perhaps feeling a little low, or bored and looking for an easy pick-me-up, it becomes a battle in our head as to whether consuming this thing we'd worked so hard to give up might not be the answer to our immediate needs. This is why a year feels like a good target to have in mind when we set about getting our taste buds to the stage where we are able to tell ourselves "but I don't even like the taste anymore" when we're battling in our head if we should give in to temptation or not.

There is no doubt that for many people good food has become one of life's pleasures (it has been the case for much longer in certain parts of the world): enjoying good food with family is an integral part of social fabric and traditions in many countries around the world. Italy, France, Spain, Greece, Mexico, India, China, Japan, Morocco and Lebanon (to name a few), all have a long tradition of family and food being central to their culture.

'We are what we eat'

It (the food we put in our mouths) is also what ends up on our hips, or expands our waistline if we eat too much of the wrong stuff or even too much of one thing:
https://www.webmd.com/fitness-exercise/what-is-waist-to-hip-ratio

It is what accumulates on the inside of our blood vessels if we eat

more fatty food than our body can process in a safe way, slowly putting us at increased risk of a heart attack:

See: https://www.mayoclinic.org/diseases-conditions/arteriosclerosis-atherosclerosis/symptoms-causes

See also: Libby, P. The changing landscape of atherosclerosis. *Nature* **592**, 524–533 (2021). https://doi.org/10.1038/s41586-021-03392-8

from a positive standpoint, if we are eating a healthy, balanced diet, this can have a massive impact on how good we feel hour-to-hour:

See: https://www.medicalnewstoday.com/articles/322268

If we include our weekly exercise in the equation, we're going to feel more energised, more confident in our appearance and very likely - happier: the assumptions here are that because we are exercising regularly, we feel more in control of our appearance and we feel more confident in ourselves as a result. Having more energy is also going to radiate through our appearance; a gentle glow, a wider smile, even choosing our outfit for the day can depend on how much energy we have as we open our wardrobe in the morning. Also - if we have more energy to do the things we enjoy doing, this is also going to promote our levels of happiness.

See also: https://www.mayoclinic.org/healthy-lifestyle/fitness/in-depth/exercise/art-20048389

exercise plays a vital role in helping us to feel good about our health and wellbeing; simply watching our diet and being care-

ful what we eat and drink will have a much more limited effect: there are two parts to this, firstly calorie counting and restricting what we eat every single day is not going to be much fun for most people, plus this could lead to health issues in later life if we're not getting all of the vitamins and nutrients within our limited calorie intake each week. The second point is that 'health and wellbeing' are more than just calorie intake; it is being in good physical and mental health, it is the absence of disease. It is not impossible to achieve this ambition through diet alone but it is much more likely that we'll address all three if we add exercise into the equation.

calorie counting can often just leave us feeling stressed:

See: https://www.health.harvard.edu/staying-healthy/stop-counting-calories

"they never put on weight; they must have a fast metabolism":

See: https://www.health.harvard.edu/staying-healthy/the-truth-about-metabolism

A high proportion of the additional energy we require as children is because we are growing but we are also much more active when we are younger:

See: https://www.nhs.uk/common-health-questions/childrens-health/how-many-calories-does-a-child-of-7-10-need/

See also: Committee on Physical Activity and Physical Education in the School Environment; Food and Nutrition Board; Institute of Medicine; Kohl HW III, Cook HD, editors. Educating the Student Body: Taking Physical Activity and Physical Education to School. Washington (DC): National Academies Press (US); 2013 Oct 30. 3, Physical Activity and Physical Education: Relationship to Growth, Development, and Health. Available from: https://www.ncbi.nlm.nih.gov/books/NBK201497/

as a growing girl or boy we were burning as many as 2,200 - 2,600 calories (per day) respectively:

See: https://www.eatright.org/fitness/sports-and-athletic-performance/beginner-and-intermediate/teen-nutrition-for-fall-sports

See also: https://www.nhs.uk/common-health-questions/childrens-health/how-many-calories-do-teenagers-need

A woman in her forties, who goes about her daily life, going to work, then coming home and getting on with family life before going to bed and doing the same thing day after day, will only need the energy equivalent of about 1,800 calories per day:

See: https://health.clevelandclinic.org/how-many-calories-a-day-should-i-eat

If said woman were to consume more than 1,800 calories per day, she would put on weight: see reference for the 'weight loss equation' (our digestive system). This is overly simplified since we know that not all calories are equal and we know that when and how we consume calories also plays a part.

See also: https://www.nhs.uk/live-well/healthy-weight/managing-your-weight/understanding-calories

if we want to avoid the ever-expanding waistline and the health risks that come hand-in-hand:

See: Mingay E, Hart M, Yoong S, Hure A. Why We Eat the Way We Do: A Call to Consider Food Culture in Public Health Initiatives. Int J Environ Res Public Health. 2021 Nov 15;18(22):11967. doi: 10.3390/ijerph182211967. PMID: 34831723; PMCID: PMC8623951.

See again:

https://www.webmd.com/fitness-exercise/what-is-waist-to-hip-ratio

The fact that we can run our normal daily lives using fewer calories as we get older also means that if we're running two or three times a week, we don't need to increase the amount we're eating: if on a non-exercise day we burn 1,800 calories, compared with 2,200 on an exercise day and we assume we exercise three days out of seven every week, we will burn a total of: (4 x 1,800) + (3 x 2,200) = 13,800 calories per week. If we average this over seven days this equates to 1,970 per day, meaning that even if we're doing pretty vigorous exercise three time a week, we don't need to eat more than 2,000 calories per day. The same holds for men, burning 2,200 calories on a non-exercise day and 2,600 with exercise: (4 x 2,200) + (3 x 2,600) = 16,600 calories per week, or 2,370 on average per day.

as we get fitter and are able to exercise for longer, or more intensively, not only do we burn more calories while we are exercising but our body will continue to burn calories faster even after we finish working out:

See: McCarthy SF, Jarosz C, Ferguson EJ, Kenno KA, Hazell TJ. Intense interval exercise induces greater changes in post-exercise metabolism compared to submaximal exercise in middle-aged adults. Eur J Appl Physiol. 2023 Oct 11. doi: 10.1007/s00421-023-05334-w. Epub ahead of print. PMID: 37819613.

afterburn effect: scientifically known as 'excess post-exercise oxygen consumption' (EPOC), or 'post-exercise metabolic rate', this refers to the phenomenon where the body continues to burn calories at an elevated rate after a workout, even while at rest. According to ChatGPT. (n.d. Nov'23) the science behind EPOC includes continued elevated oxygen consumption and calorific expenditure and varies according to the type, duration and intensity of the exercise, as well as individual factors such as age, fitness level, genetics and body composition.

See also: Børsheim E, Bahr R. Effect of exercise intensity, duration and mode on post-exercise oxygen consumption. Sports Med. 2003;33(14):1037-60. doi: 10.2165/00007256-200333140-00002. PMID: 14599232.

repay oxygen debt: because our body may not be able to supply enough oxygen to meet the immediate energy demands during strenuous physical activity, we end up with a temporary deficit in our muscles and bloodstream. When anaerobic metabolism (energy production without oxygen) is used to support our exercise (for example, when we push our body until we're out of breath), we have to 'repay' this oxygen debt/deficiency. We do this by resting and allowing our breathing to return to normal immediately after exercise and then giving our body the time (and food) to replenish depleted energy stores. Obviously the more debt we get into while exercising (perhaps doing a longer, more intense sessions), the longer it takes to repay this debt.

the rebuilding (of the energy stores in our muscles) that happens after exercise, is actually making our muscle even stronger:

See: McGlory C, Devries MC, Phillips SM. Skeletal muscle and resistance exercise training; the role of protein synthesis in recovery and remodeling. J Appl Physiol (1985). 2017 Mar 1;122(3):541-548. doi: 10.1152/japplphysiol.00613.2016. Epub 2016 Oct 14. PMID: 27742803; PMCID: PMC5401959.

deep, heavy breathing or feeling out of breath. These are both signs that our body is calling out for more oxygen: also that there is more carbon dioxide to remove due to the body's heightened metabolic activity. Our muscles are calling out for more energy and need oxygen for ATP production (energy for our cells), our heart is pumping faster to move the oxygen to our muscles, plus with all of this activity going on, our body temperature increases and the heavy breathing helps keep this in check by releasing heat as we exhale.

metabolic rate: or metabolism, is the rate at which the body converts food (calories) into energy and carries out various chemical processes necessary for life. It represents total energy expenditure over a given period of time. Our Basal Metabolic Rate (BMR) is the amount of energy the body expends while at rest to maintain the basic bodily functions such as breathing, heart pumping and regulating body temperature. Out Resting Metabolic Rate (RMR) is when we're awake but in a resting state; this then includes energy required for digestion for example. Our metabolic rate will increase during and after exercise and the more physically active we are, the higher our overall metabolic rate. Age, gender, genetics, muscle mass, hormonal fluctuations, can all effect our metabolic rate.

if we don't use the muscles once we've built them up, the muscle will deplete and we will become weaker:

See: https://www.health.harvard.edu/staying-healthy/the-muscle-bone-connection

See also:

https://www.health.harvard.edu/staying-healthy/dont-let-muscle-mass-go-to-waste

bodybuilding involves increased calorie intake to support the muscle growth... Reassuringly, when we exercise we can build up muscle as quickly as we might lose it:

See: Joanisse S, Lim C, McKendry J, Mcleod JC, Stokes T, Phillips SM. Recent advances in understanding resistance exercise training-induced skeletal muscle hypertrophy in humans. F1000Res. 2020 Feb 24;9:F1000 Faculty Rev-141. doi: 10.12688/f1000research.21588.1. PMID: 32148775; PMCID: PMC7043134.

More on the mones

the functioning of our endocrine system changes as we age and our hormone levels start to shift around...For women, our estrogen levels start to decline, not only leading to a slow decrease

in our bone mineral density but also the ability of our body to regulate our metabolism:

See: van den Beld AW, Kaufman JM, Zillikens MC, Lamberts SWJ, Egan JM, van der Lely AJ. The physiology of endocrine systems with ageing. Lancet Diabetes Endocrinol. 2018 Aug;6(8):647-658. doi: 10.1016/S2213-8587(18)30026-3. Epub 2018 Jul 17. PMID: 30017799; PMCID: PMC6089223.

(as we age) our body also becomes less efficient at burning these calories and breaking down fat:

See: Flanagan EW, Most J, Mey JT, Redman LM. Calorie Restriction and Aging in Humans. Annu Rev Nutr. 2020 Sep 23;40:105-133. doi: 10.1146/annurev-nutr-122319-034601. Epub 2020 Jun 19. PMID: 32559388; PMCID: PMC9042193.

Low-T: approximately 20% of men aged 65+ have testosterone concentrations below the normal range for young men.

See also: van den Beld AW, Kaufman JM, Zillikens MC, Lamberts SWJ, Egan JM, van der Lely AJ. The physiology of endocrine systems with ageing. Lancet Diabetes Endocrinol. 2018 Aug;6(8):647-658. doi: 10.1016/S2213-8587(18)30026-3. Epub 2018 Jul 17. PMID: 30017799; PMCID: PMC6089223.

muscle burns more calories than other tissues:

See: Wade AJ, Marbut MM, Round JM. Muscle fibre type and aetiology of obesity. Lancet. 1990 Apr 7;335(8693):805-8. doi: 10.1016/0140-6736(90)90933-v. PMID: 1969558.

See also: Methenitis S, Feidantsis K, Kaprara A, Hatzitolios A, Skepastianos P, Papadopoulou SK, Panayiotou G. Body Composition, Fasting Blood Glucose and Lipidemic Indices Are Not Primarily Determined by the Nutritional Intake of Middle-Aged Endurance Trained Men-Another "Athletes' Paradox"? J Clin Med. 2022 Oct 13;11(20):6057. doi: 10.3390/jcm11206057. PMID: 36294378; PMCID: PMC9605115.

if muscles aren't purposefully maintained to counteract the fact that they naturally degenerate as testosterone levels decrease, the amount of calories required reduces, perhaps by as much as 300 - 400 calories per day (c. 15 - 20%): a sedentary male, aged 60 or over needs on average 2,000 calories per day; an active male of the same age, who is maintaining muscle strength might need up to 2,600 calories on average each day, with 2,400 calories recommended for even 'moderately active' males over the age of 60.

See: Batsis JA, Villareal DT. Sarcopenic obesity in older adults: aetiology, epidemiology and treatment strategies. Nat Rev Endocrinol. 2018 Sep;14(9):513-537. doi: 10.1038/s41574-018-0062-9. PMID: 30065268; PMCID: PMC6241236.

See also: https://health.clevelandclinic.org/how-many-calories-a-day-should-i-eat

what isn't yet properly understood is how much our naturally being less active as we age contributes to the changes in our hormone levels versus how much is actually just due to the slowing down of our body as we age: one of the problems with measuring this is that we're all different, so what might apply for me and my hormone levels as I age, may not apply to you. What is clear is that levels of progesterone, oestrogen, testosterone, gonadotropins, DHEA, insulin clearance etc. are all decreasing naturally as we age; whereas cortisol levels become more irregular, sleep changes with a decreased circadian amplitude and ghrelin levels are also impacted by age. We also know that some of these shifts are influenced by how much exercise we do; both cardiovascular exercise and resistance (strength) training will help to slow down the changes in hormonal levels that happens as we age. What isn't clear is how our hormone levels would change if we didn't do any exercise between the age of 16 and 70 years of age, versus how much they would change if we were regularly exercising between the same ages. We know there would be a significant difference (which is why exercising is highly recommended for hormone regulation), we just don't know what this difference would be.

See also: van den Beld AW, Kaufman JM, Zillikens MC, Lamberts SWJ, Egan JM, van der Lely AJ. The physiology of endocrine systems with ageing. Lancet Diabetes Endocrinol. 2018 Aug;6(8):647-658. doi: 10.1016/S2213-8587(18)30026-3. Epub 2018 Jul 17. PMID: 30017799; PMCID: PMC6089223.

what has been proven is that regular exercise helps to slow down the decline of these vital hormones: regular exercise affects where we store fat in our body as well as how much fat we store, storing too much of the wrong fat negatively impacts our sex hormone levels, therefore exercising to stay in shape can help protect against this decline. Exercise, and in particular, resistance (strength) training, helps to maintain muscle in our body (as well as bone strength). Our sex hormone levels are positively impacted by muscle mass. In men, low oxygen capacity (weak breathing muscles) have been associated with Low-T, suggesting that keeping our cardiovascular system strong is also going to have a knock-on impact to maintaining hormone levels better into old age. Calorie restriction is also linked with better hormone regulation as we age.

See: Pataky MW, Young WF, Nair KS. Hormonal and Metabolic Changes of Aging and the Influence of Lifestyle Modifications. Mayo Clin Proc. 2021 Mar;96(3):788-814. doi: 10.1016/j.mayocp.2020.07.033. PMID: 33673927; PMCID: PMC8020896.

the health risks associated with a podgy paunch: "high waist circumference increased the risks of developing hypertension, type 2 diabetes mellitus, hypercholesterolemia, joint pain, low back pain, and hyperuricemia". See: Darsini D, Hamidah H, Notobroto HB, Cahyono EA. Health risks associated with high waist circumference: A systematic review. J Public Health Res. 2020 Jul 2;9(2):1811. doi: 10.4081/jphr.2020.1811. PMID: 32728557; PMCID: PMC7376462.

if we're running outdoors, studies suggest this helps optimise melatonin levels, regulating the sleep-wake cycle and the quality of our sleep: "acute suppression of melatonin secretion by light tends to reinforce the phase-shifting effects of light". Or more simply put - if we expose ourselves to lots of light during the daytime, this suppresses our melatonin level during the day, meaning that when darkness sets in and our melatonin levels increase, the larger variable between daytime and nighttime levels helps us to fall asleep.

See: Brown GM. Light, melatonin and the sleep-wake cycle. J Psychiatry Neurosci. 1994 Nov;19(5):345-53. PMID: 7803368; PMCID: PMC1188623.

See also: Zisapel N. New perspectives on the role of melatonin in human sleep, circadian rhythms and their regulation. Br J Pharmacol. 2018 Aug;175(16):3190-3199. doi: 10.1111/bph.14116. Epub 2018 Jan 15. PMID: 29318587; PMCID: PMC6057895.

Exercise has been listed as one of the best ways to help women manage through the adjustments and transition happening in our body during menopause:

Helping with anxiety, sleep, social interaction, energy levels, better regulating hormone levels, countering the decrease in oestrogen levels, keeping weight in-check, maintaining muscle strength, helping against hot flashes (improved thermoregulatory control), all of which is also going to help us feel a little more in control of what is happening in our body and better about ourselves!

See: Mishra N, Mishra VN, Devanshi. Exercise beyond menopause: Dos and Don'ts. J Midlife Health. 2011 Jul;2(2):51-6. doi: 10.4103/0976-7800.92524. PMID: 22408332; PMCID: PMC3296386.

See: https://www.hopkinsmedicine.org/health/conditions-and-diseases/staying-healthy-after-menopause

See: https://www.health.harvard.edu/staying-healthy/exercising-to-relax

See also: https://womensmentalhealth.org/posts/brief-exercise-helps-menopausal-hot-flashes/

with regular cardiovascular exercise, the effects on sleep and on feeling low on energy can be better regulated:

See: Ezati M, Keshavarz M, Barandouzi ZA, Montazeri A. The effect of regular aerobic exercise on sleep quality and fatigue among female student dormitory residents. BMC Sports Sci Med Rehabil. 2020 Aug 5;12:44. doi: 10.1186/s13102-020-00190-z. PMID: 32774864; PMCID: PMC7405354.

if we don't exercise as we age: the almost inevitable weight-gain can lead to insulin, ghrelin and leptin resistance, making over-eating more likely and making it more difficult for our hormones to regulate themselves:

See: Sitar-Tăut AV, Cozma A, Fodor A, Coste SC, Orasan OH, Negrean V, Pop D, Sitar-Tăut DA. New Insights on the Relationship between Leptin, Ghrelin, and Leptin/Ghrelin Ratio Enforced by Body Mass Index in Obesity and Diabetes. Biomedicines. 2021 Nov 10;9(11):1657. doi: 10.3390/biomedicines9111657. PMID: 34829886; PMCID: PMC8615809.

Other bodily benefits

The zeds: sleep and exercise, exercise and sleep

All of this physical exertion...is also going to help us sleep better... This deeper sleep gives our body (and mind) the chance to rejuvenate:

See: Alnawwar MA, Alraddadi MI, Algethmi RA, Salem GA, Salem MA, Alharbi AA. The Effect of Physical Activity on Sleep

Quality and Sleep Disorder: A Systematic Review. Cureus. 2023 Aug 16;15(8):e43595. doi: 10.7759/cureus.43595. PMID: 37719583; PMCID: PMC10503965.

exercise hormones: exercise stimulates the release of endorphins, serotonin and nonrepinephrine, which lower stress levels and anxiety and improve relaxation (so aiding good sleep). Running will however also stimulate dopamine, which induces alertness and is associated with wakefulness. It is therefore recommended that exercise cease at least one hour before going to bed, allowing dopamine levels to drop again, blood pressure to return to normal levels and allowing the positive effects of the serotonin take over.

See: Alnawwar MA, Alraddadi MI, Algethmi RA, Salem GA, Salem MA, Alharbi AA. The Effect of Physical Activity on Sleep Quality and Sleep Disorder: A Systematic Review. Cureus. 2023 Aug 16;15(8):e43595. doi: 10.7759/cureus.43595. PMID: 37719583; PMCID: PMC10503965.

See also: Fairbrother K, Cartner B, Alley JR, Curry CD, Dickinson DL, Morris DM, Collier SR. Effects of exercise timing on sleep architecture and nocturnal blood pressure in prehypertensives. Vasc Health Risk Manag. 2014 Dec 12;10:691-8. doi: 10.2147/VHRM.S73688. PMID: 25540588; PMCID: PMC4270305.

our metabolism slows down when we aren't getting enough sleep:

See: Sharma S, Kavuru M. Sleep and metabolism: an overview. Int J Endocrinol. 2010;2010:270832. doi: 10.1155/2010/270832. Epub 2010 Aug 2. PMID: 20811596; PMCID: PMC2929498.

if cortisol remains at too high a level, it will prompt our body to store fat: often referred to as our 'stress hormone', cortisol is produced by the adrenal glands in response to stress and is part of the body's fight or flight mechanism. Cortisol does also help regulate metabolism and how the body converts protein, carbs and fats into energy. Not only do high cortisol levels lead to an increase in fat storage, but during prologued stress this tends to be abdominal fat, which as we've learned, is even more high risk.

See: van der Valk ES, Savas M, van Rossum EFC. Stress and Obesity: Are There More Susceptible Individuals? Curr Obes Rep. 2018 Jun;7(2):193-203. doi: 10.1007/s13679-018-0306-y. PMID: 29663153; PMCID: PMC5958156.

Seel also: Henry M, Thomas KGF, Ross IL. Sleep, Cognition and Cortisol in Addison's Disease: A Mechanistic Relationship. Front Endocrinol (Lausanne). 2021 Aug 27;12:694046. doi: 10.3389/fendo.2021.694046. PMID: 34512546; PMCID: PMC8429905.

Immune system benefits

white blood cells can grow and mature into different types of white blood cells:

See also: https://my.clevelandclinic.org/health/body/21871-white-blood-cells

See also: Blumenreich MS. The White Blood Cell and Differential Count. In: Walker HK, Hall WD, Hurst JW, editors. Clinical Methods: The History, Physical, and Laboratory Examinations. 3rd edition. Boston: Butterworths; 1990. Chapter 153. Available from:

https://www.ncbi.nlm.nih.gov/books/NBK261/

Exercise has been shown to reduce inflammation in our body:

See: Beavers KM, Brinkley TE, Nicklas BJ. Effect of exercise training on chronic inflammation. Clin Chim Acta. 2010 Jun 3;411(11-12):785-93. doi: 10.1016/j.cca.2010.02.069. Epub 2010 Feb 25. PMID: 20188719; PMCID: PMC3629815.

See also: Effects of Exercise Training on the Autonomic Nervous System with a Focus on Anti-Inflammatory and Antioxidants Effects

See also: Daniela M, Catalina L, Ilie O, Paula M, Daniel-Andrei I, Ioana B. Effects of Exercise Training on the Autonomic Nervous System with a Focus on Anti-Inflammatory and Antioxidants Effects. Antioxidants (Basel). 2022 Feb 10;11(2):350. doi: 10.3390/antiox11 020350. PMID: 35204231; PMCID: PMC8868289.

running improves the diversity of our gut bacteria, which we now know plays a vital role in our immune function: there is thought to be an optimal level of exercise to positively impact our gut microbiota and it is likely that if we exceed that (exercising for 6 or more hours per day), the positive effects actually start to decline.

See: Monda V, Villano I, Messina A, Valenzano A, Esposito T, Moscatelli F, Viggiano A, Cibelli G, Chieffi S, Monda M, Messina G. Exercise Modifies the Gut Microbiota with Positive Health Effects. Oxid Med Cell Longev. 2017;2017:3831972. doi: 10.115 5/2017/3831972. Epub 2017 Mar 5. PMID: 28357027; PMCID: PMC5357536.

See also: Simon GL, Gorbach SL. The human intestinal microflora. Dig Dis Sci. 1986 Sep;31(9 Suppl):147S-162S. doi: 10.1007/BF012

95996. PMID: 3731990.

exercise helps reduce stress and anxiety:
See: Childs E, de Wit H. Regular exercise is associated with emotional resilience to acute stress in healthy adults. Front Physiol. 2014 May 1;5:161. doi: 10.3389/fphys.2014.00161. PMID: 24822048; PMCID: PMC4013452.

A win with the skin

Our skin…is actually a complex organ (the largest of the body) and consists of a variety of specialised cells:
See: Roger M, Fullard N, Costello L, Bradbury S, Markiewicz E, O'Reilly S, Darling N, Ritchie P, Määttä A, Karakesisoglou I, Nelson G, von Zglinicki T, Dicolandrea T, Isfort R, Bascom C, Przyborski S. Bioengineering the microanatomy of human skin. J Anat. 2019 Apr;234(4):438-455. doi: 10.1111/joa.12942. Epub 2019 Feb 10. PMID: 30740672; PMCID: PMC6422806.

the strong blood flow to the skin helps us to sweat out some of the products from our body, so cleansing our body from the inside out: sweat evaporation from the skin helps to cool us down when we exercise, sweat also plays a role in clearing waste from our body, carried in our blood (and lymph). As blood flow is also heightened during exercise, the ability of our body to cleanse itself is increased.

See: Baker LB. Physiology of sweat gland function: The roles of sweating and sweat composition in human health. Temperature

(Austin). 2019 Jul 17;6(3):211-259. doi: 10.1080/23328940.2019.1632145. PMID: 31608304; PMCID: PMC6773238.

Not the traditional baby making exercise...

exercise...can absolutely optimise our chances of a successful pregnancy. A good, strong supply of oxygen rich blood will aid the thickening of the uterine lining preparing it for implantation of the embryo: by regulating hormonal balance and enhancing blood flow, exercise can indirectly contribute to improving uterine health. A healthy lifestyle, including exercise, will positively impact overall reproductive health. It should be noted that excessive exercise, or training at an intense level (pushing ourselves to the point of exhaustion) can be detrimental to our reproductive health.

See also: Orio F, Muscogiuri G, Ascione A, Marciano F, Volpe A, La Sala G, Savastano S, Colao A, Palomba S. Effects of physical exercise on the female reproductive system. Minerva Endocrinol. 2013 Sep;38(3):305-19. PMID: 24126551.

See also: Ribeiro MM, Andrade A, Nunes I. Physical exercise in pregnancy: benefits, risks and prescription. J Perinat Med. 2021 Sep 6;50(1):4-17. doi: 10.1515/jpm-2021-0315. PMID: 34478617.

In the first weeks of pregnancy, before the placenta and umbilical cord have formed, the embryo is fully reliant on this blood flow to the lining of the womb:

See: Hempstock J, Cindrova-Davies T, Jauniaux E, Burton GJ. Endometrial glands as a source of nutrients, growth factors and cytokines during the first trimester of human pregnancy: a morphological and immunohistochemical study. Reprod Biol Endocrinol. 2004 Jul 20;2:58. doi: 10.1186/1477-7827-2-58. PMID: 15265238; PMCID: PMC493283.

See also: Marty M, Kerndt CC, Lui F. Embryology, Fetal Circulation. [Updated 2023 May 1]. In: StatPearls [Internet]. Treasure Island (FL): StatPearls Publishing; 2023 Jan-. Available from: https://www.ncbi.nlm.nih.gov/books/NBK537149/

Even once the placenta has taken over, a healthy supply of oxygen and nutrients to the growing fetus is wholly dependent on the blood supply to the uterus, so maintaining a strong, healthy blood flow is also necessary for a healthy birth:

See: Zhang S, Regnault TR, Barker PL, Botting KJ, McMillen IC, McMillan CM, Roberts CT, Morrison JL. Placental adaptations in growth restriction. Nutrients. 2015 Jan 8;7(1):360-89. doi: 10.3390/nu7010360. PMID: 25580812; PMCID: PMC4303845.

Detox:

Not only does our body process what we eat at a faster rate when we exercise, it also gets rid of the waste by-products more efficiently, speeding up our body's own detoxing processes: we know that we're using the energy in our cells at a faster rate when we exercise and that energy comes from what we consume. There will also be more waste products in our blood and lymph as a result of the metabolic processes that are happening in our body. Because exercise stimulates the flow of both lymph and blood compared to when we're sedentary, the body is able to clear the waste products, together with any toxins in our body at a much faster rate.

water (which is needed to help smooth the way along the digestive tract):
See:
https://www.nhs.uk/live-well/eat-well/digestive-health/good-foods-to-help-your-digestion

running is as good a detox as we'll get and is great at getting rid of even the last bits of waste that might be trying to hide in a little nook somewhere along our pipes: increased blood flow to the muscles in our digestive system helps with the peristalsis process, massaging our digesting food along the tract. There is also the force of gravity at work when we run; bounding along the pavement can help to loosen and expel anything caught in our pipes (as long as we're well hydrated).
See also:

https://www.axahealth.co.uk/health-information/gut-health/exercises-to-improve-digestion

Detecting illness:

This does require that we have been running regularly enough and for long enough that we know how we feel during a run when everything is 'normal': if we're running at least once a week and we've been running consistently for six months or more, we're going to have a good idea about how we feel when we run. We'll know what our pace is, we'll know at what stage in our run our legs start to feel a bit tired and we'll know at what point during our run fatigue of our breathing sets-in. Once we reach this steady state with or running, it is then easy to notice when we feel off, or more tired than normal. While having 'one difficult run' is perfectly normal every now and then, if this feeling persists during every run over a number of weeks, it is a sign that there is something else going with our body and we should seek medical advice. This assumes that there haven't been any significant changes in diet, sleeping habits or other factors that could contribute to a sudden change in energy levels.

Running for our mind

pleasure: in his book, 'The Art of Happiness', the Dalai Lama says "Happiness that depends mainly on physical pleasure is unstable, one day it's there, the next day it may not be". The "better approach to framing any decision we face is to ask ourselves 'Will it bring me happiness?'" Thus recognising that something that gives us short-term pleasure does not mean it will make us happier. See: "The Art of Happiness, HH Dalai Lama, Cutler, HC. (1998). Coronet Books"

food, drink and buying new stuff can all give us a little dopamine 'hit': a 'spike' is apparently a more appropriate term for an increase above our baseline levels of this vital hormone. Dopamine is always present within the body and along with its receptors, it plays a role in movement, emotions and the reward system in the brain.

See: Bhatia A, Lenchner JR, Saadabadi A. Biochemistry, Dopamine Receptors. [Updated 2023 Jun 22]. In: StatPearls [Internet]. Treasure

Island (FL): StatPearls Publishing; 2023 Jan-. Available from: https://www.ncbi.nlm.nih.gov/books/NBK538242

See also: Volkow ND, Wang GJ, Baler RD. Reward, dopamine and the control of food intake: implications for obesity. Trends Cogn Sci. 2011 Jan;15(1):37-46. doi: 10.1016/j.tics.2010.11.001. Epub 2010 Nov 24. PMID: 21109477; PMCID: PMC3124340.

Running on the other hand can provide both immediate pleasure and a route to feeling consistently happier in ourselves: when starting out with running, it is most likely that the pleasure of running is most strongly felt immediately after finishing the run; the feeling that we've done something really good for ourselves is going to increase our dopamine level. Once we've been running for a while and we can enjoy the run itself, or if we're running at a slower pace that allows us to look around and enjoy the run, we're also going to have this feel-good factor during the run. But the dopamine levels will drop again and within the next couple of days the pleasurable feeling will have passed. Over time however, when our body is telling us that we're fitter, when we feel better in ourselves as a result of the time and effort we've invested in our health, this compassion we've shown to ourself is an opportunity for happiness. Try, and see if you feel it.

running is well-documented in helping manage and alleviate the symptoms of depression:

See: Craft LL, Perna FM. The Benefits of Exercise for the Clinically Depressed. Prim Care Companion J Clin Psychiatry. 2004;6(3):104-111. doi: 10.4088/pcc.v06n0301. PMID: 15361924; PMCID: PMC474733.

endorphins and beta-endorphin is one of the neurochemicals associates with the phenomenon known as 'the runner's high': while it is widely acknowledged the 'runner's high' is a thing (although not everyone will experience it, or experience it equally), the cause is still a subject of research. Earlier research suggested that endorphins were the answer; more recently this has been questioned because it was stated that endorphins "couldn't cross the blood-brain barrier". In this research, it is suggested that it is in fact the release of endocannabinoids that bring on the euphoria during, and after exercise (running in particular).

See: Chaudhry SR, Gossman W. Biochemistry, Endorphin. [Updated 2023 Apr 3]. In: StatPearls [Internet]. Treasure Island (FL): StatPearls Publishing; 2023 Jan-. Available from: https://www.ncbi.nlm.nih.gov/books/NBK470306/

Seel also: Siebers M, Biedermann SV, Fuss J. Do Endocannabinoids Cause the Runner's High? Evidence and Open Questions. Neuroscientist. 2023 Jun;29(3):352-369. doi: 10.1177/10738584211069981. Epub 2022 Jan 26. PMID: 35081831; PMCID: PMC10159215.

our body also releases the hormones serotonin, norepinephrine and dopamine during exercise...these chemicals combined, help to combat depressive episodes and boost energy and alertness:

See: Basso JC, Suzuki WA. The Effects of Acute Exercise on Mood, Cognition, Neurophysiology, and Neurochemical Pathways: A Review. Brain Plast. 2017 Mar 28;2(2):127-152. doi: 10.3233/BPL-160040. PMID: 29765853; PMCID: PMC5928534.

serotonin also aids healthy digestion, good quality sleep, our brain function and our circadian rhythms:

See: Yabut JM, Crane JD, Green AE, Keating DJ, Khan WI, Steinberg GR. Emerging Roles for Serotonin in Regulating Metabolism: New Implications for an Ancient Molecule. Endocr Rev. 2019 Aug 1;40(4):1092-1107. doi: 10.1210/er.2018-00283. PMID: 30901029; PMCID: PMC6624793.

See also: Daut RA, Fonken LK. Circadian regulation of depression: A role for serotonin. Front Neuroendocrinol. 2019 Jul;54:100746. doi: 10.1016/j.yfrne.2019.04.003. Epub 2019 Apr 16. PMID: 31002895; PMCID: PMC9826732.

circadian rhythms: "physical, mental, and behavioral changes that follow a 24-hour cycle. A master clock in the brain coordinates all the biological clocks in a living thing, keeping the clocks in sync. These natural processes respond primarily to light and dark. Circadian rhythms can influence important functions in our body, such as: hormone release, eating habits and digestion and body temperature. However, most people notice the effect of circadian rhythms on their sleep patterns". As the amplitude ('range') of our circadian rhythm decreases as we age, it becomes increasingly important that we need to take the time to go outdoors during daylight hours so that we help protect the quality of our sleep.

See: https://www.nigms.nih.gov/education/fact-sheets/Pages/circadian-rhythms

Ninety-five percent of our body's serotonin is produced in our gut, and our gut bacteria play a key role in this:

See: Terry N, Margolis KG. Serotonergic Mechanisms Regulating the GI Tract: Experimental Evidence and Therapeutic Relevance. Handb Exp Pharmacol. 2017;239:319-342. doi: 10.1007/164_2016_103. PMID: 28035530; PMCID: PMC5526216.

See: Sasso JM, Ammar RM, Tenchov R, Lemmel S, Kelber O, Grieswelle M, Zhou QA. Gut Microbiome-Brain Alliance: A Landscape View into Mental and Gastrointestinal Health and Disorders. ACS Chem Neurosci. 2023 May 17;14(10):1717-1763. doi: 10.1021/acschemneuro.3c00127. Epub 2023 May 8. PMID: 37156006; PMCID: PMC10197139.

we also know (is) that regular exercise helps to boost the diversity of our gut microbiome:

See: Monda V, Villano I, Messina A, Valenzano A, Esposito T, Moscatelli F, Viggiano A, Cibelli G, Chieffi S, Monda M, Messina G. Exercise Modifies the Gut Microbiota with Positive Health Effects. Oxid Med Cell Longev. 2017;2017:3831972. doi: 10.1155/2017/3831972. Epub 2017 Mar 5. PMID: 28357027; PMCID: PMC5357536.

If we read any book about achieving happiness it will tell you that it comes from within, and that lasting happiness can be achieved through having the right state of mind: "The Art of Happiness" by Dalai Lama and Howard Cutler. "The Happiness Project" by Gretchen Rubin. "Authentic Happiness" by Martin Seligman. "The How of Happiness" by Sonja Lyubomirsky. Etc. Etc.

happiness is a 'by product' of the things we do each day: I particularly like this reference, which I heard Margaret Atwood use in the podcast 'How To Fail' with Elizabeth Day (S16, Ep10).

Going out for a run is also an opportunity for some time-out for our head. A kind of meditation, with our mind wandering where it needs to go before slowly coming back to the rhythmical sound of our feet hitting the ground: there is an argument that says that exercise 'excites' our body, whereas meditation is defined as a deep state of relaxation and calm. However there have been times during my marathon training, running at a very steady pace with my body in 'automatic mode', just getting on with doing what it knows it needs to do, that my mind most certainly achieves a meditative state.

Part Three

Absolute beginner

Because our lungs are still gaining in fitness, this limits how quickly our body can get the right amount of oxygen top our muscles: when we're just starting out, the lungs aren't as efficient at gas exchange, the cardiovascular system is having to build 'fitness' at the same time as the lungs and our muscles aren't yet well-practised in extracting the oxygen they need from the blood. Our body is having to work much harder to make everything happen when we're beginning our running mission. But it does quickly become easier.

See: Your lungs and exercise. Breathe (Sheff). 2016 Mar;12(1):97-100. doi: 10.1183/20734735.ELF121. PMID: 27066145; PMCID: PMC4818249.

by regularly 'stretching' our breathing capacity through frequent extended cardiovascular activity (exercise that makes us feel out of breath for at least twenty minutes): lung capacity increases as our respiratory muscles strengthen, also our cardiovascular system is working at a higher capacity. Our lungs are healthier due to the better blood flow. Our body becomes more efficient at oxygenating blood and removing carbon dioxide. Oxygen utilisation is improved as our heart pumps more effectively and our muscles become better at extracting oxygen from the blood.

See: Your lungs and exercise. Breathe (Sheff). 2016 Mar;12(1):97-100. doi: 10.1183/20734735.ELF121. PMID: 27066145; PMCID: PMC4818249.

Scheduling

Having effectively been fasting through the night, our body is probably already in fat-burning mode by the time we wake up:
See:

https://www.ntu.ac.uk/about-us/news/news-articles/2022/11/exercising-on-an-empty-stomach-burned-70-more-fat,-study-found

your morning routine might require some attention: some people really seem to struggle with going for an early morning run without suddenly needing to go to the toilet halfway round. If you find it impossible to adjust your morning routine, either by abstaining from coffee for 24 hours beforehand, drinking plenty of water within that same period and making sure you're eating a good balance of protein, carbs, fats and with the right amount of fibre in the preceding 24 hours, it may be you just have to force things along instead. So - drink the coffee and some water as soon as you wake up, use the bathroom and then head out. The only problem with going to the toilet before you run, so emptying your body completely, is that it may leave you feeling even lower on energy first thing in the morning and therefore having a higher risk of fainting, or feeling faint. It may be that eating a dry cereal bar beforehand may help with just enough of a boost to get you round and without causing your digestive system too much hard work.

well-balanced dinner the evening before (a morning run) carbs, protein, fibre and healthy fats: for example, a bowl of pasta (not too much pasta) with chicken, tomatoes, broccoli and pesto is a good option, or replace the chicken with chickpeas

avoiding having too big a portion: if we include protein and fibre in our meal, this is going to help us feel more full and more satisfied for longer after we've eaten; both are going to help to make sure we don't overeat. Getting our portion size right has become a big problem and many of us eat too many calories because we fill our plate and eat so quickly that we don't give our body a chance to let us know we're full. Eating fruit, vegetables, beans, chickpeas, whole grains and foods high in fibre mean we're less likely to eat too much, plus they slow down the digestion process, energy is released more gradually and we feel fuller for longer. The problem with only eating carbs is that they pass through our body so quickly we're going to be feeling hungry again within a couple of hours, plus with carbs being more calorific, we're much more at risk of eating way more calories than we need. On the other hand, because protein takes longer to digest, it also uses more energy, plus with protein keeping our muscles strong, this also helps metabolism.

Habit hacks - Tips to keep you true to your new routine

Pomodoro technique:

Evidence suggests that in this age of mobile phones, we feel the urge to pick them up to see what's going on an average of 58 times per day (with statistics suggesting it cold be as many as 344 times per day for some people: statistics vary but 'Nomophobia' is a real thing. Most of us are highly addicted to the potential of a quick dopamine hit when we see something on our phones that gives us a moment of pleasure!

See: De-Sola Gutiérrez J, Rodríguez de Fonseca F, Rubio G. Cell-Phone Addiction: A Review. Front Psychiatry. 2016 Oct 24;7:175. doi: 10.3389/fpsyt.2016.00175. PMID: 27822187; PMCID: PMC5076301.

See also: Tanil CT, Yong MH. Mobile phones: The effect of its presence on learning and memory. PLoS One. 2020 Aug 13;15(8):e0219233. doi: 10.1371/journal.pone.0219233. PMID: 32790667; PMCID: PMC7425970.

Pomodoro technique: work is broken down into short, timed intervals known as 'Pomodoros' and is separated by short breaks. It works by: 1) Choosing one specific task. 2) Set a timer for 25 minutes ('one pomodoro'). 3) Work on this one task solidly for 25 minutes, only stopping when the timer goes off. 4) Set the timer for a 5 minute break. 5) Repeat the process. 6) After completing 4 pomodoros, take a 30 minute break before starting the process again. By avoiding distractions, focus is maximised and work is more efficient. We can use this focus to ensure that getting out for our run is our sole objective in a moment of time during our day. It may take a bit longer than 25 minutes from start to finish but the strategy to get us out of the front door when the pressure is on for us to tick-off our chosen task is a good one to employ!

The kit - How to choose shoes and other clothing considerations

Running shoes

To protect our body when running, a good pair of running shoes is the most important piece of equipment we'll buy when we first start out: having cushioned running shoes is going to dampen the impact of our foot as it hits the ground, helping to protect our joints and our muscles as we run on the ever-harder concrete pavements and roads. How much cushioning we need depends on our running style, which is going to be unique to us (see below). Running shoes by their very definition should have good enough cushioning, without having to invest in an expensive pair of shoes.

our personal running mechanics: this is how we naturally move when we run and will depend on many variables, including height, body shape, leg morphology, gait, stride length, arm swing, core strength and even the size of our feet. We will all have our own running style when we first start out and once we have been running for a number of consecutive weeks, our unique body shape and running mechanics mean that we develop a style that is most economical for us as an individual.

See also: Anderson T. Biomechanics and running economy. Sports Med. 1996 Aug;22(2):76-89. doi: 10.2165/00007256-199622020-00003. PMID: 8857704.

gait analysis: in simple terms gait analysis is the study of how we (as an individual) walk, or run. It looks at the movement of our joints, the angles of our joints through the different stages of movement, the time spent in each phase of the gait cycle, the symmetry of the gait, examining which muscles are active through each phase, and if we suffer an injury it can be used to look for weaknesses in muscles or stiffness of joints.

See also: Simonsen EB. Contributions to the understanding of gait control. Dan Med J. 2014 Apr;61(4):B4823. PMID: 24814597.

how our muscles, bones, joints, and tendons work together will vary from person to person depending on many factors from genetic, to how much sport we did when we were younger and how our movement developed as we were growing up: we know that our unique running style does change slightly as we become fitter and stronger; it adapts so that we run as economically as possible, with our body exerting minimum effort for maximum effect. We also know that muscle memory means our body can adapt to exercise faster if we were active and fit in the past. With each of us then having a different start point dependent on these variables (and multiple others), we are each going to have our own unique running style.

See also: Moore IS. Is There an Economical Running Technique? A Review of Modifiable Biomechanical Factors Affecting Running Economy. Sports Med. 2016 Jun;46(6):793-807. doi: 10.1007/s40279-016-0474-4. PMID: 26816209; PMCID: PMC4887549.

a twenty-stone muscle man will wear through his shoes faster than a ballerina: the heavier man has more pressure going through each leg (and foot) with each step compared to the lighter ballerina. If they're wearing the same kind of shoe, the additional pressure of the heavier weight through the sole of the trainer will cause it to wear through faster than the lighter pressure exerted on the sole by the ballerina.

it becomes easier to tell when the sole of our shoe has lost its bounce and feels overly soft, or deflated: when running our shoe shouldn't feel 'squidgy' or as if it is 'deflating' as our foot hits the ground. Instead our running shoes should provide just enough tension and firmness with each stride that we can feel the shoe complementing our running mechanics and how our muscles create the spring in our movement.

Running socks

breathable trainer socks: proper running socks help regulate temperature and remove moisture from the surface of the foot, protecting against blisters. Most running socks use a combination of synthetic materials, including polyester, nylon and elastane, making them durable as well as more comfortable during our run.

Running top

particularly if we're sweating and our body is trying to cool itself down:
See also: Baker LB. Physiology of sweat gland function: The roles of sweating and sweat composition in human health. Temperature (Austin). 2019 Jul 17;6(3):211-259. doi: 10.1080/23328940.2019.1632145. PMID: 31608304; PMCID: PMC6773238.

However if we're going to be continuously jogging or running, even if it is cold outside, our body is going to feel really warm after five minutes: the muscles we're using while we run quickly begin to produce a lot of heat and with our blood flowing around our body faster too, distributing the heat as our body works to regulate body temperature, we're soon going to feel warm.

See: Baker LB. Sweating Rate and Sweat Sodium Concentration in Athletes: A Review of Methodology and Intra/Interindividual Variability. Sports Med. 2017 Mar;47(Suppl 1):111-128. doi: 10.1007/s40279-017-0691-5. PMID: 28332116; PMCID: PMC5371639.

See also: Molkov YI, Zaretsky DV. Why is it easier to run in the cold? Temperature (Austin). 2016 Jun 17;3(4):509-511. doi: 10.1080/23328940.2016.1201182. PMID: 28090551; PMCID: PMC5198806.

Washing

Washing straight after exercise helps to get rid of the bacteria that make our clothes (and us) smelly: fresh, 'sterile sweat' is odourless, however when mixed with the microbiomes that live on the surface of our skin, this can lead to body-odour. During exercise the sweat (now mixed with microorganisms that sit on the surface of our skin), transfers to our clothing. The sooner we can wash this off after exercise, the less likely it is settle in the material and over time leave an underlying odour that is difficult to wash away.

See: Chang Y, Wang X. Sweat and odor in sportswear - A review. iScience. 2023 Jun 8;26(7):107067. doi: 10.1016/j.isci.2023.107067. PMID: 37534139; PMCID: PMC10391722.

I'm me and you're you - Running style and technique

A twisting upper body while running reduces our stability and increase the risk of injury: as we run faster and use our arms to help propel us forwards, or as we feel more fatigued towards the end of a run and our form becomes more lazy as our core muscles lose power, if we're still building our running fitness these are moments we need to be more aware of to avoid injuring ourselves. As we build fitness and core strength we won't experience the muscle fatigue to such an extent, plus there will be other muscles that kick into gear to help us maintain good stability from head to toe, even towards the end of a marathon when our repetitive movements are all starting to droop a little bit.

See also: Kibler WB, Press J, Sciascia A. The role of core stability in athletic function. Sports Med. 2006;36(3):189-98. doi: 10.2165/00007256-200636030-00001. PMID: 16526831.

small tweaks could be the difference between coming in fourth place and winning Gold:

See: Folland JP, Allen SJ, Black MI, Handsaker JC, Forrester SE. Running Technique is an Important Component of Running Economy and Performance. Med Sci Sports Exerc. 2017 Jul;49(7):1412-1423. doi: 10.1249/MSS.0000000000001245 . PMID: 28263283; PMCID: PMC5473370.

Fuelling the habit - Food and hydration

Assuming we're eating three 'normal sized' meals a day: eat wholegrain cereal, porridge or pancakes for breakfast and add some fruit, or yoghurt with dried fruit and seeds, or an egg on wholemeal toast; any of these will keep us going until lunch time. Eating loads of bread for lunch is going to leave us feeling drained of energy by mid-afternoon. A small amount of bread for lunch is ok, combined with protein and a piece of fruit. Otherwise eat leftovers from the night before to avoid taking the easy option of a giant baguette, that digests really slowly during the inactivity of our desk bound afternoon.

With many seeing dinner as the 'main meal' of the day, the risk is it becomes a 'feast', with us feeling the need to eat like it is going to be our last meal on earth. In fact - we're probably not long off going to bed, so while we do need calories to see us through the night and to help with energy levels when we wake up, a hand-sized plate of food (fingers open wide), including our proteins, carbs and fats is not far off where we want to be aiming.

we can do full-on marathon training without needing to increase the quantity of food we're consuming: a woman consuming 2,000 calories a day, or 14,000 per week, will use approximately 600 additional calories during a steady three-hour training run and 300 - 400 additional calories during shorter training runs, equating to maybe 1,500 extra calories per week once the after burn effect is factored in. On non-exercise days perhaps 1,800 calories are burned each day (stripping out the already factored in after burn). Across the week there may be a slight calorie deficit and if this is maintained over a period of three or four months, there would be a decrease in fat in the body. If this running schedule is maintained for a longer period, diet can be adjusted slightly to ensure no loss in muscle mass as the number of fat cells deplete. During the limited time period of training for a marathon however and the number of fat cells in our body when we begin training, there is no need to adjust our calorie intake.

protein intake should be approximately 25% of our total daily calorie intake, carbs about 60%, leaving fats equating to around 15%: it takes very careful planning each day to achieve our desired calories across breakfast, lunch and dinner considering the 25% protein, 60% carbs and 15% fats split of calories. Or we can view our energy intake across a couple of days and just try and eat as healthily as possible at each meal and be careful what we're snacking on in-between. Oatmeal with berries and nuts, grilled chicken salad, salmon and veg for dinner, with fruit and yoghurt in between is going to be a good day. The next day may include some bread, or pasta mixed in with our proteins but as long as we're not eating too much of either, the balance across the two days is going to work well.

when we exercise two or three times a week, burning an additional 400 - 600 calories on these days, we can calculate that during the course of a week we will be burning as many calories as we're consuming: two or three days a week burning an additional 400 calories each time will be offset by the four or five days that we're not exercising and burning less calories than we're eating. However if we're running such that we're consistently burning an additional 1,200 calories extra each week over a longer period of time, we will need to look at rebalancing our energy consumption if we want to avoid losing muscle mass while we ramp our training up.

See also: Murray B, Rosenbloom C. Fundamentals of glycogen metabolism for coaches and athletes. Nutr Rev. 2018 Apr 1;76(4):243-259. doi: 10.1093/nutrit/nuy001. PMID: 29444266; PMCID: PMC6019055.

pasta does get mixed reviews and being carbohydrate-rich (highly calorific) it is one of the foods we should avoid eating too much of once we hit forty: 100 grams of pasta (approximately one cup) contains about 400 calories. Add a meaty or a creamy sauce and this could easily equate to a third of our total daily calorie intake and use up all of our daily carb budget, all in one-go. When we're burning fewer calories as we age and if we don't need access to as much of the 'quickly available' energy that carbs provide, the risk of eating too much is increased, with the excess calories stored as fat.

Protein plays numerous crucial roles in our everyday functioning and must be a staple in our diet: the current recommended daily intake for adults is 0.8 grams per kilogram of body weight per day. Regular endurance exercise may increase this figure to 1.0 gram (or more) per kilogram of body weight. Older adults should also consume more protein each day to help maintain muscle mass, strength and good health.

See also: Campbell B, Kreider RB, Ziegenfuss T, La Bounty P, Roberts M, Burke D, Landis J, Lopez H, Antonio J. International Society of Sports Nutrition position stand: protein and exercise. J Int Soc Sports Nutr. 2007 Sep 26;4:8. doi: 10.1186/1550-2783-4-8. PMID: 17908291; PMCID: PMC2117006.

we should eat a higher percentage of protein in our diet after exercise to help our muscles recover: when we exercise we are building our skeletal muscle as well as influencing how it adapts as it strengthens, depending on the type of exercise we're undertaking. When we mix our exercise sessions between running and resistance, we're going to see all-round improvements and reasonably quickly. Our muscles must have access to the right amount of protein so that they can transform efficiently and without leaving us feeling really tired in the days after a tough training session.

See: McGlory C, Devries MC, Phillips SM. Skeletal muscle and resistance exercise training; the role of protein synthesis in recovery and remodeling. J Appl Physiol (1985). 2017 Mar 1;122(3):541-548. doi: 10.1152/japplphysiol.00613.2016. Epub 2016 Oct 14. PMID: 27742803; PMCID: PMC5401959.

protein package: of the protein we consume day to day, many of the foods will also contain fats or carbohydrates as well. Therefore when trying to eat the right amount of protein each day we need to be careful about how much fat or how many carbs we're ingesting at the same time. This is why pork may be preferred to beef, or turkey consumed over duck. If we're eating oily-fish one day, this is great for protein, vitamins and nutrients but may mean we try and limit consuming other fats during the rest of the day. Likewise we'd avoid eating a whole container of nuts in one day; good for protein and micronutrients but also mean a lot more fat consumed in one go than we need. Also note that while animal-based proteins are generally 'complete', in that they contain all essential amino acids, some plant-based proteins are 'incomplete', highlighting the fact that it is important to eat a variety of protein sources throughout the week. Proteins can be rated using various scales; the Biological Value (BV) method looks at how efficiently the body can use the protein (eggs score very highly here), whereas the Protein Digestibility Corrected Amino Acid Score (PD-CAAS) assesses both the amino acid requirements of a human, plus our ability to digest it (casein, egg whites, soy and whey proteins score highly here).

See also: Campbell B, Kreider RB, Ziegenfuss T, La Bounty P, Roberts M, Burke D, Landis J, Lopez H, Antonio J. International Society of Sports Nutrition position stand: protein and exercise. J Int Soc Sports Nutr. 2007 Sep 26;4:8. doi: 10.1186/1550-2783-4-8. PMID: 17908291; PMCID: PMC2117006.

Salt plays a role in electrolyte balance and is therefore essential for nerve impulse transmission, muscle function as well as regulating the distribution of water in and around our cells ensuring optimal hydration:

See: Strazzullo P, Leclercq C. Sodium. Adv Nutr. 2014 Mar 1;5(2):188-90. doi: 10.3945/an.113.005215. PMID: 24618759; PMCID: PMC3951800.

Too much salt will leave us feeling dehydrated: our body is very clever when it comes to making sure we have the right concentration of sodium circulating at any one time. If we consume too much, we'll feel thirsty, prompting us to drink water and help with the dilution and expulsion of salt from our body. However the right amount of electrolytes is vital for the functioning of our body and if we're training intensively, this is when we may not be getting quite enough salt through our regular diet and we may need to top up with an electrolyte drink.

See also: Stachenfeld NS. Acute effects of sodium ingestion on thirst and cardiovascular function. Curr Sports Med Rep. 2008 Jul-Aug;7(4 Suppl):S7-13. doi: 10.1249/JSR.0b013e31817f23fc. PMID: 18843231; PMCID: PMC2871322.

more serious risks with consuming too much salt and an accumulation of this mineral in our body include hypertension and the negative impact this has on the health of our brain, heart and kidneys: too much salt is associated with an immediate increase in blood pressure, however unless we're particularly sensitive to sodium, this should pass. Overloading on salt on an ongoing basis however can lead to hypertension, putting pressure on our heart, risking cerebral haemorrhage or kidney failure.

See also: Hosohata K. Biomarkers for Chronic Kidney Disease Associated with High Salt Intake. Int J Mol Sci. 2017 Sep

30;18(10):2080. doi: 10.3390/ijms18102080. PMID: 28973979; PMCID: PMC5666762.

See also: Barnett AM, Babcock MC, Watso JC, Migdal KU, Gutiérrez OM, Farquhar WB, Robinson AT. High dietary salt intake increases urinary NGAL excretion and creatinine clearance in healthy young adults. Am J Physiol Renal Physiol. 2022 Apr 1;322(4):F392-F402. doi: 10.1152/ajprenal.00240.2021. Epub 2022 Feb 14. PMID: 35157527; PMCID: PMC8934673.

See also: Doyle AE. Hypertension and vascular disease. Am J Hypertens. 1991 Feb;4(2 Pt 2):103S-106S. doi: 10.1093/ajh/4.2.103s. PMID: 2021454.

eating fermented foods is a great way to balance out gut microbiota, which plays a crucial role in digestion, our immunity and overall health:

See: Leeuwendaal NK, Stanton C, O'Toole PW, Beresford TP. Fermented Foods, Health and the Gut Microbiome. Nutrients. 2022 Apr 6;14(7):1527. doi: 10.3390/nu14071527. PMID: 35406140; PMCID: PMC9003261.

As well as reducing any inflammation of or digestive tract and enhancing nutrient absorption, there is even emerging research suggesting a link between gut health and our mental health and well-being:

see also: Rutsch A, Kantsjö JB, Ronchi F. The Gut-Brain Axis: How Microbiota and Host Inflammasome Influence Brain Physiology and Pathology. Front Immunol. 2020 Dec 10;11:604179. doi: 10.3389/fimmu.2020.604179. PMID: 33362788; PMCID:

PMC7758428.

fermentation process: primarily used to preserve food, fermentation was probably first discovered thousands of years ago and resulted in the discovery of beer. Microorganisms in food, when combined with sugars (the primary energy source) and deprived of oxygen, produce alcohol, carbon dioxide and organic acids. The acidity level increases such that it acts as a preservative by inhibiting the growth of other microorganisms that would normally cause the food to go off.

See also: Institute of Medicine (US) Committee on Strategies to Reduce Sodium Intake; Henney JE, Taylor CL, Boon CS, editors. Strategies to Reduce Sodium Intake in the United States. Washington (DC): National Academies Press (US); 2010. 4, Preservation and Physical Property Roles of Sodium in Foods. Available from: https://www.ncbi.nlm.nih.gov/books/NBK50952/#

the dangers of consuming too much sugar…the risk of type 2 diabetes increases significantly: plus the risk of other chronic metabolic diseases increases as well. Not all sugars are the same; fruit juices are bad whereas eating a piece of fruit (which also contains fibre and slows down the digestion of the sugars) is ok. Obviously cakes, biscuits, cereals with added sugars, milk chocolate and sweets should be limited.

See also: EFSA Panel on Nutrition, Novel Foods and Food Allergens (NDA); Turck D, Bohn T, Castenmiller J, de Henauw S, Hirsch-Ernst KI, Knutsen HK, Maciuk A, Mangelsdorf I, McArdle HJ, Naska A, Peláez C, Pentieva K, Siani A, Thies F, Tsabouri S, Adan R, Emmett P, Galli C, Kersting M, Moynihan P, Tappy L, Ciccolallo

L, de Sesmaisons-Lecarré A, Fabiani L, Horvath Z, Martino L, Muñoz Guajardo I, Valtueña Martínez S, Vinceti M. Tolerable upper intake level for dietary sugars. EFSA J. 2022 Feb 28;20(2):e07074. doi: 10.2903/j.efsa.2022.7074. PMID: 35251356; PMCID: PMC8884083.

Possible health complications from high blood sugar levels and insulin resistance include cardiovascular and kidney disease, complications with our eyes and vision, numbness and pain in our legs and feet, skin diseases as well as there being evidence that type 2 diabetes increases the risk of developing Alzheimer's Disease: insulin maintains glucose homeostasis within our body, and loss of sensitivity to insulin (insulin resistance) can lead to glucose intolerance, with our body unable to process sugars. This can in turn lead to diseased arteries, increasing the risk of hypertension (high blood pressure) and damage to the brain and heart; in our smaller blood vessels the risks are carried to eyes, skin and can cause numbness.

See also: Petrie JR, Guzik TJ, Touyz RM. Diabetes, Hypertension, and Cardiovascular Disease: Clinical Insights and Vascular Mechanisms. Can J Cardiol. 2018 May;34(5):575-584. doi: 10.1016/j.cjca.2017.12.005. Epub 2017 Dec 11. PMID: 29459239; PMCID: PMC5953551.

Sugar highs, and the lows that follow, are also going to mess with our mood and our energy levels: blood sugar levels affect how we feel and poor management of blood glucose can lead to negative moods.

See also: Angela Jacques, Nicholas Chaaya, Kate Beecher, Syed Aoun Ali, Arnauld Belmer, Selena Bartlett,The impact of sugar consumption on stress driven, emotional and addictive behaviors,Neuroscience & Biobehavioral Reviews,Volume 103,2019,Pages 178-199,ISSN 0149-7634,https://doi.org/10.1016/j.neubiorev.2019.05.021.

https://www.sciencedirect.com/science/article/pii/S0149763418308613

We can get all of the sugars that we need to function by eating a piece of fruit each day and consuming a diet rich in vegetables:
See also:
https://www.hsph.harvard.edu/nutrition-source/what-should-you-eat/vegetables-and-fruits/

Eating the right mix of protein, carbs and good fat, together with drinking enough water, is going to provide enough fuel without leaving us feeling lethargic after meals or having to worry about a growing waistline:
See also: Institute of Medicine (US) Subcommittee on Military Weight Management. Weight Management: State of the Science and Opportunities for Military Programs. Washington (DC): National Academies Press (US); 2004. 4, Weight-Loss and Maintenance Strategies. Available from: https://www.ncbi.nlm.nih.gov/books/NBK221839/

whether we're running or not, we should always try and allow at least three hours between eating and going to bed: it may be that eating a 'small, nutrient dense snack' before sleep is ok, particularly if we've exercised earlier in the day. However - most research still suggests that consuming a large, mixed meal before bed is going to lead to weight gain and being more susceptible to cardiometabolic diseases:

See also: Kinsey AW, Ormsbee MJ. The health impact of nighttime eating: old and new perspectives. Nutrients. 2015 Apr 9;7(4):2648-62. doi: 10.3390/nu7042648. PMID: 25859885; PMCID: PMC4425165.

Bin the sin

Portion size and second helpings are two of the major contributing factors to our over-eating:
See also: Livingstone MB, Pourshahidi LK. Portion size and obesity. Adv Nutr. 2014 Nov 14;5(6):829-34. doi: 10.3945/an.114.007 104. PMID: 25398749; PMCID: PMC4224223.

In an ideal world, we'd chew each mouthful at least ten times while eating: actually if we were to chew our food 40 times, we'd eat about 12% less than when we chew our food 15 times. 40 times sounds a little enjoyment sapping however...

See: Li J, Zhang N, Hu L, Li Z, Li R, Li C, Wang S. Improvement in chewing activity reduces energy intake in one meal and modulates plasma gut hormone concentrations in obese and lean young Chinese men. Am J Clin Nutr. 2011 Sep;94(3):709-16. doi: 10.3945/ajcn.11 1.015164. Epub 2011 Jul 20. PMID: 21775556.

What happens to the excess (calories that we put into our body)? Well - our body deals with it by storing it as fat:

See: https://www.nhs.uk/live-well/healthy-weight/managing-your-weight/understanding-calories

Why can't I just go on a diet (again)?

The problem with dieting (typically maintaining a calorie deficit of between 500 - 1,000 calories per day): meal planning takes a lot of time and effort, as does the calorie counting itself. Then the metabolism adapts to the decreased energy output which might even lead to a plateauing weight after all of this effort! The very definition of disappointing.

See also: Kim JY. Optimal Diet Strategies for Weight Loss and Weight Loss Maintenance. J Obes Metab Syndr. 2021 Mar 30;30(1):20-31. doi: 10.7570/jomes20065. PMID: 33107442; PMCID: PMC8017325.

when we revert back to our previous way of eating we lose any benefits (of dieting) we've managed to accumulate: and then this happens... Our metabolism has slowed down because we're not active and we've adjusted our calorie intake down as well, if we were to increase our calorie intake to above the 1,000 or 1,500 calories per day again, the weight is just going to go back on.

See again: Kim JY. Optimal Diet Strategies for Weight Loss and Weight Loss Maintenance. J Obes Metab Syndr. 2021 Mar 30;30(1):20-31. doi: 10.7570/jomes20065. PMID: 33107442; PMCID: PMC8017325.

cutting out certain food groups altogether may be counterpro-

ductive in the long run: how many different types of diet are being recommended these days? I read about 'low-calorie', 'very low calorie' (aka 'very dangerous'), 'meal replacement', 'low fat', 'low carb', 'ketogenic' (very low carb intake with more protein and fats), 'high protein', 'paleo', 'low GI' and the list goes on. Because I've always run I have never been on a weight-loss diet. Yes - I suffered the initial weight gain when I first went to university (before I learned how to cook the right amount of food for one person and got over the fact I could eat whatever I wanted, whenever I wanted). I yo-yo'd a bit around the injuries that forced me to rest for a few weeks here and there, and yes - I too suffered the shock of the overnight body shape change that turning forty brings with it. Having been through a 'fertility diet' however, I have since adapted what I eat and drink because I learnt that cutting out gluten, sugar and alcohol made a big difference not just to my waistline, but also to how I felt waking up and then throughout the day. (I consume considerably less of all three now). And because we're all different we need to test different strategies for controlling our weight and learn what works best for us.

But it is difficult to maintain strict diets over a long period of time and as our body gets used to eating less, or not eating certain food types, our body will adjust our energy levels to suit that diet. If we do eventually cave-in and eat something we're not supposed to, our body probably isn't going to be very happy about it and it is very likely that it will let us know in one way or another.

Cutting out certain foods altogether also risks us not eating sufficient micronutrients and the knock-on effects to our health over time.

Of all the diets, the one that is recommended over all others time and again is the Mediterranean diet, consisting of lots of fruit and vegetables, fish, poultry and with very limited red meat.

See also: Kim JY. Optimal Diet Strategies for Weight Loss and Weight Loss Maintenance. J Obes Metab Syndr. 2021 Mar 30;30(1):20-31. doi: 10.7570/jomes20065. PMID: 33107442; PMCID: PMC8017325.

Research that measures the different levels of ghrelin in people of different body weights and in those who fast, seems to suggest that ghrelin is involved in the long-term regulation of body weight:

See: Chao AM, Jastreboff AM, White MA, Grilo CM, Sinha R. Stress, cortisol, and other appetite-related hormones: Prospective prediction of 6-month changes in food cravings and weight. Obesity (Silver Spring). 2017 Apr;25(4):713-720. doi: 10.1002/oby.21790 . PMID: 28349668; PMCID: PMC5373497.

the evidence is that ghrelin also helps to maintain healthy muscles, bones, metabolism, cardiovascular health and plays a role in mediating memory and stress: ghrelin was discovered in 1999 and is a unique 28-amino-acid peptide. Not only does this hormone let us know when it is time to eat, it has so many functions, effecting all body systems, it is even being researched for its therapeutic properties as well as how it might be used to treat diseases in respective body parts.

See also: Akalu Y, Molla MD, Dessie G, Ayelign B. Physiological Effect of Ghrelin on Body Systems. Int J Endocrinol. 2020 May 25;2020:1385138. doi: 10.1155/2020/1385138. PMID: 32565790;

PMCID: PMC7267865.

research identifying the signalling pathways of the ghrelin system may even lead to new treatments for neurological diseases:
See again: Akalu Y, Molla MD, Dessie G, Ayelign B. Physiological Effect of Ghrelin on Body Systems. Int J Endocrinol. 2020 May 25;2020:1385138. doi: 10.1155/2020/1385138. PMID: 32565790; PMCID: PMC7267865.

here comes the argument against any fad diets, yo-yo dieting and carbohydrate free diets. These are all going to mess with our ghrelin levels, increasing production of our hunger hormone meaning any weight we've lost by cutting out carbs, or by crash dieting will quickly go back on once we return to eating our regular meals: any 'abnormal' eating behaviours are going to affect secretion of ghrelin, which over time is not only going to influence the body's normal reaction to food but because ghrelin is vital for so many bodily functions, we risk causing ourself all kinds of other health issues.

See also: Inui A, Asakawa A, Bowers CY, Mantovani G, Laviano A, Meguid MM, Fujimiya M. Ghrelin, appetite, and gastric motility: the emerging role of the stomach as an endocrine organ. FASEB J. 2004 Mar;18(3):439-56. doi: 10.1096/fj.03-0641rev. PMID: 15003990.

See also: Ma Y, Zhang H, Guo W, Yu L. Potential role of ghrelin in the regulation of inflammation. FASEB J. 2022 Sep;36(9):e22508. doi: 10.1096/fj.202200634R. PMID: 35983825.

cutting out certain food groups completely for a period of time

will only confuse our body when we go back to eating those food types; our body isn't used to having to digest these foods and will have more difficulty processing the food: our diet has changed quite significantly over the decades and we now eat more processed and ultra-processed foods. This also means that we're asking our body to digest different substances, as well as a much wider mix of foods in one go than our body would have had to deal with a 150 years ago. In fact, looking at the Victorian era and if we strip out infant mortality, the average life expectancy for an adult was around 75 years, even taking into account the lack of medicines back in the 1900s. Death by heart disease, stroke or cancer was extremely rare. If we were to eat the same diet (and be as active) as people in the 1900s, while degenerative diseases wouldn't disappear completely, the occurrence would decrease significantly. Likewise for cancer, it is very likely that the diagnosis of many types of cancer would drop in number significantly. So it is what we put in our body, it is the manmade foods and it is the fact that we put so many different ultra-processed ingredients in our body in one go that puts this additional stress on our bodily systems and causes these 'modern day' diseases. Our body is amazing at what it can do and how it adapts over time, however it is no wonder we feel tired and lacking in energy and drive after eating rubbish 'food'.

See also: Clayton P, Rowbotham J. An unsuitable and degraded diet? Part one: public health lessons from the mid-Victorian working class diet. J R Soc Med. 2008 Jun;101(6):282-9. doi: 10.1258/jrsm.2 008.080112. Erratum in: J R Soc Med. 2008 Aug;101(8):390. PMID: 18515775; PMCID: PMC2408622.

See also: Clayton P, Rowbotham J. An unsuitable and degraded diet? Part two: realities of the mid-Victorian diet. J R

Soc Med. 2008 Jul;101(7):350-7. doi: 10.1258/jrsm.2008.080113. PMID: 18591688; PMCID: PMC2442131.

See also: Rowbotham J, Clayton P. An unsuitable and degraded diet? Part three: Victorian consumption patterns and their health benefits. J R Soc Med. 2008 Sep;101(9):454-62. doi: 10.1258/jrsm.2008.080114. PMID: 18779247; PMCID: PMC2587384.

Instead, in order to manage ghrelin levels, we should eat a diet that includes healthy carbohydrates and lean proteins:

See: Adamska-Patruno E, Ostrowska L, Goscik J, Pietraszewska B, Kretowski A, Gorska M. The relationship between the leptin/ghrelin ratio and meals with various macronutrient contents in men with different nutritional status: a randomized crossover study. Nutr J. 2018 Dec 28;17(1):118. doi: 10.1186/s12937-018-0427-x. PMID: 30593267; PMCID: PMC6309055.

The 16/8 fasting method...with reported benefits including weight management, improved insulin sensitivity, reduced blood pressure, reducing inflammation and...could it even improve our longevity...Fasting may negatively affect our sex hormones: there is ongoing research to validate if the benefits are due to the 16 hour break in eating, or if the tendency to eat less while on the 16/8 diet also plays a part in the reduced risk of hypertension and improved glucose metabolism. Fasting isn't recommended for people with hormonal imbalances, diabetics or people with a BMI under 18.5.

See: Malinowski B, Zalewska K, Węsierska A, Sokołowska MM, Socha M, Liczner G, Pawlak-Osińska K, Wiciński M. Intermittent

Fasting in Cardiovascular Disorders-An Overview. Nutrients. 2019 Mar 20;11(3):673. doi: 10.3390/nu11030673. PMID: 30897855; PMCID: PMC6471315.

Water, water, water, water, water

Being well-hydrated means our red blood cells can replace themselves at the rate they need to: also that our red blood cells have a healthy water content, keeping them supple and able to move through our blood vessels more easily, promoting healthy blood flow. If we don't drink enough water, our blood cells become stickier and can't move as freely through the body.

See also: Gallagher PG. Disorders of erythrocyte hydration. Blood. 2017 Dec 21;130(25):2699-2708. doi: 10.1182/blood-2017-04-590810. Epub 2017 Oct 19. PMID: 29051181; PMCID: PMC5746162.

approximately 60% of the human adult body (is) composed of water:

See: Mattoo TK, Lu H, Ayers E, Thomas R. Total body water by BIA in children and young adults with normal and excessive weight. PLoS One. 2020 Oct 8;15(10):e0239212. doi: 10.1371/journal.pone.0239212. PMID: 33031479; PMCID: PMC7544096.

being well-hydrated helps optimise our digestion, and it washes away toxins from our body:
dehydration...can leave us feeling so tired and fatigued that we feel ready to go to bed by 7pm every day:

See: Popkin BM, D'Anci KE, Rosenberg IH. Water, hydration, and health. Nutr Rev. 2010 Aug;68(8):439-58. doi: 10.1111/j.1753-488 7.2010.00304.x. PMID: 20646222; PMCID: PMC2908954.

Inadequate hydration can impair ATP production, thus contributing to our feeling mentally and physically fatigued and a general sense of exhaustion: water is a crucial component in the metabolic reactions that produce ATP (the primary molecule used for energy in our cells) and dehydration can lead to reduced production, manifesting as a decrease in both our physical and mental energy levels. Chronic, or even significant dehydration can lead a feeling of exhaustion.

See also: Owen L, Sunram-Lea SI. Metabolic agents that enhance ATP can improve cognitive functioning: a review of the evidence for glucose, oxygen, pyruvate, creatine, and L-carnitine. Nutrients. 2011 Aug;3(8):735-55. doi: 10.3390/nu3080735. Epub 2011 Aug 10. PMID: 22254121; PMCID: PMC3257700.

If we're not getting enough water it adversely affects our blood pressure:

See: Riebl SK, Davy BM. The Hydration Equation: Update on Water Balance and Cognitive Performance. ACSMs Health Fit J. 2013 Nov;17(6):21-28. doi: 10.1249/FIT.0b013e3182a9570f. PMID: 25346594; PMCID: PMC4207053.

We should aim for at least one and half litres of water per day, or two litres if we've exercised: we also absorb water from our food (approximately 0.7L), and via metabolic processes (0.3L), taking total water 'input' to circa 2.5 litres per day on a non-exercise day and 3.0 litres if we're also rehydrating after working out.

See again: Riebl SK, Davy BM. The Hydration Equation: Update on Water Balance and Cognitive Performance. ACSMs Health Fit J. 2013 Nov;17(6):21-28. doi: 10.1249/FIT.0b013e3182a9570f. PMID: 25346594; PMCID: PMC4207053.

Beware that we don't want to drink too much water in one go as this will over-dilute the natural level of electrolytes in our body and can actually be harmful:

See again: Riebl SK, Davy BM. The Hydration Equation: Update on Water Balance and Cognitive Performance. ACSMs Health Fit J. 2013 Nov;17(6):21-28. doi: 10.1249/FIT.0b013e3182a9570f. PMID: 25346594; PMCID: PMC4207053.

the diuretic affect of caffeine means we will be going to the toilet more often. So while coffee may give us a short boost, we're also losing the liquid at a faster rate, limiting the hydrating effect of coffee: caffeine isn't only cause us to go to the toilet more often, losing the liquid we're drinking more quickly, it also affects bodily functions in the kidneys and liver, causing more sodium to be lost from the body (sodium being important for cell osmolality), with high consumption also increasing risk of disease or pathological conditions. It is likely that coffee consumption affects different people in different ways, with 'fast metabolisers' of coffee seeing less of a detrimental affect than 'slow metabolisers', meaning there is a genetic disposition on the effect caffeine will have on the kidneys.

Guidelines for caffeine consumption vary from country to country, with the majority consensus being that two or three small cups per day is fine (400mg of caffeine per day for an adult, with pregnant women advised to limit consumption as much as possible). Some countries still point to the risk factors however, with Poland discouraging the consumption of black tea and Latvia of both tea and coffee, stating the increased risk to mental health and heart disease.

See also: Marx B, Scuvée É, Scuvée-Moreau J, Seutin V, Jouret F. Mécanismes de l'effet diurétique de la caféine [Mechanisms of caffeine-induced diuresis]. Med Sci (Paris). 2016 May;32(5):485-90. French. doi: 10.1051/medsci/20163205015. Epub 2016 May 25. PMID: 27225921.

See also: Giontella A, de La Harpe R, Cronje HT, Zagkos L, Woolf B, Larsson SC, Gill D. Caffeine Intake, Plasma Caffeine Level, and Kidney Function: A Mendelian Randomization Study. Nutrients. 2023 Oct 18;15(20):4422. doi: 10.3390/nu15204422. PMID: 37892497; PMCID: PMC10609900.

See also: Reyes CM, Cornelis MC. Caffeine in the Diet: Country-Level Consumption and Guidelines. Nutrients. 2018 Nov 15;10(11):1772. doi: 10.3390/nu10111772. PMID: 30445721; PMCID: PMC6266969.

Sugary energy drinks are the real enemy here however, with the regularly induced spikes in blood sugar levels leading to inflammation, fatigue, hunger, cravings and ultimately, through prolonged consumption, increasing the risks of stroke, heart disease, liver disease and type-2 diabetes: the fact is that it is probably only the caffeine that has any beneficial 'performance enhancing' properties in an energy drink. Whereas caffeine has been proven to improve alertness and reaction time, boosting performance if ingested before certain types of exercise, the rest of the ingredients probably have very little effect and if consumed in large quantities, are just going to wreck our liver. Then there is the sugar content to consider in many of the available energy drinks; that's type 2 diabetes waiting to happen right there. As for the sugar replacement in the 'sugar-free' drinks, this is just going to add to the load being put through our liver and other organs.

See: Jagim AR, Harty PS, Barakat AR, Erickson JL, Carvalho V, Khurelbaatar C, Camic CL, Kerksick CM. Prevalence and Amounts of Common Ingredients Found in Energy Drinks and Shots. Nutrients. 2022 Jan 13;14(2):314. doi: 10.3390/nu14020314. PMID: 35057494; PMCID: PMC8780606.

See also: Jagim AR, Harty PS, Tinsley GM, Kerksick CM, Gonzalez AM, Kreider RB, Arent SM, Jager R, Smith-Ryan AE, Stout JR, Campbell BI, VanDusseldorp T, Antonio J. International society of sports nutrition position stand: energy drinks and energy shots. J Int Soc Sports Nutr. 2023 Dec;20(1):2171314. doi: 10.1080/15502783.2023.2171314. PMID: 36862943; PMCID: PMC9987737.

Even those (energy drinks) that claim to be healthy are said by the medical profession to have possible side-effects of nausea, bloating, adverse blood-pressure and hormone disruption:

See: https://www.nccih.nih.gov/health/energy-drinks

See also: Alsunni AA. Energy Drink Consumption: Beneficial and Adverse Health Effects. Int J Health Sci (Qassim). 2015 Oct;9(4):468-74. PMID: 26715927; PMCID: PMC4682602.

See also: Trapp GS, Hurworth M, Jacoby P, Maddison K, Allen K, Martin K, Christian H, Ambrosini GL, Oddy W, Eastwood PR. Energy drink intake is associated with insomnia and decreased daytime functioning in young adult females. Public Health Nutr. 2021 Apr;24(6):1328-1337. doi: 10.1017/S1368980020001652. Epub 2020 Jul 29. PMID: 32723415; PMCID: PMC10195404.

we definitely shouldn't be consuming these (energy drinks) on a daily basis:

See: Costantino A, Maiese A, Lazzari J, Casula C, Turillazzi E, Frati P, Fineschi V. The Dark Side of Energy Drinks: A Comprehensive Review of Their Impact on the Human Body. Nutrients. 2023 Sep 9;15(18):3922. doi: 10.3390/nu15183922. PMID: 37764707; PMCID: PMC10535526.

Building fitness

by the time we are moving consistently and maintaining a high heart rate for anything more than twenty minutes, our muscles are screaming for more energy. It is at this twenty-minute tipping point that the fat our body is burning is accelerated: when exercising such that our breathing is in a state of both forced inhalation and forced exhalation (breathing a lot deeper and more frequently, almost to the point of feeling out of breath), this is a sign that our cardiorespiratory system is being worked outside of its nice, relaxed, everyday comfort zone. This is good. This is going to keep our heart, lungs, brain, organs, muscles, bones, blood vessels, (yes - everything), in good working order. Obviously it depends how fit we are as to how soon during our run we feel our breathing reaching this work-rate but the real advantages to our health come when we are able to maintain this high heart rate (60 - 80% max HR) for at least twenty minutes. Cardiac output improves, as does oxygen uptake capacity and blood flow to the muscles (and around the rest of our body post exercise).

Note that if you have any health concerns or existing heart problems, your doctor should perform the standard checks (blood pressure, heart rate, patient review) to check whether this type of training is suitable, or whether a lower intensity is suggested.

See: Chen H, Chen C, Spanos M, Li G, Lu R, Bei Y, Xiao J. Exercise training maintains cardiovascular health: signaling pathways involved and potential therapeutics. Signal Transduct Target Ther. 2022 Sep 1;7(1):306. doi: 10.1038/s41392-022-01153-1. PMID: 36050310; PMCID: PMC9437103.

See also: Joyner MJ, Casey DP. Regulation of increased blood flow (hyperemia) to muscles during exercise: a hierarchy of competing physiological needs. Physiol Rev. 2015 Apr;95(2):549-601. doi: 10.1152/physrev.00035.2013. PMID: 25834232; PMCID: PMC4551211.

See also: Braun LT. Exercise physiology and cardiovascular fitness. Nurs Clin North Am. 1991 Mar;26(1):135-47. PMID: 2000315.

This might be because we've used up the energy from one source in our body and now it has to start providing fuel from one of our alternative energy stores meaning there is a small gap in the energy supply to our muscles: energy production and where in the body we source our energy from depends on the intensity and duration of our run, as well as our fitness level, diet and hydration level. For short, intense bursts (sprinting), the primary source of energy is our ATP-CP system, for longer runs our body will rely more on glycolysis (breaking down glucose for energy) then for long-distance running we switch to aerobic metabolism, burning carbs and fats. When we switch from one every source to another, we may experience a temporary drop in energy, after the transition however we experience a 'second wind'. We might experience these energy highs and lows several times throughout our run (again depending on the above factors) but if we can keep running through the low, we will come out the other side.

See also: Mul JD, Stanford KI, Hirshman MF, Goodyear LJ. Exercise and Regulation of Carbohydrate Metabolism. Prog Mol Biol Transl Sci. 2015;135:17-37. doi: 10.1016/bs.pmbts.2015.07.020. Epub 2015 Aug 20. PMID: 26477909; PMCID: PMC4727532.

See also: Salazar-Martínez E, Santalla A, Valenzuela PL, Nogales-Gadea G, Pinós T, Morán M, Santos-Lozano A, Fiuza-Luces C, Lucia A. The Second Wind in McArdle Patients: Fitness Matters. Front Physiol. 2021 Oct 15;12:744632. doi: 10.3389/fphys.2021.744632. PMID: 34721068; PMCID: PMC8555491.

Have you heard the saying 'muscle burns more calories than fat'? It's true; because muscle consumes energy (calories) even at rest, when we start to build-up our muscles through repeated exercise, we're also speeding up our metabolic rate: muscle tissue is more metabolically active than fat tissue, so even at rest consumes more calories. Then when we move and put this muscle tissue to work, the energy requirement for these muscle cells increases again. Because the energy in our muscle cells is easier for our body to access, we use this energy source first, before our body calls on the energy from our fat cells (which is not so readily available because the process of breaking down the fat for energy is not as immediate). Muscle cells also contain more mitochondria, which is where ATP (energy) is produced. This also adds to the efficiency of muscle cells for producing and using energy. So when we increase muscle mass, the metabolic rate of our muscles improves and we burn more calories when at rest.

See also: McPherron AC, Guo T, Bond ND, Gavrilova O. Increasing muscle mass to improve metabolism. Adipocyte. 2013 Apr 1;2(2):92-8. doi: 10.4161/adip.22500. PMID: 23805405; PMCID: PMC3661116.

On an exercise day, not only will our 'active calories' burnt be approximately 200 calories for every twenty minutes of running we do, but our elevated heart rate immediately after exercise, plus the impact on our resting heart rate for the rest of the day means that, depending on how long we keep our heart rate raised during exercise, we will burn an additional 400 calories per day. This figure increases for every additional minute of exercise we do above the twenty minutes at approximately 10 calories per minute of exercise: we have active calories burned during the run, plus the afterburn effect of exercise (EPOC), with our muscles in recovery mode and needing energy to replenish themselves. Even once our heart rate has dropped back down to resting rate, the repair work in our muscles continues. The harder we worked out (running further or faster) the more calories we'll burn during the post workout hours.

See also: Lagerwaard B, Keijer J, McCully KK, de Boer VCJ, Nieuwenhuizen AG. In vivo assessment of muscle mitochondrial function in healthy, young males in relation to parameters of aerobic fitness. Eur J Appl Physiol. 2019 Aug;119(8):1799-1808. doi: 10.1007/s00421-019-04169-8. Epub 2019 Jun 8. PMID: 31177324; PMCID: PMC6647177.

By pushing past week nine and on to week thirteen...the benefits we're going to see and feel, mentally and physically, are going to be life-changing, making all of the pain of our efforts worthwhile: our heart is going to be stronger and be more efficient at pumping blood around our body, circulation is better and the increase in oxygen supply is going to help us feel more energised in our day-to-day activities. Our body composition is changing, metabolism is improved, our muscles are becoming stronger, movement is easier, we're more flexible and we're feeling good about our body! To top this off, dedicating this time to ourselves each week, making sure that we have two or three hours out of the 112 waking hours* to look after our own health, is going to help with sleep, reduce stress and anxiety, increase happy hormones and therefore with our mental well-being. Our immune system is stronger, blood sugar control is better, our brain is more alert, energy levels are higher. We're going to feel on top of the world!

*112 waking hours assumes we sleep eight hours per night, seven days a week

See also: https://health.clevelandclinic.org/the-many-benefits-of-a-cardio-workout

Dodging the running rut – Taking our training to the next level

We are no longer pushing our body as hard as we were in our early running days, meaning we'll also see our weight plateau (at best): when we exercise our body goes through a number of changes, including how we store and use nutrients, the amount and the type of metabolic enzymes, the amount of proteins in our muscle and how our muscles and connective tissues move. If we keep repeating the same exercise, at the same intensity, the body isn't pushed to continue to make these adaptations. If we keep pushing a little more each time, or include other exercise as well, our body will continue to make these mitochondrial adaptations and the benefits to our body and mind.

See also: Hughes DC, Ellefsen S, Baar K. Adaptations to Endurance and Strength Training. Cold Spring Harb Perspect Med. 2018 Jun 1;8(6):a029769. doi: 10.1101/cshperspect.a029769. PMID: 28490537; PMCID: PMC5983157.

Mixing it up

'Fartlek' is a training method developed in the late 1930s by Swedish Olympian Gösta Holmér. The literal translation is 'speed play' and the nature of it means this training can be done anywhere:
See also:

https://www.runnersworld.com/uk/training/a36362823/fartlek-run

The intensity of speedwork…we're putting a high demand through the entire length of the muscle and activating our 'fast-twitch' muscle fibres:

See: Gibala MJ, Little JP, van Essen M, Wilkin GP, Burgomaster KA, Safdar A, Raha S, Tarnopolsky MA. Short-term sprint interval versus traditional endurance training: similar initial adaptations in human skeletal muscle and exercise performance. J Physiol. 2006 Sep 15;575(Pt 3):901-11. doi: 10.1113/jphysiol.2006.112094. Epub 2006 Jul 6. PMID: 16825308; PMCID: PMC1995688.

See also: Dudley GA, Abraham WM, Terjung RL. Influence of exercise intensity and duration on biochemical adaptations in skeletal muscle. J Appl Physiol Respir Environ Exerc Physiol. 1982 Oct;53(4):844-50. doi: 10.1152/jappl.1982.53.4.844. PMID: 6295989.

Our fast-twitch fibres have a lower concentration of blood vessels running through them (they're able to make their own quick source of energy):

See: Ferraro E, Giammarioli AM, Chiandotto S, Spoletini I, Rosano G. Exercise-induced skeletal muscle remodeling and metabolic adaptation: redox signaling and role of autophagy. Antioxid Redox Signal. 2014 Jul 1;21(1):154-76. doi: 10.1089/ars.2013.5773. Epub 2014 Mar 6. PMID: 24450966; PMCID: PMC4048572.

See also: Vigh-Larsen JF, Ørtenblad N, Emil Andersen O, Thorsteinsson H, Kristiansen TH, Bilde S, Mikkelsen MS, Nielsen J, Mohr M, Overgaard K. Fibre type- and localisation-specific muscle glycogen utilisation during repeated high-intensity intermittent exercise. J Physiol. 2022 Nov;600(21):4713-4730. doi: 10.1113/JP2832 25. Epub 2022 Sep 18. PMID: 36030498; PMCID: PMC9825866.

In contrast, jogging relies first on our 'slow-twitch' muscle fi-

bres, which not only have more blood vessels running through them but also contain more of the protein 'myoglobin', whose main function is to supply oxygen to the cells in our muscles:

See again: Ferraro E, Giammarioli AM, Chiandotto S, Spoletini I, Rosano G. Exercise-induced skeletal muscle remodeling and metabolic adaptation: redox signaling and role of autophagy. Antioxid Redox Signal. 2014 Jul 1;21(1):154-76. doi: 10.1089/ars.2013.5773. Epub 2014 Mar 6. PMID: 24450966; PMCID: PMC4048572.

No one needs to get hurt... Avoiding injury

Our muscles shorten when we don't regularly stretch them:

See: Shellock FG, Prentice WE. Warming-up and stretching for improved physical performance and prevention of sports-related injuries. Sports Med. 1985 Jul-Aug;2(4):267-78. doi: 10.2165/00007256-198502040-00004. PMID: 3849057.

See also: Arntz F, Markov A, Behm DG, Behrens M, Negra Y, Nakamura M, Moran J, Chaabene H. Chronic Effects of Static Stretching Exercises on Muscle Strength and Power in Healthy Individuals Across the Lifespan: A Systematic Review with Multi-level Meta-analysis. Sports Med. 2023 Mar;53(3):723-745. doi: 10.1007/s40279-022-01806-9. Epub 2023 Jan 31. PMID: 36719536; PMCID: PMC9935669.

A frequent cause of muscular injuries these days is due precisely to the fact that as well as the natural age-related muscle loss, our muscles weaken to the point of the maximum exertion we put through them:

See: Aagaard P, Suetta C, Caserotti P, Magnusson SP, Kjaer M. Role of the nervous system in sarcopenia and muscle atrophy with aging: strength training as a countermeasure. Scand J Med Sci Sports. 2010 Feb;20(1):49-64. doi: 10.1111/j.1600-0838.2009.01084.x. PMID: 20487503.

See also: Larsson L, Degens H, Li M, Salviati L, Lee YI, Thompson W, Kirkland JL, Sandri M. Sarcopenia: Aging-Related Loss of Muscle Mass and Function. Physiol Rev. 2019 Jan 1;99(1):427-511. doi: 10.1152/physrev.00061.2017. PMID: 30427277; PMCID: PMC6442923.

Something has to take the strain when we run and because our glutes have become 'lazy', we risk overloading our hamstrings. Welcome knee pain, lower leg injury, or even hip pain, depending on how far the transference of workload has travelled: weirdly (or so I thought at the time) my weak glutes caused a tiny stress fracture in my pubic bone. It took seeing several doctors and physios to figure out why I had such bad pain along my pubic bone every time I went for a run (and at the end, in-between runs too). Apparently the weakness was transferred from glutes to hamstrings, eventually putting too much force through the tendons attached to my pubic bone. The problem went away after a few weeks of hardcore glute strengthening exercises and with ongoing strength training I've been able to keep it at bay ever since. My story aside, keeping our buns strong is going to make such a massive difference in avoiding injury and because we all sit down so much these days, butt muscles flaccid and uncaring, investing thirty minutes bum-time every week is wholly advisable.

See also: Buckthorpe M, Stride M, Villa FD. ASSESSING AND TREATING GLUTEUS MAXIMUS WEAKNESS - A CLINICAL COMMENTARY. Int J Sports Phys Ther. 2019 Jul;14(4):655-669. PMID: 31440415; PMCID: PMC6670060.

The more stable we are when we run...the better protected we are against jarring our back, or again – any imbalance through our hips, or forced over-compensation by muscles further down our legs:

See: Rivera CE. Core and Lumbopelvic Stabilization in Runners. Phys Med Rehabil Clin N Am. 2016 Feb;27(1):319-37. doi: 10.1016/j.pmr.2015.09.003. PMID: 26616187.

Muscle damage is generally caused when we suddenly put heavy strain on the muscle as a result of physical exertion:

See: Schoenfeld, Brad J.. Does Exercise-Induced Muscle Damage Play a Role in Skeletal Muscle Hypertrophy?. Journal of Strength and Conditioning Research 26(5):p 1441-1453, May 2012. | DOI: 10.1519/JSC.0b013e31824f207e

The damage can cause a small amount of bleeding within the muscle itself, manifesting as tenderness and swelling:

See also: Clarkson PM, Hubal MJ. Exercise-induced muscle damage in humans. Am J Phys Med Rehabil. 2002 Nov;81(11 Suppl):S52-69. doi: 10.1097/00002060-200211001-00007. PMID: 12409811.

Sometimes taking a paracetamol, or having a steroid injection

will take the swelling down such that the pain goes away completely (if the pain was due to the swelling):

See: https://www.nhs.uk/medicines/hydrocortisone-injections/

Post run injury prevention

The cooldown jog

For any speedwork sessions, or competitive races, where our pace was faster than normal, making time for a jog immediately afterwards will help our heart rate return to resting level more gradually as well as metabolise lactic acid at a faster rate, enhancing our recovery:

See: Bangsbo J, Graham T, Johansen L, Saltin B. Muscle lactate metabolism in recovery from intense exhaustive exercise: impact of light exercise. J Appl Physiol (1985). 1994 Oct;77(4):1890-5. doi: 10.1152/jappl.1994.77.4.1890. PMID: 7836214.

Stretching after a run

Stretching also helps our body to process the bi-products of exercise (including lactate); transporting these away from the muscle so they can either be used elsewhere or be expelled from the body: an 'active cooldown' (gentle jog, or walking), post-exercise stretching, sleep, nutrition, hydration, foam rolling, self-massage, compression clothing (for some) etc. are all going to help our body to recover and relax after a tough run. Importantly there is a psychological effect of calming the mind and body down after exercise as well; 'the work is done, now my body can relax and recover'.

See also: Braun-Trocchio R, Graybeal AJ, Kreutzer A, Warfield E, Renteria J, Harrison K, Williams A, Moss K, Shah M. Recovery Strategies in Endurance Athletes. J Funct Morphol Kinesiol. 2022 Feb 13;7(1):22. doi: 10.3390/jfmk7010022. PMID: 35225908; PMCID: PMC8883945.

Inbetween runs

Complementary exercises

Body & mind, mind & body

These days professional athletes and sports people understand the benefits of strengthening their body through Pilates and many will have at least a couple of sessions each week: you can search online for the long lists of professional sports people who include Pilates as part of their weekly training schedule.

Pilates and yoga work different muscles...Once you know the moves however (and importantly – how to breathe through the movements): requiring centring, concentration, control, precision, rhythmic breathing and flowing movements, emphasis is placed on alignment of body posture. The muscle strengthening properties associated with Pilates means it is recommended time and again for combating back pain as well.

See also: Eliks M, Zgorzalewicz-Stachowiak M, Zeńczak-Praga K. Application of Pilates-based exercises in the treatment of chronic non-specific low back pain: state of the art. Postgrad Med J. 2019 Jan;95(1119):41-45. doi: 10.1136/postgradmedj-2018-135920. Epub 2019 Jan 12. PMID: 30636192; PMCID: PMC6581086.

See also: Fernández-Rodríguez R, Álvarez-Bueno C, Cavero-Redondo I, Torres-Costoso A, Pozuelo-Carrascosa DP, Reina-Gutiérrez S, Pascual-Morena C, Martínez-Vizcaíno V. Best Exercise Options for Reducing Pain and Disability in Adults With Chronic Low Back Pain: Pilates, Strength, Core-Based, and Mind-Body. A Network Meta-analysis. J Orthop Sports Phys Ther. 2022 Aug;52(8):505-521. doi: 10.2519/jospt.2022.10671. Epub 2022 Jun 19. PMID: 35722759.

The power of resistance

Resistance training (also called strength, or weight training) is "the use of resistance to muscular contraction to build strength":

Quoted from: https://www.betterhealth.vic.gov.au/health/healthyliving/resistance-training-health-benefits

See also: Figueiredo VC. Revisiting the roles of protein synthesis during skeletal muscle hypertrophy induced by exercise. Am J Physiol Regul Integr Comp Physiol. 2019 Nov 1;317(5):R709-R718. doi: 10.1152/ajpregu.00162.2019. Epub 2019 Sep 11. PMID: 31508978.

Acupuncture

The underlying principle is based on the concept of Qi (pronounced "chee"), which is the energy that flows through pathways in our body known as meridians. According to Chinese medicine, if the flow of Qi is disrupted or imbalanced, it can lead to illness or pain:

See: Marshall AC. Traditional Chinese Medicine and Clinical Pharmacology. Drug Discovery and Evaluation: Methods in Clinical Pharmacology. 2020 Mar 2:455–82. doi: 10.1007/978-3-319-68864-0_60. PMCID: PMC7356495.

if we have an injury, acupuncture is said to both influence the nervous system including helping with pain management but also to trigger the body's self-healing processes and restore the Qi around the place of the injury:

See also: McDonald J, Janz S. The Acupuncture Evidence Project: A Comparative Literature Review (Revised Edition)

The benefits of this ancient medical practice (acupuncture) are well documented and there is plenty of research that demonstrates the positive effects for various conditions, including chronic pain, migraines, osteoarthritis:

See also: Fan AY, Miller DW, Bolash B, Bauer M, McDonald J, Faggert S, He H, Li YM, Matecki A, Camardella L, Koppelman MH, Stone JAM, Meade L, Pang J. Acupuncture's Role in Solving the Opioid Epidemic: Evidence, Cost-Effectiveness, and Care Availability for Acupuncture as a Primary, Non-Pharmacologic Method for Pain Relief and Management-White Paper 2017. J Integr Med. 2017

Nov;15(6):411-425. doi: 10.1016/S2095-4964(17)60378-9. PMID: 29103410.

Running myths

Running myth # 1: 'I will ruin my knees if I run'.

Running is going to strengthen our quadriceps (front thigh muscles), calves and glutes, all of which help support and stabilise our knee joint and reduce the stress going through the joint itself. Not only this, but running improves the strength of the surrounding tendons and ligaments, as well as the density of all of our weight-bearing bones:

See: Abulhasan JF, Grey MJ. Anatomy and Physiology of Knee Stability. *Journal of Functional Morphology and Kinesiology*. 2017; 2(4):34. https://doi.org/10.3390/jfmk2040034

See also: See: Di Rosa M, Castrogiovanni P, Musumeci G. The Synovium Theory: Can Exercise Prevent Knee Osteoarthritis? The Role of "Mechanokines", A Possible Biological Key. J Funct Morphol Kinesiol. 2019 Jan 23;4(1):11. doi: 10.3390/jfmk4010011. PMID: 33467326; PMCID: PMC7739218.

Running myth # 2: 'Running causes arthritis and this will cause me problems into old age':

See: Stone RC, Baker J. Physical activity, age, and arthritis: exploring the relationships of major risk factors on biopsychosocial symptomology and disease status. J Aging Phys Act. 2014 Jul;22(3):314-23. doi: 10.1123/japa.2012-0293. Epub 2013 Jul 22. PMID: 23881509.

See also: Brooks JM, Titus AJ, Polenick CA, Orzechowski NM, Reid MC, MacKenzie TA, Bartels SJ, Batsis JA. Prevalence rates of arthritis among US older adults with varying degrees of depression: Findings from the 2011 to 2014 National Health and Nutrition Examination Survey. Int J Geriatr Psychiatry. 2018 Dec;33(12):1671-1679. doi: 10.1002/gps.4971. Epub 2018 Sep 19. PMID: 30229563; PMCID: PMC6422526.

See also: Castrogiovanni P, Musumeci G. Which is the Best Physical Treatment for Osteoarthritis? *Journal of Functional Morphology and Kinesiology*. 2016; 1(1):54-68. https://doi.org/10.3390/jfmk1010054

Running myth # 3: Running ages us

For the average adult, the ability to process oxygen declines by about 10% each decade after the age of twenty-five; this increases to 15% every ten years once we reach the age of fifty:

See: Kim CH, Wheatley CM, Behnia M, Johnson BD. The Effect of Aging on Relationships between Lean Body Mass and VO2max in Rowers. PLoS One. 2016 Aug 1;11(8):e0160275. doi: 10.1371/journal.pone.0160275. PMID: 27479009; PMCID: PMC4968829.

Running myth # 4: I'm too old to start running now!

Tell your doctor that you want to start being more active, working up to a gentle jog; ask them to check your heart rate and blood pressure and get their opinion if there is any medical reason you can't begin to exercise. Once you have the OK from the doctor, just start very slowly; fast-walking is a great way to begin. If you're able to arrange a couple of one-on-one training sessions with a personal trainer with experience working with older people, ask them to show you a few simple exercises to help get you started and set you on your way.

It is hypothesised that we exercise in a more body-friendly way when we age anyway, more conscious of our movements and looking after our joints, so enabling us to reap all of the benefits while minimising any risk of injury.

See: Borgia B, Dufek JS, Silvernail JF, Radzak KN. The effect of fatigue on running mechanics in older and younger runners. Gait Posture. 2022 Sep;97:86-93. doi: 10.1016/j.gaitpost.2022.07.249. Epub 2022 Jul 25. PMID: 35914388; PMCID: PMC10170943.

Part Four

Meal ideas

the 25%/60%/15% split of protein, carbs and fats is a good guide to be working with: when looking at what we eat, we can break this down into micro and macronutrients. Macronutrients are the overarching food categories of proteins, carbohydrates and fats. When we get into micronutrients, we're looking at the vitamin and mineral level of what's in our food and we're including fibre content. The percentage split of our protein, carbs and fats will depend on what our goal is. If we're looking to put on muscle we'll eat a higher percentage of protein and healthy fats in our diet and fewer carbs, however if we want to lose fat and we're exercising at the same time, the 25%/60%/15% split (protein/carbs/fats) is what we want to be aiming for on average each day (or across every couple of days). By maintaining the carbs at a slightly higher percentage of our daily calorie intake, we are ensuring we have enough energy to recover after exercise and this will help us avoid feeling fatigued by the middle of the week.

A study found that regular endurance training (e.g. running), or strength training leads to specific changes in the blood's chemical composition versus those who don't exercise. The changes relate to how energy is produced and used in the body, how muscles and other tissues are built and maintained, as well as how cells communicate and function. Because exercise changes how the body's cells produce energy (mitochondrial energy metabolism), how it processes amino acids (the building blocks of protein), and how it breaks down fats (fatty acid oxidation), we can understand why optimising our diet at the same time is a win-win for both getting into shape and giving our body exactly what it needs to do so.

See: Parstorfer M, Poschet G, Kronsteiner D, Brüning K, Friedmann-Bette B. Targeted Metabolomics in High Performance Sports: Differences between the Resting Metabolic Profile of Endurance- and Strength-Trained Athletes in Comparison with Sedentary Subjects over the Course of a Training Year. Metabolites. 2023 Jul 10;13(7):833. doi: 10.3390/metabo13070833. PMID: 37512540; PMCID: PMC10383823.

See also: Murray B, Rosenbloom C. Fundamentals of glycogen metabolism for coaches and athletes. Nutr Rev. 2018 Apr 1;76(4):243-259. doi: 10.1093/nutrit/nuy001. PMID: 29444266; PMCID: PMC6019055.

Limit ultra-processed foods as much as possible...for example, high-fructose corn oil, hydrogenated or intensified oils, hydrolysed proteins, flavours, flavour enhancers, colours, emu-

lsifiers, emulsifying salts, sweeteners, thickeners, anti-foaming, bulking, carbonating, gelling or glazing agents: see also: Monteiro, C., Cannon, G., Levy, R., Moubarac, J., Louzada, M., Rauber, F., . . . Jaime, P. (2019). Ultra-processed foods: What they are and how to identify them. *Public Health Nutrition, 22*(5), 936-941. doi:10.1017/S1368980018003762

Some research also suggests that how we have altered modern wheat over time may be linked to an increase in wheat intolerance and the digestive issues associated with the inflammation this causes:

Wheat was modified in the early 1970s, first so that the wheat contained more seeds, then when this caused the crop to fall over, the stem also had to be strengthened. Hormones were used, then more hormones, and what isn't fully understood is what impact these modifications had on how we digest wheat, the possible inflammatory effects, or on hormonal imbalances. See: "Endometriosis, A Key To Healing And Fertility Through Nutrition. Shepperson Mills, D & Vernon, M. (2002), HarperCollins".

Plus with the latest available allergy testing, more people are finding out that it is the yeast in regular bread that is the issue:

See: https://www.intolerancelab.co.uk/bread-intolerance-symptoms/

See also: https://www.nhs.uk/conditions/food-allergy/

'An apple a day keeps the the doctor away':

With all of the various ailments we suffer from these days, this statement was quickly disproved by researchers. However it was noted by the same research that people who ate an apple a day did tend to be healthier. Attributed to fibre content and essential vitamins and minerals, an apple a day really could help keep disease at bay.

See: Davis MA, Bynum JP, Sirovich BE. Association between apple consumption and physician visits: appealing the conventional wisdom that an apple a day keeps the doctor away. JAMA Intern Med. 2015 May;175(5):777-83. doi: 10.1001/jamainternmed.2014.5466. PMID: 25822137; PMCID: PMC4420713.

Printed in Great Britain
by Amazon